CRAN   M6/534636
DU 740.42 .J66 1
C. 1
JOSEPHIDES
PRODUCTION

EAST KOOTENAY COMMUNITY COLLEGE

D0722123

47.28   870304

JOC

East Kootenay Community College
BOX 8500
CRANBROOK, B.C.   V1C 5L7
PHONE 489-2751

The
Production of Inequality

THE
PRODUCTION
OF INEQUALITY

Gender and exchange
among the Kewa

Lisette Josephides

Tavistock London and New York

E.K.C.C. LIBRARY

First published in 1985 by
Tavistock Publications Ltd
11 New Fetter Lane,
London EC4P 4EE

Published in the USA by
Tavistock Publications
in association with Methuen, Inc.
29 West 35th Street
New York, NY 10001

© 1985 Lisette Josephides

Typeset by
Rowland Phototypesetting Ltd
Printed in Great Britain at
The Cambridge University Press

All rights reserved. No part of
this book may be reprinted or
reproduced or utilized in any form
or by any electronic, mechanical
or other means, now known or
hereafter invented, including
photocopying and recording, or
in any information storage or
retrieval system, without
permission in writing from the
publishers.

*British Library Cataloguing in
Publication Data*
Josephides, Lisette
  The production of inequality:
    gender and exchange among
    the Kewa.
  1. Kewa (New Guinea people)
  I. Title
  305.8'9912   DU740.42

  ISBN 0-422-79720-0
  ISBN 0-422-79730-8 Pbk

60-878-643

Contents

Preface   vii
Introduction   1

Part One: Structures, groups, and processes   13
1 Group formation I: Idioms and practices   15
2 Group formation II: 'Base-men of the place' and
   women sojourners   41
3 Change and continuity: Colonial and post-colonial
developments   68

Part Two: The production of inequality   ·   95
4 Concepts and models   97
5 The construction of gender categories   115
6 The ideology of equality and the politics of power   140
7 Exchange and the pig kill   172
8 Maximizing control: Alienation and the production of
   exchange values   203
9 Conclusion   216

Glossary and note on pronunciation   222
Appendix: Wars involving Yala   224
References   226
Name index   232
Subject index   235

To my mother

Preface

The field research on which this book is based was conducted during 1979–81 while I was a graduate student in the Department of Anthropology at University College, London. I prepared for fieldwork by learning Melanesian pidgin while still at University College, and from January to April 1979 I did library research on Kewa language materials in the New Guinea Collection at the University of Papua New Guinea. My first attempts at learning Kewa benefited also from conversations with Kewa speaking students at UPNG. As a result of a recommendation from one of these students, I made an exploratory trip to Kagua in the Southern Highlands, where I visited a number of villages. In Sumbura I was taken over by the local Councillor, Rake, who accompanied me to various locations while I tried to decide where to have a house built. One of these walks took us to the settlement of Yakopaita. After a chat in the porch of the men's house, when Rake explained to those gathered there that I intended to spend two years in one of the villages in the area, we took our leave. We had walked only a hundred yards when Rimbu, clearly the most prominent man in the settlement, ran after us, followed by three or four other men. 'Why don't you stay in our settlement?' he asked. It was built snugly at the foot of a woody ridge not far from the banks of the river Sugu, which twisted and turned in the valley. All around was green and clear and still, and a longhouse stood in preparation for a pig kill. I arranged to have a house built there.

For almost six weeks I lived in a derelict shack by the court-house and the market, waiting for my house to be built. Eventually an uninvited and unidentified nocturnal visitor demonstrated conclusively how well-founded were the villagers' many warnings that it was unsafe to live so close to the main road and so far from other houses, so I moved to Kagua for a few days until the house was finished. Throughout this period I concentrated on language learning, but though I acquired a fair working knowledge of the Kewa language and used it in conversation with non-pidgin speakers, I always needed the assistance of pidgin speakers during difficult and intricate discussions.

Rimbu was my patron and major informant throughout my fieldwork period. Marc Schiltz joined me for independent research during breaks from his teaching at the University of Papua New Guinea, but the rest of the time I lived alone. I lived only in Yakopaita, though I spent much time in other villages and visited many outlying areas. Usually Rimbu was my guide for the more distant excursions. I did not pay Rimbu for his services, but we had a mutually beneficial exchange relationship. I used one assistant whom I paid; he recorded women's market transactions. Apart from this work, and some quasi-formal interviewing of migrants, my data comes from participant observation, discussion, and informal interviews. I did much recording of people's autobiographical reminiscences, their descriptions of warfare and cult practices, and their renderings of myths and songs. All this I later translated from the Kewa with the help of pidgin speakers. Some of it has been published by the Institute of Papua New Guinea Studies.

In the Kewa area it would have been difficult to do fieldwork without having a sponsor and forging exchange relations with him. Being associated with one person and one group naturally imposed from restrictions on one's field of operations; but being associated with no group would have made all operations impossible. This relationship culminated in a pig kill when Marc Schiltz and I finally left the village.

In Mendi and Kagua, Marc Schiltz and I did archival work, ploughing through mountains of unclassified material and taking meticulous notes on the Kagua and Erave patrol reports from 1956 to 1980. We also made a number of trips to various other parts of the Highlands and to coastal areas, where we interviewed Kewa migrants and generally observed their working conditions. In Port Moresby, where I spent a total of thirty months, I became aware of the wider political and economic context within which Kagua and its people had to be understood; while at the same time I strove to keep in touch with Kewa speakers living in the capital.

As is usual in these cases, I incurred a number of debts while pursuing my research. My grateful thanks must first go to the British Social Science Research Council, who supported my research with a major award, and to the Central Research Fund of the University of London, who assisted with a smaller grant for equipment. To Andrew Strathern I owe my first introduction to the Highlands, which fired my interest in the area. As my teacher and supervisor at University College, and good friends at all times, he gave invaluable help towards the preparation and organization of the fieldwork leading to my PhD dissertation of 1984, of which this book is a revised version. I bear a lasting gratitude to him for directing me to Kagua, and for his stimulating help and encouragement both in London and in Port Moresby.

In Papua New Guinea, my grateful thanks goes to the University's Anthropology and Sociology Department for affiliating me during my stay in the field; to UPNG cartographers for helping with mapping; to Kewa students, notably Su Rambe and Martin Yakopa, who helped me choose a field site and discussed many ethnographic and linguistic points with me; and to the Premier of the Southern Highlands for granting me permission to do research. Many people have offered help and hospitality while I travelled (often with Marc Schiltz) from Port Moresby through Mt Hagen to Kagua and Yakopaita. In Mt Hagen, Lois and Ken Logan always had a bed for us when we were stranded; in Kagua the Catholic mission at Karia offered language material as well as hospitality, while High School staff were free with much needed lifts. Staff at the Health Centre and District Office were consistently kind and helpful. Paul and Liese Fearman did much to ease my settling into the village, and Paul's practical help was invaluable while he was District Officer in Kagua during 1979. Consistent hospitality and many lifts were also offered by George and Linda Kelley, missionaries at Katiloma, and Anne and John Sharp, who damaged their vehicle while driving us over a bridge with low headroom. John also showed us around the tea plantations in Kagua, which he managed.

My debts to villagers in Kagua, and especially in Yakopaita, Aka, Poiale, and Puliminia, are too numerous to list. They are all gratefully acknowledged for their warmth, hospitality, and communicativeness. Many appear by name throughout the pages of this book, and my debt to them is implicit. However, three at least merit a very special mention: Rimbu, my closest friend and main informant, who was so free and generous in all his dealings with me; Lari whose warmth and sensitive intelligence made so many strange things pleasant and intelligible; and Wapa, who provided information on pre-contact days and whose death in the field grieved us deeply.

To Sacha Josephides I am much indebted for many critical comments and practical assistance while this work was in its thesis stage. My thanks also to my examiners, Rosemary Harris and Alfred Gell, who received my thesis so well and offered constructive comments. My debt to Marilyn Strathern is also considerable. Apart from our many discussions (mostly by correspondence) on issues central to this work, I have been much influenced generally by her ideas, expressed in the many papers which she has always been kind enough to send to me.

A final acknowledgement goes to Marc Schiltz, for all his mapping and measuring; for having a home for me on my return visits to Port Moresby; for his involvement in fieldwork, data analysis, and the development of the major arguments in this book. His contribution in all these areas is not quantifiable.

The 'false generic'

Throughout this work the words 'man', 'he', and 'his' refer only to people of the male sex, to their attributes, attitudes, and possessions. I never include women in the category 'man'. The false generic is a soft option and a subterfuge, but though it sounds simpler and more elegant to the ear it has always been analytically woolly and is fast becoming politically unacceptable.

Lisette Josephides
University of Papua New Guinea, 1984

Introduction

Social inequality has been written about from a number of perspectives. Many social scientists have looked for its origins, and have puzzled over how an assumed original state of equality could have allowed for the development of inequalities. Often such inequalities have been tied to specific institutions, economic forms, and political organization. My perspective differs in that I assume that all social systems, whatever their structure, contain the seeds of inequality. My concern therefore is not with historical origins of institutions and statuses, but rather with understanding how inequalities are engendered and perpetuated within social practice.

Though New Guinea Highland societies have been described as egalitarian, having no paramount chiefs or hereditary statuses, many studies have also shown that inequalities exist among men as well as between men and women. This book describes these inequalities and attempts to locate their source. The issues of gender and exchange feature prominently in this analysis. Production is relevant in both these areas, openly in the case of gender relations (in their domestic form), but played down in exchange relations. The interplay between these – production, exchange, and gender relations – and the way they are socially validated is crucial to our understanding of inequality. While the exchange sphere is said to be egalitarian, the productive domestic sphere is one of interdependence. Yet the egalitarianism of exchange is false, precisely because of its unacknowledged relationship to production; and the interdependence in production really supports hierarchical domestic relations. The enquiry then proceeds from obvious and acknowledged inequalities to subtle, covert ones. While a major division on gender lines is both the demarcation line between the politically dominant and the politically and economically dependent, and the idiom in which power differentials are perceived and validated, an examination of the source of men's power over women devolves on the control of their labour power. This perspective leads to the appraisal of the big man status as one affording unequal access to the labour pool not only of all women in the community, but also that of less prominent men. An enquiry beginning with the concepts of gender and prestige structures thus ends with those of alienation and labour control. This is not a paradigmatic shift, but the outcome of a methodological approach that is concerned with the analysis of social practices rather than with making inferences from structures and formal statuses. Social inequality is produced in social interaction, but the choice of words in the title of this book alludes also to the misrecognized role of production in the creation of inequalities.

In common with other groups in the area the Kewa did not have a name by which they referred to themselves, but were given this name by administration officers and linguists. When Kewa speakers say 'Kewa' they refer to people living more southerly than themselves. 'Kewa' now denotes a linguistic group of some 50,000[1] people who inhabit an area of approximately 1,500 square kilometres in the southern part of the Southern Highlands Province (*Maps 1 and 3*). They are bounded on the north-west by the Magi and the Mendi, on the north by the Imbonggu, on the east by the Wiru, on the south by the Polopa and the Sau, and on the south-west by the Foi. The majority of Kewa speakers falls within the present political unit of Kagua district (*Map 2*).

The Southern Highlands is one of nineteen provinces in Papua New Guinea, the eastern half of a Pacific island which is the second largest in the world. Its western half was a Dutch colony before being ceded to Indonesia in 1963 and given the name of Irian Jaya. The eastern half of the island gained its independence from Australia in 1975 and became the nation state of Papua New Guinea, with an elected Parliament and Prime Minister on the Westminster model. Its seat of government is in Port Moresby on the south coast. While English is the official language of politics, business and education, Melanesian pidgin is the more widely-used lingua franca. The Kina, containing 100 toea and worth 88 UK pence in 1984, is the national currency.

There are three major dialects in the Kewa language, one of

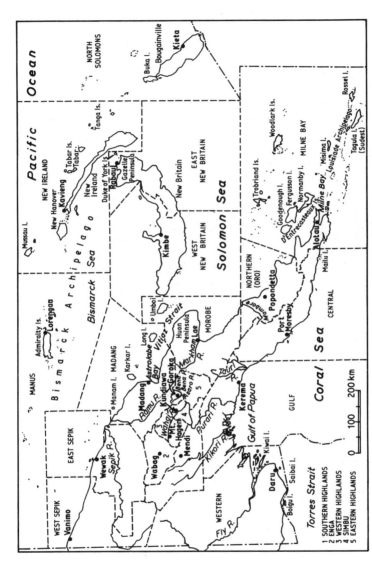

Map 1 *Papua New Guinea: provinces, provincial headquarters and general features*

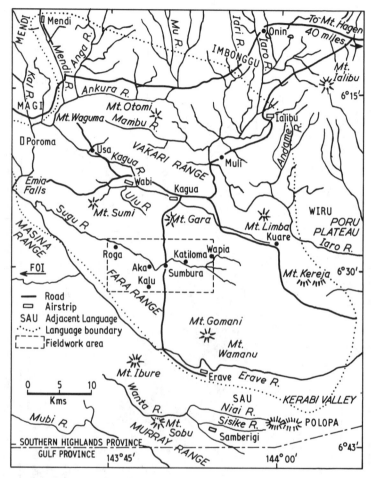

Map 2   *Kewa language area*
Source: K. J. Franklin 1978

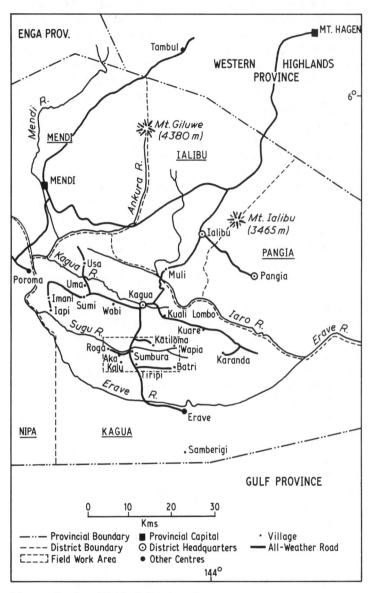

Map 3 *Southern Highlands Province: Eastern Districts*

which has a sub-dialect of its own. Extensive linguistic work on these dialects has been carried out by K. J. and J. Franklin, whose major work *A Kewa Dictionary* (published in 1978) includes various anthropological materials. Other notable anthropological publications on the area are those of John LeRoy (1975, 1979a, 1979b, 1981) who in the 1970s conducted substantial fieldwork at three different locations: in Koiari village in the south, Kuare in the east and Iapi in the west.

The Sugu River Valley where I conducted fieldwork is in the southern half of the Kewa language area (*Map 2*). In terms of social organization and ecology this area belongs neither to the 'grasslands' nor to the 'forest' Kewa (a distinction made in LeRoy 1975), but has features of both. The Sugu River Valley is formed largely of freshwater lake deposits overladen with brown clay soils.[2] Vegetation ranges from primary and secondary montane rain forest to *kunai* grassland. The rugged and generally steep valley walls are formed by limestone and are also covered by clay soils. These soils are poor, supporting only stunted trees and grasses. The valley walls reach an altitude of 1,800 metres, while the altitude in the valley ranges between 1,600 metres at the river Sugu headwaters and 1,300 metres at the confluence with the Erave river. Rainfall figures (available only for Kagua) give an average annual rainfall of 310 cm. There is no marked wet or dry season, although there are dry periods of variable durations and long, extremely wet periods during which the rain is torrential and constant at night. Most rain tends to fall in the afternoon and during the night. Temperatures range from 17–27°C by day to 9–17°C by night.

From the river headwaters to the vehicular road at Sumbura the Sugu flows through a relatively broad and open valley. At this point it begins to narrow westwards. At some parts the valley floor disappears altogether, and limestone ridges descend directly into the river in steep gorges. This funnel-like topography widens and narrows alternately until, on the north-west, it becomes consistently broader.

The Yala people with whom I lived are located where the valley narrows and gorges are formed. The soils here are alluvial, clay-like loams, particularly fertile in the many karst holes which are a common topographical feature. In the past these karst holes (in Kewa called *katupi*) were reserved for the planting of yams (*pira*) and indigenous taro (*ma*), while nowadays they have mostly been turned into coffee gardens. Yam and indigenous taro are now rarely planted and are eaten mostly on special occasions. Sweet potato remains the staple, while Hong Kong taro fills in as a second best when sweet potato harvests are poor. Many varieties of bananas (*kai*) and sugar cane (*wali*) are eaten, as well as various grasses (*alamu, padi*; pidgin *pitpit*), greens (*rani*; pidgin *kumu*), the fruit and nuts of the pandanus (*aga*) and other wild fruit and nuts. Nowadays maize corn, pumpkins, cabbages, cucumbers and tomatoes are also part of people's diets.

Many varieties of sweet potato (*modo, sapi*) are grown in mounds in plots of irregular sizes (varying between 150 and 1,500 square metres) which in people's living memories were used for upward of twenty years without fallowing. The result of this is crops of tiny tubers very unlike the huge ones which people go to Mount Hagen in the Western Highlands to purchase. Elderly informants insisted that they never fallowed in the old days and that they considered the small tubers, which they called *modo kuli*, 'sweet potato bones', extremely tasty.

The Kewa have three types of gardens. The kitchen garden which is found around most houses is called *yamanu* and has mixed cropping. The *modo mapu* contains mainly sweet potatoes although it is sprinkled also with pitpit, sugarcane and various greens. *Emapu* are usually made further away from settlements and are planted mainly with greens and edible grasses. As opposed to the two other types of gardens, the *emapu* are burnt at the end of the year and allowed to fallow. Yala households were found to have an average of half a hectare under cultivation each.[3] Since there are no marked seasons in the area, planting as well as cropping took place throughout the year.

Fauna in the area appears to be scarce. While people insisted that in the past marsupials and cassowaries were plentiful, this is certainly no longer the case. Small marsupials may still be found fairly frequently but cassowaries are a rare treat indeed. Usually they are obtained south of the Erave river, where populations are sparser and wildlife better preserved. Wild pigs are also scarce, although bush rats and birds abound. Another source of protein is wild fowl eggs and river fish, while children especially often eat grubs and termites. As in the rest of the Highlands, the pig is the domesticated animal. In recent years the pig has been joined by cattle and chickens in some households.

The Kewa do not live in villages, but in dispersed nucleated settlements. Population density for the Yala tribe in 1981 was 25 persons per square kilometre. This figure must not be taken to apply to the whole of Kewa area: densities are likely to be higher in the grasslands in the north and lower in the more forested south. Land belongs to the tribe and the clan, and garden land is held in the name of individual men. Women do not own land but garden on their fathers' land when girls and move to their husbands' when they are married. Although residence on marriage is virilocal, women may not stay on in their husband's settlement once they are divorced or widowed.[4] This fact has important implications for the position of women.

The Kewa have no chiefs or hereditary statuses, but in common with other Highlands societies they organize politically around a big man and a cycle of exchange events which, together with warfare in pre-contact days, defined and ranked political groupings and persons. Although men may achieve various gradations of prominence as a result of their personal efforts and charisma, Kewa have no hard and fast social categories which differentiate men. All men may (and in most cases do) achieve economic independence on maturity and marriage, although inequalities continue in the political arena, and this makes possible the control of the group's activities and through that the control of people and their labour power. In the case of male/female relations, differentiations clearly exist and are institutionalized. Although compared to many other Highlands groups Kewa have only mild fears of female pollution and today practise very little sexual separation, women are clearly politically subordinated to men and economically dependent on them. This is the other side of the male 'egalitarian ethos' coin.

The central event in the Kewa social cycle is the periodic pig feast. The frequency of this event for each group varies, depending on inter-group relations and intra-group politics. Of the first sorts of relations, rehabilitation of groups and individuals following warfare is an important example. Reparation payments are still important in this connection. The second consideration – intra-group politics and the concerns of individual men – seems to gain in importance in the pacified Kewa country. In seventeen years (1964–81), the Yala of Agema have killed pigs five times in three different settlements. The events were hosted by three different groups of men, with two groups killing pigs twice in the same settlement, at eleven and thirteen years' intervals.[5]

Although these events cannot be compared in scope and magnificence to their counterparts in other parts of the Highlands where as many as 2,000 pigs may be killed on one occasion, they do nevertheless perform the same function on a humbler scale.

The Kewa are one of the most recently contacted Highlands groups and therefore one of the least 'developed', which in this connection appears to mean 'exploited agriculturally or minerally'. Within the Highlands, the Southern Highlands Province (not only the Kewa) is the poor relation whose young people migrate to the Western and Eastern Highlands and further for cash labour on plantations. They have taken over the position of the Central Highlanders, who in earlier years migrated to rubber and copra plantations and stood in relationship to coastals as the Southern Highlanders now stand to them. Nevertheless there is a sort of Highlands ideology which presents Highlanders as an interest group opposed to coastals, whom they distrust more than Europeans, fearing that they will be less impartial. For their part, many coastals fear that Highlanders are violent and 'uncivilized', and oppose the extension of the Highlands Highway to the south coast for this reason. A Highlands separatist movement did develop in the early 1970s, known as the Highlands Liberation Front (see Standish 1982; Mel 1982; May 1982); but Kewa villagers had little knowledge of this. The parliamentary National Party, although it has its base and origin in the Highlands, is not specifically supported by Kewa villagers who vote for personalities or for kinspeople (when they vote at all) rather than for parties.

Locally the Kewa are administered by the District Office in Kagua and the Kagua Council. In Kagua there is also a High School, a Health Centre, a Post Office, a gaol, and representatives from the Business Development Office and the Department of Primary Industry. There is an airstrip, which is used mostly by missions. People normally fly from Mt Hagen or Mendi if they want to leave the Highlands. Alternatively they can take a truck to Lae in Morobe Province and then a boat to any port. Although Mendi is the provincial capital, many Southern Highlanders look on Mt Hagen as their major town. It is a busier centre, and the gateway to the rest of the country which is inaccessible by road.

Southern Highlanders in general have one of the highest rates of outmigration in the country, but their pattern of migration is 'oscillating' and therefore difficult to quantify (see Josephides and

Schiltz 1980, 1981). The opportunity to work outside their village and Province, though it has precipitated many social problems, has also given many Kewa men and some women an idea of the wider world, as well as a grounding in pidgin. Since the late 1970s the Southern Highlands has had its own Integrated Rural Development Project (launched with a US$ 21 million loan from the World Bank) which includes agricultural, educational and health components. In Kagua two tea plantations owe their birth to this project. However they are doing badly, and there is no indication that they are discouraging young people from offering their labour to employers outside the Province. At the same time, economic developments both within and without the Province have not turned people away from involvement in their own indigenous gift-exchange economy. This may be a reason why village-based business enterprises have so far tended to miscarry.

The book is divided into two parts. Part I provides background materials to Kewa social organization and elaborates the social context in which unequal relations become possible. A historical analysis of group fission and fusion through the activities of warfare and exchange, both pre-eminently carried out by men, illustrates that the figment of agnatic descent which prevails in these conditions renders women peripheral to group ideologies of male solidarity. A closer focus on residence and co-operation as markers of group identity corroborates historical evidence that agnatic ideologies gloss many accretions and genealogical discontinuities. A section on marriage elaborates the position of women and shows that in addition to being ideologically peripheral they are also considered to be sojourners in respect of any group. The argument that they are sojourners is given by men as both the reason and the justification why women may not own land. This inability of women to own land, together with the practice of virilocality and the ideology of agnatic descent groups, is shown to subordinate women to men. Though considerable social changes have taken place in recent years as a result of European contact, the indigenous gift economy remains the dominant mode of social interaction, and therefore the inequalities embedded in it still prevail.

Part II weaves theory with ethnography in an attempt to elucidate gender relations and power relations. These are issues with which a number of anthropologists are currently preoccupied, and the materials in Part I now call for contextualization within this body of literature. Kewa gender relations and idioms undergo analysis, and it is concluded that though an examination of gender categories is necessary in the analysis of the social relations of inequality, it must be undertaken as part of a wider analysis of social relations. Facets of these relations do not make use of gender idioms; nor do all unequal relations operate on divisions informed by sexual differences.

For this reason, the discussion next considers the steps by which inequalities are engendered in practice, rather than the *de facto* position of one social category. It is shown that in spite of the so-called egalitarian ethic, the extent to which 'rights' can be claimed is a function of political influence. This influence is achieved by some men who are successful in convincing the rest of the community that they can provide practical solutions to day-to-day problems. Though allowed an unequal control of group activities, such men can be toppled when they are too blatant in their control, or too consistently unsuccessful in keeping the community running smoothly. Yet the big man's position, though supported by the community, has a hidden aspect. This is the fact that through his control of the political activities of the group the big man also gains some control over the group's labour power.

The political activities of the group concern primarily exchange relations, both within the group and between groups. The periodic pig kill is the most important of these activities, but it has a dual and contradictory function. While it is the occasion on which the group trumpets to the world the solidarity and magnificence of its members, it is also the forum in which male group members compete for prestige. At the same time, the multiple exchanges leading to it provide a smokescreen in which the link between labour and its product is lost. It is the occasion on which the value of women as wives and producers is acknowledged by payments made to their kin, while the products of their labour are quietly appropriated and ceremonially reallocated.

This appropriation and reallocation leads finally to a discussion of how objects may be alienated from producers by being circulated in the exchange system, and how, in this way, labour power may be controlled and inequalities created. The specific processes by which this comes about forms the central theme of this book.

Notes

1   Figure obtained from Franklin 1978.
2   Source of the following two paragraphs: Kagua Patrol Report of 1968–9, Area Study of East and West Sugu Census Division.
3   This was the result of a survey done by Marc Schiltz.
4   Except in cases of late widowhood.
5   In 1964 and 1975, Pisa, Rama and Pupula killed pigs in the old settlements on the ridge. In 1966 and 1979, Mapi and Roga killed pigs in Aka. In 1981, Rimbu and Yadi killed pigs in Yakopaita.

Part One
Structures, groups, and processes

1
Group formation I:
Idioms and practices

A historical presentation of group formation in this chapter highlights the interplay between descent and residence, fission and
fusion, inclusiveness and exclusiveness, and demonstrates that
despite the fact that Kewa groups were perceived within an
overall ideology of agnatic descent they were in practice contingent on warfare and exchange. Since both these activities were
pre-eminently the business of men, the material in this chapter
elucidates women's ambiguous position in group ideologies as
well as in group formation itself.

The *ruru*

The generic name for a social grouping in Kewa is *ruru*, of which
repa is a dialectical variation. The Kewa may refer to their tribe,
their clan, their patrilineage or their family as their *ruru*. The word
is now extended to new political forms: the tribes in the East and
West Sugu census divisions are 'Sugu *ruru*', government officials
and white people are '*kadipi ruru*', and missionaries and church
officials are '*missini ruru*'. *Ruru* organization is extremely varied
and defies classification in terms of labels available to us in
anthropological literature. LeRoy (1975: 16) has described this
difficulty as arising out of a double complexity: geographical
('*repa* are dispersed as a result of group fission') and organizational
('*repa* of different orders of inclusiveness are combined or opposed
within a single community'). Many elements of my own discussion of group structure agree with LeRoy's analysis, but there are
also some divergences. These divergences do not at all invalidate

his analysis; rather, they add more facets to the complexities to which he referred.

LeRoy defines *repa* as 'the elements of Kewa community or "district"' (p. 479). Although a district is composed of several *repa*, its territory is associated with only one or two of these; the rest are related to the land as immigrants (*epea ali*: men who came). The status of immigrant does not imply discrimination as far as access to land is concerned (p. 482). Whereas single immigrants will eventually accrete to the host group and shed their immigrant status, larger groups are likely to retain their original *repa* name and become an element in the *repa* pair or *ruru* cluster. (It is not clear if in such a case an immigrant *repa* would ever lose its immigrant status.) Although LeRoy treats 'forest' and 'grasslands' Kewa separately, the differences are variations which at times he brings under a common denominator. More space is given to the grasslands *ruru* organization because of its greater complexity, and this is the group to which the Kewa south and east of the Sugu river seem more akin, though in dialect and ecology, they diverge. For the sake of simplicity I shall always use the term *ruru* rather than *repa* in my discussion, except where I cite LeRoy directly.

LeRoy describes *ruru* as groups whose members are related through male patrifiliation (though actual links are not always demonstrable), and with a supra-lineage common mythic and historical background (p. 16). They may or may not be subdivided, depending on their size. When they are so divided no word exists to denote the groups formed, but *ruru* may be prefixed by *oge* (small) when it is desired to make the distinction. Two *ruru* may form a pair, or a cluster of *ruru* a 'super-*ruru*', and its members adopt sibling terms. Again, there is no word for such a cluster, but it may be referred to as *ada ruru* (large *ruru*). Depending on the size of the groupings, *ruru* clusters, *ruru* pairs and single *ruru* may be on a par. LeRoy concludes that 'group affiliation inevitably expresses the combined effects of both patrifiliation and transactional relationships' (p. 490), and that

> '*repa*-structure reflects two opposing processes: (1) accretion of other *repa* migrants, which produces a tendency to complexity of structures, and (2) conversion of these migrants, which produces a tendency to simplicity of structure.'
>
> (p. 492)

LeRoy is concerned here with actual group composition, which is an important dimension in the analysis of group structure. I shall adopt his approach when I come to discuss the diachronic aspects of group formation in the case of the Sugu Kewa. At this stage, however, rather than start the discussion at the level of the putative lineage (as LeRoy does) and then characterize the over-arching political unit as a *ruru* cluster, I shall begin instead with the larger political unit, which I shall call the tribe. I employ this approach because the people themselves stress the larger group, so that if you ask a man 'What is your *ruru*?' he will reply giving the name of the largest group to which he belongs, which is unlikely to be his clan or patrilineage. He will call this his 'big name' (*ada ruru*; pidgin, *biknem*). Although in terms of historical formation the tribe may resemble LeRoy's *ruru* cluster, ideologi-cally members do not think of it simply as an alliance between groups but as a higher, more encompassing, and somehow more powerful form.

The tribe, then, is a congeries of clans with varying *de facto* links affected by physical proximity and perceived propinquity in relation to an apical ancestor. This perception, however, is itself a function of political alliance and is subject to revision and reversal. In anthropological discussions, the tribe has been described as 'a politically or socially coherent and autonomous group occupying or claiming a particular territory' (*Notes and Queries* 1960: 66). As well as being associated with a territory, the Kewa tribe shares an ideology of brotherhood encapsulated in the tribal name by which individuals make themselves known. The tribe contains a number of clans, also named, but how widely these names are used depends on the size and complexity of the tribe, and on how far the clan's relations with others in the tribe are necessary for that clan's survival or political identity. Clans are exogamous and claim agnatic descent from a common ancestor, but in-formants were usually unable to trace actual genealogical links at this level. Many clans are subdivided into sections contain-ing one or more patrilineages (*apara*). Often it is impossible to demonstrate genealogical links between patrilineages in a single clan section. When lineages were absorbed from other tribes within living memory this demonstration was not even attempted.

When the tribe is large it is more dispersed, a heterogeneous group which has little in common apart from an overarching name and an ideology of kinship resting on a common story of origin (which may, however, be disputed). Often it may have a history of co-operation in past wars and pig kills. When the tribe is small it will have closer *de facto* connections, especially co-residence. In this case lower subdivisions may be collapsed and the 'big name' become coterminous with some of the levels below it. The tribe comes together for compensation payments, pig kills and the deaths of important members. Land disputes and local minor deaths normally involve only the localities concerned. Involvement in warfare was a more complicated matter, and will be dealt with in a separate section.

Most bushland is held in common by the tribe, and any member may hunt in it or cultivate it. Bushland may also be held by the clan, in which case members of other clans may use it only by permission of the owners. Cultivated land always bears the name of the man who last gardened there, and his permission must be obtained by any other man wanting to use it. Land can also be inherited by individual men: the land on which their father gardened passes on to them. There is some evidence which suggests that in the days before contact, when warfare was endemic, tribal land boundaries were fluid and changing with routed groups moving elsewhere, forging new alliances and receiving new land from their allies. Elderly informants often insisted that in the past there were no land disputes.[1] Enemy land was never appropriated or settled in by a victorious group; it was only devastated and abandoned.

Writing in the early days of the Melanesianists' rebellion against African lineage systems in the New Guinea Highlands, Andrew Strathern was concerned to show the distinction between 'the descriptive statements and idioms in terms of which Hageners refer to the solidarity, continuity and segmentation patterns of their main social groups' and 'the rules which they say apply to processes of recruitment to these groups' (1972: 2). It is difficult nowadays for writers on Highland societies to ignore this well-documented and eloquently argued distinction between ideologies of group formation and constitution and the practical necessities governing actual recruitment to group. Here I want to trace those 'processes of recruitment' by looking at the historical organization of one tribe as it moved through wars and alliances yet retained always a group ideology of continuity.

Yala origins: myth and reality[2]

The Yala tribe consists of about 600 people spread over the three main localities of Agema, Kalu and Wapia, with smaller pockets in Erave in the south, Ita in the north-east, and elsewhere. Altogether there are fifteen clans, some linked by a common story of origin and others through later accretion. Even in the cases where a putative common ancestor is postulated, genealogical links leading to him cannot be demonstrated, since Kewa genealogies are normally no more than four generations deep. Although there is much telescoping, this is not disingenuous. Informants seemed well aware of the places where fudged links existed, and were open about them. Some clans and clan sections are dispersed within the three localities, while others live together in just one (*Figure 1*). There are three major stories of origin, with three corresponding places of origin. The Paripa clan claim they were begotten by Pipi, a huge tree, in Genoka (Aliwi); the Tiarepa clan insist that all Yala descend from Rau of Samberigi; while the Yarepa, Ausparepa, Sularapola and Palerepa cluster of clans have as ancestor Yala, who came from Kuare. Only the first two stories present themselves as mutually exclusive and contradictory, and the groups that tell them adopt antagonistic attitudes. By contrast, the third group is unassuming and offers its story as an

Figure 1   *Yala clans, claimed place of origin, and present residence*

tribe	clan	place of origin	present residence
	Paripa	Aliwi	Agema
	Waluaparepa	Usu	Agema
	Tiarepa	Samberigi	Agema, Ita, Erave
	Yarepa	Kuare	Agema, Kalu
	Ausparepa	Kuare	Agema, Kalu
	Sularapola	Kuare	Kalu
	Palerepa	Kuare	Wapia
	Mapopidipia	Kalu	Agema, Kalu
Yala	Kopereyala	Kalu	Kalu
	Yalapala	Samberigi	Erave
	Sunale	Samberigi	Erave
	Lodorepa	Kuare	Wapia
	Kewai	Kuare	Wapia
	Kalopo	Kuare	Wapia
	Rugialirepa	Kuare	Wapia

addition, not an alternative, to one of the other stories. In Agema this group sees itself as closer to the Paripa clan than the Tiarepa. The stories, briefly, are as follows:

THE STORY OF GENOKA PIPI

At this time the Yala and Perepe tribes did not exist. Three sisters, Ribanu, Wenu and Kamarenu lived in Genoka where they slept in the open because they had no man to build them a house. One day after working hard gathering the edible nuts of the pandanus and making string for their netbags, they grew tired, and sat down to rest. They were in the clearing where the sun beat down on them mercilessly, so Ribanu was happy, when suddenly she felt a certain coolness. She called to Wenu: 'Sister, this place where I am sitting is very pleasantly cool. Come and try it.' Wenu did so, and in turn called Kamarenu who also tried it. Thus all three sisters were impregnated by Pipi, the tree, who had only just then begun to thrust himself out of the ground. Wenu and Kamarenu stayed in Genoka and gave birth to two Perepe clans while Ribanu went to Aliwi and bore the Paripa clan, the Yala core group into which other clans were later married.

THE STORY OF RAU OF SAMBERIGI

Rau lived in Samberigi. He lived only on water; when he saw possums and other game, as well as wild plants, he did not know that they were food for him so he left them. Another man, of Ripurepa, saw him sleeping like a pig and living only on water, so he took him to his house and prepared a feast for him. But since Rau neither ate nor defecated, he had no anus. He became very uncomfortable when his stomach was full of food which he could not discharge, so his new friend tricked him into sitting on a sharp stick which opened his anus. Rau then married this man's sister and was the begetter of all Yala.

THE STORY OF YALA OF KUARE

Two brothers called Yala and Anona left their home in Kuare in search of game. Yala forded the Sugu river at Wakiapada, while Anona did his hunting over the other side. After killing many marsupials Yala wanted to return, but found that the river had swollen, and was no longer fordable. So he threw half of the marsupials to the other side for Anona and walked to Aliwi. There he was befriended by Yala tribespeople who gave him gardens and a girl to work with him as his sister. One day some years later Yala and his sister were preparing to attend a courting session (*romedi*). Before setting off, Yala climbed up a banana tree in order to bind the fruit. His sister looked up at him and saw his genitals. Improper thoughts came to her. 'Why should I leave my nice gardens, and why should my brother marry another woman?' she mused wistfully, and threw a yam up at him, hitting his genitals. Yala was shocked at the thought of marrying his sister but other Yala men thought nothing of it. They divided themselves into wife takers and wife givers, and Yala and his sister were married. They gave birth to the following clans: Yarepa, Ausparepa, Sularapola and Palerepa.

The story of Genoka Pipi, told by elders of the Paripa and Umba clan sections, links the Yala to the Perepe tribe living on adjacent land. The phonetic closeness of the names Perepe and Paripa is naturally of interest, and leads to speculation as to whether in fact the Paripa clan is a group broken off from this tribe. What is also of interest is the fact that when members of the Perepe tribe tell the story of Pipi they leave out Ribanu and mention only two of the sisters, Wenu and Kamarenu, who gave birth to the Perepe clans. These Perepe clans, Maita and Malipu, do acknowledge a special relationship with the Paripa but call this a 'cousin' relationship (*kai*) and explain it in terms of a bride given to a Paripa leader three generations ago (the grandfather of a man still living in 1980). Though most other Yala clans accept the Pipi story of origin as 'probably true', the Tiarepa are vociferous in rejecting it in favour of their own account of Rau and argue at the same time that the Paripa story is of recent coinage, circulated only after the Yala and Perepe started disputing land boundaries. (Both the Perepe and Yala claim the tract of land adjacent to Aliwi, where Ribanu is said to have moved to when she conceived by Pipi.) It was well-known that Pipi was the ancestor of the Perepe, Tiarepa say, but Ribanu is a new and opportunistic addition to the story.

Yet the Tiarepa's own story does not square with other acknowledged facts. It is accepted by all that some generations ago a man called Riesi of Wapiripa tribe fled from warfare in Samberigi and came to Agema, where he married a Paripa clan woman named Popanu. They had a son, Ulu, who in turn had Liwa, who bore Mara. Mara bore Yokoto and Yokoto bore Gapea, an elderly man still living in 1980. These acknowledged events are inconsistent with the claim that 'all Yala came from Samberigi, begotten by Rau', especially since Riesi[3] came of a clan known as Wapiripa, remnants of which are still found in Samberigi. Another fact to be noted is the existence of a tribe adjacent to the Yala and their traditional enemies, the Tiarepa of Yagore. When relations between the Paripa and Tiarepa are at a low ebb the Paripa will sometimes say:

'They are really another *ruru*. We are not sure where they came from. We know only that Gapea's *ruru* came from Samberigi and married Popanu [*Figure 2*]; others came from Yagore, became friends (pidgin *putim wanbel*, became of one belly) and called themselves Tiarepa.'

This view is reinforced by the fact that only one generation ago Likasi of Tiarepa Yagore joined the Tiarepa Yala and his sons are now incorporated into the Tiarepa clan and known as Yala. The Tiarepa Yala themselves, noting the existence of the Tiarepa of

Figure 2   *Tiarepa and Paripa clan sections, origins and intermarriage*

clan	Tiarepa		Paripa	
clan section	Yalinai	Ulu	Umba	Paripa
			RIBANU = PIPI	
			KAIMA	
		Riesi =	Popanu	
clan→ fission	Yalinai	Ulu	Duni	Poya ←clan fission
	Oropo	Liwa	Yamanu	Sepa
	Ali	Mara	Yawi	Perea
	Koya	Yokoto	Kogalepa	Awei
	Kodo	Gapea	Wapa	Rama

Yagore, the Tiarepa of Kuare and the Perepe Tiarepa, will
sometimes say that they used to be one group in the past but have
now split up. They cite as an example of this process what is
presently happening in the nearby village of Mugiri, where two
sections of the resident tribe have begun to call themselves by two
different place-names.

Finally, the Rau story itself has the structure of a *lidi*, a narrative
form not generally believed to be true but laughed off as a mere
myth, without rhyme or reason. The first time the story was
narrated to me it was in fact typified as a *lidi*, and only subsequently was the status of *re agele* (story of origin) claimed for it. Riesi's
marrying into Paripa, on the other hand, is a fact of a different
order. Both clans remember learning from elderly men how in
Yawi's time the Tiarepa clan, already growing in numbers,
obtained a piece of land from the neighbouring Kamarepa tribe,
for which they paid with a prized pearlshell (*kalusekere*). Yawi was
the grandfather of a living Paripa elder (Wapa) and his name has a
special significance for the clan. It serves as a temporal marker
between what can be known and what can only be guessed at. 'In
the time of Yawi' means that the event to be recounted is really
true, but it is as far back as truth can reach. Anything before that is
a popular story whose complete veracity can never be completely
ascertained. While there is obvious telescoping between Riesi and
Liwa (Ulu is the ancestor of a Tiarepa clan section), and Yawi
probably did not live at the same time as Ulu and certainly would
not have known Riesi (see *Figure 2*), the fact remains that invoking
the name of Yawi gives the account a truth value which is
unassailable.

The story of Yala from Kuare is the most uncontroversial one,
being a straightforward account of how one set of clans originated
and joined an existing group by means of double recruitment: first
by filiation and then by marriage. Although origin from Yala is
claimed consistently only for the set of clans indicated in *Figure 1*,
all Wapia Yala tell a variant of this story. They do not claim that
this is the origin of all Yala everywhere, and nobody draws any
conclusions from the fact that the Kuare ancestor's name was
Yala. This is almost like a conspiracy of silence: when questioned
on the origins of the tribal name[4], all narrators confess to per-
plexed ignorance.

My information about the Yala is not evenly detailed, mainly
because of the dispersal of the tribe. Since I lived in Agema this

section was the focus of my analysis, for two reasons: because my links with it were more intimate, and because the other sections themselves associated me with the Agema which possibly encouraged them to present Agema-focused information about their own origins and organization. It may well be that *Figure 1* is too simplified in respect of sections living in Wapia and Kalu, and that in different circumstances these may present different stories of origin linking them with other clans. I am uncertain also in specific cases whether forces of fission or accretion were involved in the formation of new clans and clan sections. In the following

Figure 3   *Agema clans, clan sections and lineages*

clan	clan section[1]	lineage
Paripa[2]	Paripa	no distinctions
	Umba	inchoate distinctions[3]
Tiarepa	Ulu	Yokorepa / Repotorepa[4]
	Yalinai	Koyarepa
	?	Likasirepa[5]
Waluaparepa		no distinctions
Yarepa		no distinctions
Ausparepa		Remorepa[6] / Yembirepa / Rurirepa
Mapopidipia		Roalirepa / Kagarepa

Notes
1 Some clan sections/ lineages created by accretion, others by fission; not always known which
2 Umba and Paripa are on the way to becoming differentiated clans, more so, for instance, than Ulu and Yalinai
3 Inchoate distinctions from Umba lineages include a group living in a different settlement from the rest of the Umba and another man who threatens that his children 'will go a different way' (Kiru)
4 Repotorepa is large and dispersed, some sections living in Ita. They are the sons of three brothers
5 Likasi joined the Tiarepa only in the last generation, coming from Yagore
6 Although I have named the lineages which have no links, they are not necessarily referred to by those names by the people except for the purposes of specification and clarification

discussion, then, I shall concentrate in more detail on the Agema Yala.

Six clans are represented in Agema: the Paripa, Tiarepa, Waluaparepa, Yarepa, Ausparepa and Mapopidipia. *Figure 3* sets out the relations among them, their clan sections and lineages. A continuous line linking clans to clan sections or lineages represents cases of fission where two brothers, descendants of an apical ancestor, split to form two groups.[5] Telescoping and fiction may be involved here, but the point is that there is an attempt to make the link. Where a dotted line appears, however, no such attempt is made and the groups linked in this way may come from different backgrounds.

Although genealogical links between the clan sections of Umba and Paripa are close, the two are on the way to becoming differentiated clans; much more so, for instance, than the two Tiarepa clan sections. Also, within Umba itself there are inchoate distinctions. The clan section consists of six, normally undifferentiated, two-generation lineages: those of three true brothers (Areli, Yamola, Wapa) and those of three fathers' father's sons – that is, both to each other and to the set of brothers (Noyopa, Adawi and Perapu: see *Figure 4*).

Following a disagreement over a pig kill in 1966, members of Yamolarepa[6] joined the Tiarepa clan with which they are now living, and the rift has never been healed. A member of another lineage, Noyoparepa, has had disagreements with Waparepa for a long time, and threatened that his children would go a different way after the 1981 pig kill.

Within the Tiarepa clan, Repotorepa can demonstrate no genealogical link with Yokorepa in Ulu clan section, while Likasirepa is known to have come from the neighbouring Tiarepa of Yagore in the last generation. The Waluaperepa and Yarepa are poorly represented and therefore more homogeneous, although within Agema they tend to have closer links with some clans than

Figure 4 *Umba lineages*

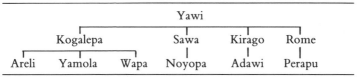

with others. Ausparepa is also small, consisting of three *repa* claiming common ancestry yet unable to demonstrate genealogical links. Mapopidipia, the bulk of which lives in Kalu, is represented by two men, also unable to show links. All clans are exogamous. No cases of intra-clan marriages were recorded. People often claim that marriage within the tribe is incestuous, and that such marriages should not take place ideally and did not take place in the past. However, this is not borne out by fact. The relationship between Tiarepa and Paripa, founded on the initial marriage of Riesi and Popanu, has been reduplicated by a number of marriages. Yet people were careful to point out that Paripa may not marry into that particular lineage which descended in a straight line from Riesi. Paripa also may not marry into Yarepa and Ausparepa, because Yarepa and Ausparepa do not intermarry, nor do they marry into the Waluaparepa with whom they have been living too closely. Mapopidipia, because of the Kalu connection, does not marry Yarepa or Ausparepa, or, by extension, Paripa. (In fact, the last three clans shared in the bridewealth when a Tiarepa boy married a Mapopidipia girl.) Within Agema, then, only sections of Tiarepa will marry into other clans. Following from the foregoing discussion, three factors appear to inform marriage prohibitions: clan membership, close relations as a result of co-residence over time, and past marriages. The first two factors directly relate to the next topic to be discussed: that is, the practice and effects of warfare.

This account of one tribe has given an indication of the variety of processes involved in group formation. Accretion, fission and fusion all play a part in the constant restructuring and redefinition of the group. However, this state of fluidity cannot be acknowledged in group ideologies which require a solidarity based on a firmer, fixed bond. Hence the necessity for a stable idiom to refer to the relationship binding members of a group together.[7] This is the idiom of kinship, and especially agnatic descent. According to this idiom all same generation group members are brothers who must demonstrate their siblingship in their everyday relations, especially by sharing and exchanging goods.[8] At the time of large accretions this 'siblingship' is expressed in the joint pig kill, when the celebrating group defines itself as a group and distinguishes itself from others, to which it may make war reparation payments. Internally, exchange among participant 'brothers' consolidates their relationship as agnates and glosses their true genealogical links. Thus the idiom of agnatic descent does not exclude non-agnates from being full members of the group; it does, however, exclude women (see Lederman 1982: 118), who cannot pass as 'brothers'; and this is an important function of this ideology. Another aspect of this ideology, that is, that all male group members are in a position of 'equality', has implications for the exercise of political leadership within the group. This question will be developed further in Chapter 6.

Warfare

War alliances and movements as a result of warfare were very important in processes of group fission and fusion. At the same time, the constraints governing this activity illustrate how it was itself affected by group structure and inter-group cross-cutting kinship relations and loyalties, as well as by the indomitable restraints imposed by the spatial organization of these groups and the awareness that the statuses of friend and foe were transient. (Often people would say that in the old days there were no friends, only enemies.) An overview, then, of the general conduct of war will precede a discussion of some actual wars fought by the Yala.

In his article 'The Adaptive Significance of Systems of Ceremonial Exchange and Trade in the New Guinea Highlands', C. J. Healey (1978: 200–01) draws a contrast between the sort of war waged by the Maring on the one hand, and the Melpa and Mae Enga on the other, linking the differences to ecological and demographic as well as social, factors. Healey cites evidence that 'most Maring wars were motivated by a desire to extract vengeance for killings and other aggressive acts by enemies, rather than for territorial expansion', such expansion being 'inhibited by a taboo on consuming the pigs and crops abandoned by fleeing enemy, and through fear of the spirits or harmful sorcery of the enemy lurking on their abandoned land'. In these wars deaths were generally few, and routed populations split into smaller groups seeking refuge with allies. These groups usually reformed and reoccupied their ancestral land. Thus

> 'While Maring warfare resulted in periodic redistribution of people between territories and territories between local populations, the outbreak of war does not appear to correlate

with demographic pressure on the land . . . Land was probably more frequently redistributed between local populations by peaceful means.'

(Healey 1978: 200–01)

Among the Mae Enga, on the other hand, 'encroachment of one local population on the land of another, or the desire to gain control of more land, was the immediate cause of over half of all wars'. This did not necessarily mean that the encroaching group was short of land; the overriding aim 'was to destroy the occupying group so that it could never re-form and recover its land' (Meggitt, cited in Healey 1978). While Melpa groups were not as a rule destroyed as groups when routed, Healey says that warfare in their case, as with the Mae, 'appears to have been less circumscribed by formal rules of battle and, potentially at least, considerably more bloody'. Also, no taboo on harvesting enemy gardens appears to have operated, and the two groups were not loth to occupy enemy territory.

Healey's larger thesis, a typology attempting to show an inverse relationship between elaborate ceremonial exchange dominated by big men, high population density and territorial expansion through war on the one hand and emphasis on trade on the other, cannot be proven in the case of the Kewa; but we shall see that the comments made about Maring warfare could apply equally well to them.

Strategies and motivations in warfare

According to elderly informants, the Sugu Kewa never went to war over land.[1] Although victorious groups would pillage gardens and seize pigs, plunder was never the motive for warfare. No hostages were ever taken (though sometimes nubile women were taken as wives), and enemy land was burnt and left to return to bush. The most common cause for war was vengeance. If a clan member is killed the clan must retaliate. Thus war was usually a punitive expedition. A second stated aim of war was for the group to establish a reputation as fierce warriors and therefore forestall possible attacks, while a third was for individuals to gain prestige by the high head counts of adversaries killed. This was a highly competitive area among men within groups.

Formal warfare was governed by rigid rules which informants claimed were never infringed. These concerned mainly the timing and duration: warning of impending attack was always given, sometimes by a wife from the group to be attacked or by a man who had matrilateral links there, or sometimes by the aggressors themselves *en masse*. On one occasion the Yala made a declaration of war on the Tiarepa of Yagore in the following way: another two tribes, the Kamarepa and Koiari, were killing pigs in the village of Roga and had invited both the Yala and Tiarepa to eat. The Yala arrived in their war decorations (*yada au*), and singing the war cry of *uuu*, followed by the chant *Yakitesi kari kibu robenuri adopiripa*. (The Tiarepa big man will see the trees on their mountain cut down; that is, men will be killed.) After the declaration of war was delivered both sides would erect palisades around their settlements, up to five in all. The following morning at first light the aggressors would put on their war paint, approach the enemy settlement and start on the war dance, meeting the enemy in a pitched battle. Within every group there was a war leader (*muduali*) who organized the battle and led the warriors into the field. Another function was that of the big man (*amoali*) who watched the hostilities from a nearby hill, a strategic position which enabled him to intercept retreating or wounded warriors with fiery words calculated to send them back to the battlefield. Once the war leader was killed, however, the battle was over. The warriors scattered about in confusion and were easily overpowered.

When the attackers broke through the third palisade the defenders would give orders to vacate. A tiresome pig would be abandoned first and a tiresome child soon after. 'We can beget more', the men would say. A second rule of warfare was that at nightfall hostilities should cease so that combatants could eat and sleep in peace. However, if the outcome of the battle was already decided the victors would freely roam the settlement of the vanquished looking for food, and kill anyone who came their way. This rule of night-truce was not followed in the case of smaller skirmishes, as in raids or ambushes. A group usually resorted to these tactics when it did not feel strong enough to win a battle, notably after it had already been routed and scattered, and was now seeking to avenge a death sustained in that defeat.

Wives from enemy groups were not victimized at the time of war; they were considered to be part of the group into which they married. Often they acted as go-betweens to notify their natal group of hostile intentions. The husbands of such women always avoided killing their in-laws, but if such deaths nevertheless occurred the husband would return home and hand his wife his bloodied axe. He then had to stay and mourn with her, for if he left her in her sorrow and rejoined the battle misfortune would strike. If his wife was pregnant the child would not be normal; if they already had children they would come to grief; their gardens would not be fertile.

Women claimed to be ignorant of, and unconcerned about, the reasons for wars, which they said were men's affairs. They often hid in the bush with their children when their husbands were on the attack. They would be concerned, however, if the battle was with their natal group. One Tiarepa woman married into Yala had just had a baby girl when the Yala attacked the Tiarepa. She said that she would have thrown the baby into the river[9] if her brother had been killed. But she had never heard of a man killing his *pali* (wife's brother).

The decision to go to war was never a unanimous one among allies, or even within one tribe or clan. This is the key to the intriguing question of why a warring group should take the trouble to warn another group that it is about to attack. This lack of unanimity was the result of the inextricable and intricate affinal and consanguineal relations linking neighbouring groups. The man who has such links will take care not to be in the van of the warring party in case his matrilateral cousin or affine kills him by mistake. If he himself came across one of these people he prepared his bow and made as if to shoot, but directed the arrow into the air at the last moment. If he killed his wife's brother she and his children would die if they accepted food from his hands.

Thus although war was endemic, killing was not indiscriminate. Warfare was imperative as an expression of political and territorial integrity, an ideological source of prestige and power both within and without the group, a warning and an assertion of aggression. As part of the wider inter-group social relations, it delineated the group and determined its social organization. But although war was imperative, and its call must always be obeyed, there operated also a set of binding personal loyalties that could be ignored only on pain of great misfortune. It may be more correct to characterize these loyalties as a set of taboos: in-laws and matrilateral kin were on no account to be killed.

The Kewa did not conduct war expeditions to faraway places, but fought mainly with their neighbours. Alliances were constantly shifting and wars easily sparked off. 'We did not fight our neighbours when they were being neighbourly', Yala men say. 'But when they stole our pigs, vegetables or women we went to war with them.' This proximity of the enemy coupled with the transience of enemy status is one factor towards explaining why Kewa never took hostages or seized land. Marriage by capture invariably had to be made good when relations were normalized with erstwhile enemies. Likewise, hostages would have become an embarrassment when peace was restored, or even impeded the restoration of peace. In any case, the status of 'slave' or second-class kinsman was not developed in the area.

Peace was referred to as 'time of no war' (*go yapi yada dia*). A group never thought itself at peace while it was dispersed and living with allies away from its own ancestral land. The small units into which it was forced to split felt weak and dependent and easily became roped into the wars of their hosts, wars to which they may have felt scant commitment. Real peace was a regrouping and a return to the ancestral lands. These regroupings, it must be pointed out, were never complete, or at least were never of exactly the same people as had fled before, especially if the flight had lasted many years. Pockets of clan members may have taken root elsewhere and chosen to stay, while refugees from other tribes may have been assimilated and taken back. This is where war can be seen to reshape groups and redraw tribal boundaries. These redefinitions must then be consolidated and given the stamp of permanence. Longhouses (*neada*) were built, pigs were killed, and reparation payments were made to allies at this time. Another war would not normally be embarked on before these things were done.

Some major Yala wars

The following account is drawn from the narratives of six different men (Wapa, Pupula, Gapea, Rama, Rambe, Koai). I employed various manoeuvres in constructing a historical sequence for the wars, but none of these was completely foolproof. Nevertheless, I do not believe that any slip-up in the sequence or spacing of events would lead to a significant misreading or misrepresentation. *Map 4* will make the narratives easier to follow, while the Appendix at the end of the book gives a chronological list of the wars, together with the ostensible reasons for their outbreak.

Famous wars are usually referred to by name. *Mena lo yada* (war over pig's belly), fought in the 1930s, was the prelude of a major clan dispersal. At the time a number of small *ruru*[10] brought together by warfare and living close to the Yala had built long-houses in preparation for a joint pig kill. They invited to the feast people from as far south as Samberigi and as far north as Kagua. When the feast was over and everyone was returning home a man of Amburupa *ruru* from Tiripi, goaded by his wife, killed another guest from Samberigi. The men of Samberigi complained to their hosts, and all the host *ruru* waged war on the Amburupa in consequence. The Perepe and Ala tribes, then living in Katiloma in the east Sugu area, went to the aid of the Amburupa, at the time their co-residents. The Yala divided themselves in the following way: the Ausparepa, Tiarepa and Yarepa clans helped the Perepe, the Waluaparepa helped the Koiari, and Paripa split itself in half and fought on both sides. The division was actually on residence lines: Naguri and Papolata, that is, Paripa, Ausparepa, Tiarepa and Yarepa clans, were for the Perepe; and Popa, Agema and Awari, that is, Paripa and Waluaparepa clans, for the Koiari. And so the Yala fought on opposite sides the whole day without killing each other (cf. Meggitt 1977: 18), and in the evening came to rest in their joint settlements. This, informants claimed, did not create tensions or hostilities among the Yala themselves. The realities however may have been somewhat more complicated, as the following incident illustrates:

'Yanyali, a Yala helping the Perepe, was killed by the Koiari. Sawa, another Yala but helping the Koiari, heard of this and lay in wait to avenge Yanyali's death. As the Koiari, battle-weary, were returning home, Sawa drew his arrow and shot down Koiari Rudu.'

This death was not forgotten or forgiven, as the next war shows. This was *mena yada* (war over a pig). Two friends, a Yala and a Kabia, caught a pig belonging to the Tiarepa of Yagore and tethered it near Yokoto's cemetery on Yala land. The pig made a mess, and in a fit of anger Yokoto killed it. The two men who had caught the pig then cooked and ate it, taunting the Tiarepa with its

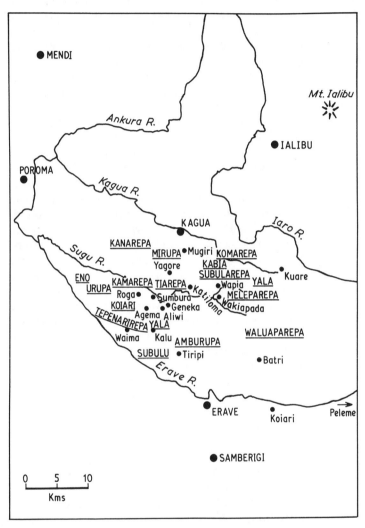

Map 4 *Approximate locations of some Sugu ruru*

bones. The Tiarepa recruited various *ruru* with a grudge against the Yala and waged war on them. These included the Koiari, still nursing a grievance for the unavenged killing of Rudu in the *mena lo yada*; and the Yaka, Eno, Komarepa, Paisa, Mirupa, Tepenarirepa, Kamarepa and Subulu, against whom half of Yala had fought in the previous war. The Perepe and the Amburupa, who might have helped the Yala, had been chased out in the same war, and the Kambia had been vanquished earlier. (This was why the Kambia man was living with the Yala.) The Yala, with no allies, were consistently beaten back until there was no more room to retreat, so one night they stole out to Wapia.[11]

While the Agema Yala were staying with the Wapia Yala, war broke out between the neighbouring two groups, Wabea and Waluaparepa. The Agema went to the assistance of the Waluaparepa, while the Wapia fought with the Wabea, Yala clansmen again taking care not to kill one another. For this reason the war is known as *Wapia rekele pi yada*, (war in which Wapia was split in half). Many Agema Yala then fled to Bala near Battri, while some stayed on in Wapia. In Bala they were again pursued by war; three neighbouring groups, the Adai, Enali and Yatupa, were attacked by the joint forces of the Kamarepa and Waluaparepa, whom the Yala had assisted while in Wapia. However, the Yala now ranged themselves on the opposite side, fighting against Waluaparepa. The Yala were defeated (they suffered five deaths) and wandered about for months sleeping on rocks and in caves until they reached Kanada, the new home of the Amburupa since they were beaten at *mena lo yada*. However the Perepe, who had a grievance against Yala on account of some unavenged deaths at the time of the *mena lo yada*, heard that they were in Kanada and came armed. The Yala were trapped inside the men's house and many girls sitting outside were killed. Two Yala men died in the ensuing battle, and the rest fled down the Erave river to Peleme, past the present government station. It was a different language area where they had no kinspeople, but they stayed for four months.

The Yala were now dispersed. Some were in Wapia, some in Peleme, a small rump in Alepea near Puli, and one man, Tupa, of Tiarepa clan, was living in Katiloma. Tupa had quarreled with his clan brother Sawa over a valuable pearlshell, so when the rest of his clan went to Wapia he stayed in Katiloma. Here he was killed in a night raid by the Ala, at the time living with the Meleperepa of Wakiapada. In the meantime one Tepenarirepa man, Maisa, was in Erave recruiting Kewa (i.e. southern) dancers for a pig kill prepared by the Tiarepa of Yagore (who had initially chased the Yala out of Agema in the *mena yada*). Maisa was sorry for the Yala's predicament and asked them to accompany him to his home in Wata. So the Yala came north again, hiding in the ranks of the Kewa dancers going to Yagore. However, before long there was trouble in Wata, where the Tepenarirepa were living together with the Paisa. A Paisa man, Peawi, was killed by the *kopayo* spirit. Since the neighbouring Eno were the owners of the *kopayo* cult, they were held responsible for the death, and the Paisa retaliated by killing Eno Karia. As a result, the Eno, Yala, Komarepa and Pamarepa placed Wata under siege. Two Yala men were killed and the rest fled again to Wapia.

To some extent regrouped in Wapia, the Yala now learnt of Tupa's death. In an unsuccessful attack on Wakiapada they suffered another casualty when the Meleparepa killed a Paripa Yala, Regepea. In retaliation, a small Yala raiding party burnt down a Meleparepa spirit house, killing one man. But now Regepea was unavenged. Some time later the Kanarepa and Waluaparepa attacked the Meleparepa and killed Yakema, the slayer of Regepea. Instead of rejoicing, the Yala joined forces with the Meleparepa against their attackers. [12]

Although the Kabia and the Yala were normally friendly ('brothers', they said), Raisi, a Kabia man, provoked a Yala attack. Yala Karia was cutting some bamboo shoots (*kelekele malo*) for Raisi when the latter mocked him, saying that with this valuable bamboo-head pearlshell (*kalusekere*) he would compensate the Yala for the death of Regepea. This was a taunt to the Yala for leaving their dead unavenged; it smarted so much that the Yala sacked Ragu, the home of the Kabia. But later they joined the Kabia, Kamarepa, Subularepa, Eno, Kanarepa and Perepe in order to sack Pagore.

In the meantime the Kamarepa had chased the Koiari out of their land in Roga and now invited the Yala to return to their own territories in Agema. This marked the end of the Yala wanderings. Immediately preparations started for a pig kill. Hardly were the pigs eaten than the Pamarepa waged war on the Kamarepa, the Eno, and the Urupa. Pamarepa had the upper hand and Kamarepa Gapea called out for assistance to the Yala. Only three men, of Paripa and Ausparepa clans, responded; the rest were for Pamarepa. Within the Paripa there was disagreement about whom to support, and when Paripa Malupa was mortally wounded by the Pamarepa he blamed the war leader, Wapa, who made him fight against them when in fact he wanted to support them. The war leader said: 'Never mind, we'll get handsome compensation for you from our allies.' Then he (Wapa) killed Ralu, the Pamarepa war leader, and the war was over. A joint pig kill was held with the Kamarepa, Eno, Urupa and Perepe, where compensation was received for Malupa. A few more battles were fought, most notably with the Tiarepa of Yagore, before Pax Australiana was established in the 1950s.

This overview of some Kewa wars has been necessarily eclectic, perhaps at times even somewhat misleading. For instance, the section opens with a general discussion of warfare which is probably idealized, in that the rigid rules referred to there may not have been adhered to in all types of wars. I would be reluctant, on the other hand, to liken these formal wars to the tournament-type joustings described by Meggitt (1977) for the Enga: for they were certainly earnest wars, not rehearsals or sporting events.

The description of some actual wars fought by the Yala perhaps redresses the balance between the ideal and the real, though here too there may be biases. For instance, the ostensible reasons given for wars may sometimes be only partial ones, while at other times (when Yala went to the assistance of other groups) the original reasons for the outbreak of the war (*yada re*) were not known by Yala informants. Yet there is overwhelming evidence that most wars were concerned more with the rights of, and rights to, people, than with the 'politics of property'.[13] In other words, in so far as the distinction can be made, they were political rather than economic.

Whatever inaccuracies of the sort referred to may be contained in these accounts they nevertheless do not affect the main point of this exposition, which is to examine the alignments in each subsequent war. In Meggitt's (1977) discussion of warfare, in spite of the fact that clans of the same phratry may fight against one another, there is always an appeal to larger groups in wars with clans of other phratries. Among the Kewa there can be no such appeal, for there really are no permanent larger groups, only shifting alliances. This is what the study of warfare tells us about the constitution and restructuring of groups, as it shows the same groups ranged on different sides in a sequence of wars, sometimes seemingly quite irrationally. At the same time the eventual regrouping in tribal territories and the retention of tribal names conceals the fact that the composition of the group may have changed, that pockets may have been shed in various places and new adherents amalgamated. A paradox should perhaps be made explicit here. Although the motive for going to war was never the acquisition of land or other property but rather the routing of the enemy and his destruction as enemy (not, I hasten to say, his extermination), the historical outcome of battles could and did lead to a redistribution of land and changing boundaries. When a group was scattered, its solidarity was unavoidably weakened, and whether it could rebuild that solidarity on the same lines again depended largely on the time span – the period of its enforced dispersal and the sort of refuge it had taken. The imposed peace of the 1950s froze any further movement in the Sugu area, apart from a return to tribal territories by some groups living in exile. The present distribution of the Yala and other tribes is in fact attributable to this freezing of settlement within tribal territories; in the absence of such a peace it is unlikely that localities would have congealed in the way they have.

Yet in spite of the cessation of warfare and the end to the constant displacement of whole tribes or clans at one stroke, settlements are still 'pulsating' within tribal territories and allegiances continue to be transient and changeable. Chapter 2 will discuss these 'pulsating' settlements and demonstrate that they are created by the demands of the periodic pig kill; while in Chapter 7 a more detailed analysis of the significance of the pig kill will be undertaken.

The enquiry into the nature of Kewa groups has led, in this chapter, to an historical analysis of group formation. Groups proved refractory to a model of social organization that posits absolute and static categories with neat boundaries and regular configurations. While the group was fluid and its recruitment open (a condition necessitated by the exigencies of warfare), the figment of agnatic descent bolstered a male group solidarity which had at least two important implications. One was that male group members, as 'brothers', enjoyed a certain equality (this affects questions of leadership to be discussed in Chapter 6). The other was to render women ideologically peripheral. This position of women was suggested almost by omission, because female organization and aspirations do not inform the accounts tendered by either sex as being determinant of the structure, organization and activities of the group. Thus in this chapter there has been little direct discussion of women's roles. In the following one the idea of women's marginality will be further developed, while their physical membership of groups as residents will be considered in the light of this peripheral status.

Notes

1 It is true that since pacification there have been a number of land disputes; but I would maintain that in the past fighting was not over gaining access to another group's land, and that no land disputes existed of the type that exist today. I have this evidence to cite:

   a I have details of twenty wars, not one of them having land as given reason (see Appendix).

   b All plots of land disputed nowadays are strategically or commercially important in modern ways: they are near vehicular roads, in valleys, planted with coffee or suitable for coffee. Nobody is fighting over settlements on ridges. In Erave Patrol Report 3 (1971), two such disputes are discussed. Both concern 'economically useful areas', with cattle, coffee and chillies.

   c Most boundary disputes are between groups which were allies at the time of independence and living together on the land concerned. It is of interest here that when warfare chased out one group in the old days the refugees would not simply go and settle in land vacated by another group in a previous war. They would settle only with other groups in established settlements. Likewise the victorious group would not move (or expand) and settle in the land of their routed enemy, but celebrate with their allies, rejoicing in the fact that they still inhabited their tribal land. There was pride in inhabiting one's own father's land, rather than another man's father's land.

2 Marie Reay (1968) has the following to say about the definition of 'myth' in Melanesia:

   'A myth is a story expressing a theory about the unknown which is taken seriously – either as historical fact or as some kind of mystical or moral truth . . . In calling a story a "myth" we do not imply anything about the truth or falsity of it.'

   (Reay 1968: 464)

3 *Rie-si* means 'tree's son', or 'little tree', and Tiarepa therefore 'the tree clan'. The letters T and R easily slide into each other. In the Sugu Kewa dialect the normal word for tree is *repena*, for which reason Tiarepa is also referred to as Repenarepa.

4 As to tribal names, it must be noted here that many recur consist-

ently among Kewa tribes and clans, while others are phonetically very similar (e.g. Paripa/Perepe).

5 In his article 'Siblingship and descent in Kewa ancestries', LeRoy elaborates on the recurrent theme of pairs of brothers featuring in Kewa ancestry. He interprets this not as factual history but as what he calls 'the idea of sociality' (1981: 35). The listing of ancestors is then seen as a statement linking the past to the present, legitimizing male group solidarity now.

6 For analytic reasons I have named lineages in *Figure* 3 which cannot demonstrate genealogical links to clans. This does not mean that these lineages are significant social groupings necessarily differentiated and named by the people themselves in normal circumstances. On the contrary, glossing is the norm. Only for the purposes of specification and clarification will a minute breakdown be given, and then only if it is known.

7 It is interesting to note how the enduring Kewa metaphoric songs such as *tupale* avoid exposing this disjuncture between group continuity and recruitment to group by never referring to large tribal territories and tribal names. Instead they sing about small bush areas and use alternative group names, which can then be interpreted in a number of ways (for examples of *tupale*, see Josephides 1982a).

8 Writing about Kewa reciprocity, LeRoy (1975) distinguishes between co-operation and exchange and argues that exchange is a relationship between affines while co-operation characterizes the relations among agnates. This thesis cannot be sustained by social practices observed in my fieldwork area, where brothers co-operated little but exchanged frequently. Although myths circulate which stress co-operation, and men themselves claim that in an ideal situation, co-operation should prevail, actual instances of co-operation are limited, as Chapter 2 will show. In Chapter 7 I discuss in some detail the many exchanges entered into by brothers. The tables of transactions produced there demonstrate clearly that most exchanges at the time of the pig kill were among agnates.

9 An older woman recounted how she had killed her baby daughter when her husband, fighting at the time, failed to visit her in the *rameada* (birth hut) three days after she had given birth. Her husband beat her for it, but if the baby had been a boy he might have killed her. Both husband and wife were berated by the big man.

10 Including: Koiari, Kamarepa, Eno, Subulu, Pamarepa, Tepenarepa, Yaka, Mamarepa, Paisa, Mirupa, Urupa.

11 I asked why the Yala performed such a provocative act when they knew they were in a weak position. The war was not planned, I was told. The two rubbish men (*tieboali*) who stole the pig did not consult anyone, and Yokoto killed it in a fit of anger because it had fouled the cemetery.

12 According to Regepea's brother Rama (in his fifties in 1980), the Yala helped the Meleperepa avenge Yakema, Regepea's slayer, for

two reasons. First, because the Meleperepa were closer neighbours; if they had gone to the assistance of the other two the Meleperepa would have raided their undefended homesteads. Second, the Yala thought, quite rightly, that if they helped the Meleperepa they would eventually receive compensation for Regepea's death. They finally did, in 1980.

13   'Many, perhaps most, of these clashes are expressions of the politics of property; that is, they concern the rights claimed by particular people to control or utilize particular commodities' (Meggitt 1977: 12). For the Enga, the list of these commodities is headed by land. The Kewa fought over stolen pigs and women, but mainly in order to avenge homicide.

2
Group formation II: 'Base-men of the place' and women sojourners

This chapter focuses on the settlement patterns and composition of residential groups, as well as the degree to which their members co-operate. The aim of this investigation is to bring into sharper relief the position of women in social groups. Rules and practices according to which women are recruited to groups are important here. Descent is mentioned only in passing, for daughters do not normally remain in the group after reaching adulthood. Marriage is discussed as the major form of recruitment, and the status of wives in their husbands' clans is scrutinized with a view to establishing the cultural variables which determine gender relations.

Residential groups: settlement patterns and composition

Traditionally, Sugu Kewa did not live in nucleated villages but in dispersed clusters of homesteads spread over the tribal territory. I shall refer to these as 'settlements'. A reconstruction of some of these is given in *Figure 5*. The dwellings were built around a ceremonial or 'dancing' ground known as *yawe kama*. They consisted of a long men's house (*tapada*),[1] low tube-like food-houses (*neada*)[2] and clusters of women's houses (*wenada*). A common pattern was to have the *tapada* at one end flanked by two *neada*, or a *neada* and a *pokala*. The *pokala*, a lean-to longhouse, is a less permanent structure and easier to build than a *neada*. It substituted the *neada* when there was pressure on time, or labour was short. A little further off, obscured by groves or discreet bushes, were the spirit and cult houses. Kitchen gardens (*yamanu*)

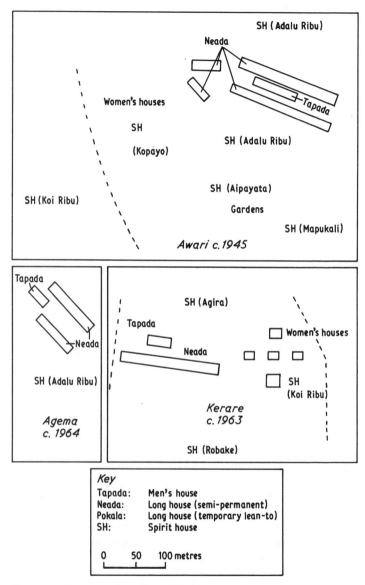

Figure 5 *Reconstruction of three Yala settlements prior to a pig kill*

were planted behind the *neada* and beyond the *yawe kama*, close to the women's houses.

Men normally slept in the *tapada* or, if there had been a sacrifice, in the spirit house. Women, with their daughters and young sons, slept in the women's houses where pigs were also given nights' lodging. Incompatible co-wives would have separate houses built for them, but often a large house, divided into a number of rooms, did the job. In the front room wives usually entertained their husbands while further in were separate sleeping chambers for themselves and their children.

In the old days, when war was a constant threat, settlements tended to be built high on ridges, with gardens on the slopes and valleys. Even discounting moves enforced by war, however, these settlements were not permanent but tended to disband and regroup, often in a different permutation, every few years. Rappaport's (1968) description of Maring 'pulsating settlements' fits the Kewa case well. When a pig kill was being planned all the neighbouring settlements would congregate in the land of the pig kill initiating clan and help build the *tapada* and *neada*, each man building his own rooms in the *neada* according to his capacity in pigs.

After the event was over the various family groups would return to their homesteads and soon another group would perhaps start planning its own pig kill, attracting all the other groups to it for a spell. When pigs had been killed in a certain settlement two or more times even the hosts might decide to move a little further off and build a new settlement.[3] At such a time residence patterns may change, one man choosing to live with a different clan brother in the new settlement or even with a man from a different clan (but usually of the same tribe). Two reasons were given by men for this movement: first, that if a place became too crowded they were afraid that disagreements, inevitably arising out of close cohabitation, might escalate to violence, which would be bad among 'brothers'; second, that pigs must be killed on as much of their land as possible instead of always on the same spot. Men said that their fathers would tell them on which pieces of land pigs had yet to be killed so that they could keep this in mind and rotate their settlements. This suggests a strategy of consecrating with pig kills as much residential land as possible, in order somehow to claim it and differentiate it from bush. As one Yala big man said:

'You know what *we* mean by "development" (in Kewa, *ada ma rekato*, to raise or awaken the village): building a 'house line' (*neada*), a men's house (*tapada*), killing pigs (*yawemena*). This we have done . . .'

(Josephides and Schiltz 1982: 82)

While the old Yala residences on the ridges were known collectively as Agema, the present settlements on the valley floor are conveniently referred to as Aka; this being the first area to be settled when the downward move started in the 1960s. In 1979 Aka consisted of four major settlements – Aka proper, Poiale, Yakopaita and Puliminia. In addition one elderly man with his wives and some of his children still inhabited the old settlement of Kerare on the ridge, while another man kept a house in Popa, another ridge settlement, where he retired whenever he quarrelled with his sons living in Yakopaita (a pretty frequent event in which this move was his recurring threat). Between 1979 and 1981 a fifth settlement, Paipada, was established, while some men of Yakopaita and elsewhere started building houses a little removed from the hub of the main settlement (if 'hub' could possibly be applied to the centre of such a small community). In addition, a number of single homesteads are scattered about in more out of the way places. This trend has become more prevalent in recent years, when fear of attack is no longer a factor dictating settlement patterns. Conversely, semi-permanent houses in the bush and near gardens, formerly a common feature for hunting parties or extended garden work, are no longer found.

Only one women's house, inhabited by an old widow, still survived in Poiale in 1981. Since the establishment of missions (which coincided with the movement down from the ridges) the Yala, like most Sugu Kewa, discarded women's houses and birth huts (*rameada*) at the same time as they demolished cult houses and started building Christian churches. Families now live in newstyle nuclear homes, often a little raised and with plaited cane walls in place of the old-style beaten bark sides resting directly on the ground. Men's houses (*tapada*) continue to be built for social and ceremonial purposes but there is no longer a ban on women living in them. In fact, the Aka *tapada* has been occupied exclusively by women and children since the men vacated it soon after the pig kill. Often men try to kill two birds with one stone: they build a small *tapada* which functions as a family house but can also double up as a men's house on ceremonial occasions or for entertaining guests in the porch (*polo*).

Aspects of the 'pulsating settlement' pattern merit mention here. In 1979, when preparations for the Aka pig kill were at their height, 68 people were resident in that settlement, while the figure dropped to 48 in the following year. In Yakopaita, on the other hand, there were 29 residents in 1979, 40 in 1980 and 57 in 1981, when the pig kill was held. The oscillation included movement out of old settlements into new ones and an influx from the outside occasioned by returning migrants. *Figures 6* and *7* illustrate these population movements.

Although much tribal land is divided up into discrete clusters for each clan, this does not necessarily indicate that clan members always lived together in the past. There were also at any given time a number of fugitives from other tribes resident with land holders and gardening on their land. These days residence may sometimes be outside the individual's garden area and cluster of clan land. Residence changes are perhaps indicative of the fact that political alliances between members of different clans often do not coagulate into permanent liaisons. In fact co-operation on most projects is by no means mandatory even within the clan, in spite of much rhetoric from men that they must help their 'brothers'. In present-day Aka the Tiarepa clan is predominant and lives with sections of Paripa, Waluaparepa and Mapopidipia. In Poiale the Tiarepa again live with the Ausparepa and Paripa, while the Paripa only inhabit Yakopaita. In Puliminia sections of Paripa, Yarepa and Waluaparepa live together. The new settlement of Paipada was established by three Tiarepa men who moved out of Aka after killing pigs there in 1979. Kerare, the settlement in old Agema, is inhabited by a Paripa family.

Informants denied that any group or individual living on tribal land and bearing the *ruru* name had an 'immigrant' status and was referred to as *epea ali*, 'men who have come', as LeRoy (1975: 482) found in Koiari village, south-east of Kagua. All resident men in the Yala settlements were known as *ada re ali*, 'base-men of the place'; only visitors resident elsewhere were *ada re ali meda*, 'base-men of another place'. Concerning Koiari village, LeRoy states further that immigrant status does not bestow disadvantages *vis-à-vis* access to land. For the Sugu Kewa, the group having equal access to a tribal territory is readily assimilated into the *ada re ali* category, and no further formal distinctions are

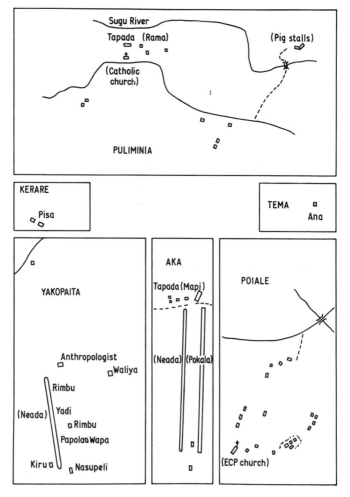

Figure 6   *(Sugu) Yala settlements in 1979*

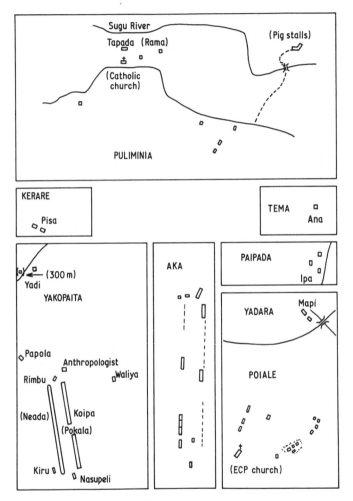

Figure 7   *(Sugu) Yala settlements in December 1981*

made. Nonetheless, the untidy pattern of Tiarepa clan land of Yala *ruru* betrays this group's more recent absorption. Unlike other clans, the Tiarepa have pockets of land scattered throughout all clan territories, a circumstance which a Paripa clansman explained in the following way:

'When the Tiarepa man Riesi first married the Paripa woman Popanu our big man gave the couple some garden land. However, they had many children and soon they needed more land. Yawi, our big man, was angry and told them to buy a plot on the hillside belonging to the Kamarepa *ruru*, which they did with the payment of a valued pearlshell. But their numbers grew and grew, so over the years the rest of us, the Paripa, Yarepa and others, have been giving pieces of our land to the Tiarepa. Now they have expanded so much that they have overtaken us all.'

Some chagrin and bitterness charge this account. These feelings, however, do not have to do specifically with land, but with a Paripa resentment against the political eminence of the Tiarepa big man and a deep-seated fear that they may be swallowed up by sheer numbers. But another, new factor, is perhaps also at work here, which has to do with a perception of modern uses of land. A recent disagreement over 'common' land (it did not go far enough to merit the name 'dispute') will perhaps clarify this. As already mentioned, the tribe as a whole holds bushland which may be cultivated by any member without permission having to be sought. (Speaking in pidgin, informants referred to this as 'public ground'.) Recently the Tiarepa big man, Mapi, attempted to clear some of this land for coffee planting. Immediately members of other clans protested: this was common bushland, not to be appropriated by an individual. If he had wanted to plant sweet potato or other traditional food crop people claimed they would not have protested. But the planting of a commercial perennial crop such as coffee would take the land out of circulation for ever, and fix it in perpetuity in his name and the names of his descendants. Such fixing would have been unlikely in the past when commercial crops were not known.

Thus changes in attitudes towards land are clearly taking place as the potential of land within a changing economy comes to be recognized. It is not clear at this stage however whether this hardening of attitudes is to the disadvantage of individual non-agnates, of whom only two exist in Aka (a sister's son and a mother's brother's son), both brought up as Yala from infancy. Non-agnatic lineages are not, as pointed out earlier, differentiated in any way, and in fact the agnatic status of many lineages is not known. Different degrees of co-operation may however be found among clans and lineages. It is to this that I now turn.

Residential groups: co-operation

No co-operation exists in everyday production beyond the domestic unit. In the past men worked jointly during ceremonial yam planting, and sometimes grouped together to clear large tracts of land of primary forest. Big men may still sponsor working parties (*ki kogono*, hand-work) when they want to prepare large gardens, especially for commercial purposes. But assistants are paid with pork on these occasions, just as they were in the past, so this is not considered a case of co-operation or joint production. In their everyday garden tending and harvesting women do not normally help one another but each works separately on her own plot. Young unmarried men, often having no substantial gardens of their own, are the one category of people who may attach themselves to married men and assist them in production in return for their keep and eventual help with bridewealth. Unmarried or divorced women also work in the households of their fathers and/or brothers.

In matters pitting the in-group against the out-group – that is, other *ruru* – there is usually some political cohesion, but it may depend on the issue and on the personal relationships of the personalities involved in the conflict. The case of a Council by-election in 1979 will illustrate this. There were three candidates for the position: the Perepe *ruru* nominated a Perepe man, while the Yala put forward two candidates, both nominated by Paripa Yala. One was Rimbu, a Paripa Yala himself, but the other was a man of Perepe *ruru* called Kegeai. Roga, the man who nominated Kegeai, was of that section of Paripa which had quarrelled with the rest of the clan and was living with Tiarepa clan. Nonetheless, Roga's action seemed odd, especially at a time when the Yala were locked in a boundary dispute with the Perepe.

But Roga was not the only one with ambivalent loyalties. Mapi's section of the Tiarepa clan failed to cast their vote, while some Paripa clan members resident in Yakopaita (Rimbu's residence), rather than upset anyone, rose very early in the morning and went to their gardens. As a result of these abstentions and desertions, Rimbu lost to Kegeai, by 57 votes to 59.[4]

This sort of *ruru* divisiveness is unheard of in the case of land disputes. All Yala stick together in claiming the disputed territory on which Aliwi stands (where Ribanu is said to have given birth to the Paripa and therefore to all Yala), even those who challenge the Pipi story of origin. The Perepe on the other side are also unanimous in claiming the land as theirs. Although land is not yet scarce in the area, it is inextricably linked to *ruru* identity and therefore has powerful ideological meaning. Two neighbouring tribes, the Koiari and the Kamarepa, have been disputing for some years the land on which the settlement of Roga and a large coffee garden stand. On at least two occasions armed fights have erupted over it, and in these some men received arrow wounds and others were gaoled (there were no fatalities). The Koiari *neada* was also set on fire. The dispute arose after coffee planted on the land began to bear fruit. Before the planting, Koiari ownership was apparently not disputed, and Kamarepa men were in fact hired to help in the preparation of the garden, being paid in the traditional way with a feast. When the Kamarepa saw the 'profit' that their labour was bringing in they decided they should have a share in it. It was only later that they laid claim to the land itself.[5] Yet both Koiari and Kamarepa have said to me that the dispute was not really over the coffee but over the place name: Roga, they say, is established, it appears on maps, people have heard of it. If they lost the name and settled in another territory they would lose part of their identity and prestige, and would have to start again from scratch building up another place.

These statements are not totally convincing, for coffee and the revenue it brings are clearly important. Moreover, there is evidence that some pressure on land may be developing in that particular area. Nonetheless, the political dimension cannot be ignored as an important contributory factor in land disputes.

Compensations for homicide are another important event bringing the *ruru* together, whether these are to be received or paid out. The clan and residential group of the victim or perpetrator are the most deeply involved in such cases, although members of the whole *ruru* will contribute or receive something. They will in any case turn up in large numbers to show support and to intimidate, in case the *ruru* responsible fails to compensate as expected. It may be that this cashing-in far and wide of all *ruru* clans is a recent phenomenon, as a speech made by a Yala big man on one occasion indicated. It was made by Mapi of Tiarepa clan during a marriage settlement, and referred to a compensation payment received for a Yala woman killed by her husband in a fight in Erave:

> 'While this sister was living in Erave all of us brothers of Wapia Yala, Kalu Yala and Agema Yala never went to see her, never did anything for her. But as soon as she dies we remember she is a sister and go crying to Erave to receive compensation for her. This is exactly what you men of Yakopaita and Puliminia are doing now: you never bothered about Yapaname before, but now that she is married you have come to receive bridewealth for her!'

Nevertheless a big turn-out on such occasions is an important show of strength, for the *ruru* and close relatives of the victim do appreciate the support. Nor are *ruru* members the only participants in such an event; the victim's maternal lineage (*agira*) is an important recipient, while friends and partners will also get their share. Thus, apart from some large sums kept by very close kin, the bulk of the payment may be broken down into tiny denominations distributed to a large number of people.[6]

Funerals are another occasion calling for group action. Only the local group (plus any other close relatives or friends of the deceased) will normally be involved in the case of the death of a person considered unimportant such as a woman or a child. But when a man dies, especially if he is important or old, much more fuss is made. A wake (*komada*) is held for at least two days, during which mourners come from afar with their gifts of food. A little while after the interment pigs are killed in the name of the deceased and pork is given to the mourners who contributed food during the *komada*. At the next major pig kill the names of these recently dead will be recalled, and it will be said (and sometimes sung) that the pig kill is in their honour. But in fact the pig kill is attributed to such a variety of causes that it really suffers from overdetermination. Very elaborate or recurrent mortuary payments as described elsewhere in the Highlands (e.g. in Sillitoe 1979; Lederman 1982; A. Strathern 1982b) are not a feature of Kewa social relations.

Religious denomination coincides with settlements. The goal of many settlement founders is to build their own church; this in fact is fast becoming the focus of the pig kill in many areas, as well as the idiom for unity.[7] In Poiale there is the Evangelical Church of Papua (ECP), attended by the surrounding settlements of Aka, Paipada and Yakopaita. In Puliminia there is a Catholic church, attended also by the people of Kerare. Traditional cults were similarly supported according to settlements. Usually a cult was bought from a neighbouring group by a wealthy man, especially at a time when deaths or sicknesses occurred and it was thought that the established cult was of limited efficacy, being overtaken by a more powerful one. A big man would usually officiate concurrently at a number of cult houses.

Pig kills were predominantly the affair of the resident group, which in the old days contained a conglomeration of tribes and clans thrown together by warfare or celebrating a victory. Nowadays the core group is invariably a group of co-resident brothers assisted by the rest of the settlement as well as sections of clans from other settlements, and to a lesser extent unrelated partners. *Ruru* members from all localities will try to attend the pig kill and expect to be given pork.

We have seen that the resident group co-operates minimally in everyday production. Garden work is done separately by each household except when some tasks require more intensive labour, and then the working party is paid for its contribution. Funerals, compensation payments and pig kills invariably involve the whole settlement, as do land disputes with outside groups. In national elections resident groups may offer block votes, but this is not necessarily the case with more local politics. Although everyday production requires little co-operation, the sphere of exchange, which redistributes that production, has not been examined; in a later section we shall see that there is in fact a fair amount of interaction in it, not only limited to the resident group.

Daughters and sisters

Daughters are automatically members of their father's clan, with residential rights in their settlements and gardening rights in their land. However, the knowledge that they will eventually marry and leave colours the way their residence with their natal clan is perceived, so that they are always thought of as transient, which affects their role and influence. They are not considered adults before they marry, whatever their age, so that their life as adults invariably starts in their husbands' settlement. Unmarried daughters, then, are socially 'children' in the village. But grown-up sisters must be thought of differently.

In 1980 there were twelve adult women living in Yakopaita.[8] Nine were wives of resident men, one was the mother of one of these wives, and only two were sisters. These two women had been married before, but one was divorced while the other had left her husband (following pressure from her brothers) because he did not complete bridewealth payments. For almost a year these two women were in and out of the settlement, staying with friends and relatives in various villages or with their brothers in Yakopaita. Their presence in Yakopaita was casual; they did not have their own gardens but worked in those of their brothers' wives. They had no productive base in the community and no say in its affairs, and everyone knew it. They were erratic and not to be depended upon, and no-one expected them to be different: they were only sojourners, biding their time. Eventually one went off to employment in municipal roadworks in Erave, while the other returned to her husband who promised to complete his bridewealth payments.

Marriage and the position of wives

As for the Mendi, for the Kewa 'the range of potential spouses is determined . . . by personal genealogy' (Ryan 1969: 163). Ego may not marry into his patrilineage (*apara*), maternal lineage (*agira*) or father's maternal lineage (*ayara*). Ryan calls these 'antigamous lineages' in respect of any individual, and limits the applicability of the prohibition to marry into 'any lineage into which a member of one's own lineage has married' to five or six generations. The Kewa case may be slightly different. To begin with, there is no antigamous rule in the same generation, and brothers are sometimes found marrying sisters, or a brother and sister may marry a sister and brother. Second, the prohibition usually lapses after the second generation, except in very special cases when the apical ancestress of a lineage was an agnate of ego's lineage. For instance, Paripa Yala may not marry into that section of Tiarepa Yala which descended in a straight line from Popanu, a Paripa woman. She is remembered because she is the link joining two groups, at the head of the formation of a new clan. Other marriages of lesser structural importance will not be remembered after the third generation and therefore the prohibition will lapse. Another antigamous rule arises out of co-residence and association. At a recent marriage (1980) between a Mapopidipia girl and a Tiarepa boy the rest of the Yala clans arranged themselves into wife-givers and wife-takers. When I asked about the rationale for this I was told the following:

'In the old days the clans of Kalu [which includes Mapopidipia] always went around together with the Ausparepa and Paripa. They fought on the same side in wars, while the Yarepa and Waluaparepa clans sided with the Koiari *ruru* and the Tiarepa clan sided with the Perepe *ruru*. So our big man at the time made it a rule that the clans which have associated so closely should never intermarry.'

Although as we saw in the previous chapter war alignments are more complicated than this, it is true that the clans mentioned do not intermarry as a result of what they perceive to be their close association over a number of years. Often lip service is paid to the ideal that members of the same *ruru* should not marry, but this is merely rhetorical.

Since marriage, as in Mendi (Ryan 1969) usually follows on an initial attraction between a boy and a girl who attend courting parties together (formerly *romedi*, now *kununa yaisia*), spouses are often taken from neighbouring clans. Sometimes specific conditions result in brides coming from further away, as when, for instance, forced 'community' labour at contact brought people of both sexes from as far as Kuare to work on the road in Sumbura. A number of marriages were contracted at this time.

Whether the boy has picked out the girl himself, or his father has suggested her to him, the next stage is usually for the boy's father to entertain the girl so that he and his wife can observe her at close quarters. They will invite her to eat with them, send gifts of food to her, observe her in her gardening, food preparation and distribution, and general diligence. It is not thought proper for either the boy or the girl to express inordinate fervour for the match, but to acquiesce modestly. If the bridewealth is acceptable to the girl's parents she will be shown a garden by the groom's mother and will begin work on it. The boy's father considers himself her protector at this initial stage, even against his son, and continues to bring her food. The boy will wait for a few days or weeks before consummating the marriage stealthily in the garden, to avoid merciless teasing from his age-mates.

A number of informants' accounts indicate that many marriages did not follow this ideal pattern in the old days any more than now. Older people tell stories of casual cohabitation which did not lead to the payment of bridewealth and therefore a permanent liaison. They were trial marriages that simply did not work, and breaking them off presented little problem, especially as in almost all cases recorded there were no children. Many men insist that their wives chose *them*, by simply moving into their mothers' houses. There was never excessive polygyny; even very important men hardly ever had more than four wives, and more commonly two (discounting casual liaisons). For this reason perhaps great discrepancies between the ages of husbands and wives were not observed. By all accounts women were not forced into marriage by their fathers as in neighbouring Pangia (A. Strathern, personal communication), but exercised a reasonable freedom of choice, as they do now.[9] So also with divorce: brothers and fathers do not stand in a woman's way if she really wants to leave a man. They say that if the woman is not happy they cannot force her to stay with the man, as the marriage would always be unstable. If separation takes place soon after marriage bridewealth must be returned, but this is not a problem if the woman has another prospective husband lined up. It is the responsibility of the new husband to pay off the old, rather than her brothers' responsibility. In this case the brothers will not receive additional bridewealth. If there are any children the mother's natal group will try to keep them but they are likely to be successful only if the father has died. It is thought that the new husband will not care much for the children and that they will probably die if they go to him. For this reason the woman is usually encouraged to wean the children before she remarries. Nevertheless, I did record a number of cases where children lived with their mother at her new husband's place, and apparently thrived.

In spite of the rather liberal attitudes outlined above, women were never free from the threat of violence from their husbands. In the old days men often demonstrated their authority over women in physically aggressive ways. They would parade up and down the settlement and threaten to put an arrow or spear in the woman's thigh. (They sometimes also threatened recalcitrant children in this way.) However, no elderly woman that I interviewed had suffered this punishment, although I know of one instance when a runaway wife was killed by being speared. Nor are women safe from violence today, although they can no longer be killed with impunity. In recent years a man ambushed and killed his ex-wife and her sister. On recounting this episode men commented grimly to me: 'We do not like our wives to leave us. They show publicly their dislike of us when they do this, and we lose face.' This particular murderer served a ten-year prison sentence, and his clan had to pay compensation to the women's clan.

Lederman (1982) has described the active exchange networks of young unmarried people in Mendi. Young men marrying for the first time are expected to raise most of their own bridewealth from these networks. Some elderly Kewa men insisted that they also did this, although on the whole the extent of the groom's contribution itself was in the old days the fruit of patronage, when a young man depended on an older, established man to furnish him with his first sow. Married sisters were (and are) a valuable source of wealth at this time. One old man explained how he raised bridewealth by making gardens and presenting his sister with the harvest. The sister and her husband responded with pigs and pearlshells.

The marriage exchanges that I witnessed in the field ranged from almost total financing by the bridegroom to total subsidization by his agnatic group. An older man marrying for the second time invariably bears the brunt of the payment while younger men will get some assistance. Those without a living father often say that they have raised bridewealth themselves by working on plantations and tilling gardens, but in this claim they usually fail to acknowledge their mother's or sister's labour in tending to the bridewealth pigs while they work for a wage. Some young men may be totally subsidized by their parents for the initial payment,[10] but usually this will be below expectations and must be made up later by the groom.

Bridewealth exchanges do not have to involve the whole of the agnatic group; they are largely elective, and although close agnates will usually participate so may more distantly-related people. The girl's guardians will normally be the main recipients of bridewealth, but this is not a category necessarily determined by kinship. Sometimes mature, established men will take notice of young nubile girls, making them gifts of money and of food, in order to acquire bridewealth rights in them. The full description of one bridewealth exchange witnessed will illustrate the sorts of transactions involved.

On the first day of the proceedings the boy's father presented the girl's father with two pigs and three pearlshells, pledging Kina 800 to follow 'in the coffee season'. On the second day interested parties were invited to participate in a *rekele pu laapo mealo* ('I break [a pig] in half and receive two.') This exchange usually takes place with a marriage settlement (*wena ragele*), except when the parties do not have many participating members and contributions are small. In these cases the settlement is limited to *ragele* or *wena nu laapo* (woman-netbag-both) or, as the men say in pidgin, *baim meri tasol* (just paying for the woman).

A number of men identified as 'wife givers' first tether their pigs to the stakes, jeering at the wife takers to match them. Protesting that they are bested, the wife takers eventually bring out their pigs and the bidding starts. Individual men have all sorts of reasons for participating in these exchanges. On this occasion, the wife givers had brought large pigs which they wanted to exchange for smaller ones to fatten for their pig kill the following year, while at least one man on the wife takers' side wanted to exchange his small pigs for a large one to give as a wedding gift (*yagi*) to his sister who was to marry soon. In the 'matching' that followed each of the wife giver's large pigs was exchanged for two (except for one pig, which was smallish); this was *rekele*. In addition, each wife taker gave an extra pig or some cash to the wife giver with whom he had exchanged pigs; this was *ragele*, bridewealth proper. The *rekele* exchanges were seen as fair, answering people's different needs; the 'extra' was the *ragele*. But the two are not unconnected, for (with the exception of the bride's father) only those participating in *rekele* received *ragele*. When these exchanges were over the bride's father presented his daughter with a large endowment sow, known as *yagi*.

An account of some of the verbal exchanges on the occasion (selected from a tape transcript) gives some flesh to the above skeleton. It also tells us something about the women's part in all this as expressed by the idiom of war in which most of the proceedings were conducted. WG stands for wife giver, WT for wife taker.

WG1: My brother, I see that they are lying in wait for you up there. They will beat you, kill you. Many men have come and are watching by the base of this banana tree, do it quickly.

WT1: There is only one of me, I am no match for you. Take them [your pigs] back home.

WG1: If you take my pig rope you have to return K2 [two kina]

WT1: What shall we two say? You looked to me and came.

WG2: If my brothers do not get a good return I withdraw my pigs.

WT2: (to WT1) You talk as if you were the only one involved, and the rest of us were just rubbish men (*tieboali*).

WG3: If this man's spear [WT1's] wounds my brother's [WG2's] chest, I wouldn't just leave him and go [i.e.: all our pigs must be exchanged, or none at all].

WT1: All of us Yala went to claim compensation when the woman died [in Erave]. You men of Yakopaita and Puliminia are doing exactly the same thing now. It is as with Lu's sister.[11] We've talked enough I think, you men. You, father of the bride, don't try to run away: I will hold you. Go fetch your large shields [*kaga*, here standing for pigs] and bamboo sticks with wealth (*kepa*), all of you who live with me. I don't think we can match their pigs; we will have to ask them to go.

WT3: (to WG4) I give two pigs for your one. The extra K40 is for brideprice (*wena yapa*, woman-possum).

WT4: I am shooting a small three-pronged spear. What shall I get for it later?

WG1: You will receive the large decorated shield (*yamo rugili*) only if you hold his small shield (*ritiyapara*) next to your skin. I watch, and exhibit wealth. As other men line up theirs, we line up ours [that is, we match them]. If you can't afford this large pig, I have small ones, two or three. You can have whatever size you want – we are lining them up.

WT1: We don't have the spears to shoot you with.

WG1: We've come from Agema Kana, we've come from Omatoyo, we've come from Riakera to try at Manayawa. [These are the paternal lands of the present transactors.] Just the three of us have come [i.e. WGs1,2,3].

WT4: Just the three of you – with what spears shall we shoot you? And if we shoot you and the others come [i.e. their friends] how shall we shoot them? We have no spears, so you'd better go back.

(Much bantering follows)

WG1: You can't win my pig.

WT1: Your pig will die [i.e. will be well-matched].

WG1: Your pig doesn't make me die [i.e. I am not satisfied].

WT1: Your pig is not big enough. Will you buy a bigger one?

WG1: If you are talking about money, I have money. If you want pigs, I can give you two or three pigs. You must return two pigs and K40 for my pig.

WT1: I have nothing (*ni papi*) and you come showing your pigs to me. Take your pigs and go. I think you've come to laugh at us.

WT4: You go and get some pigs. This man is laughing at us!

WT1: My daughters are there. Marry them! (*Lamua! Lamua!*) Marry our daughters. We are always marrying yours, you marry ours!

WG2: You are like pigs or dogs. We won't marry your sisters. You look at our sisters and tremble with desire. But when we look at your sisters we think of pigs, shells, money and other wealth that they will fetch for us. You don't think of this wealth. We can't follow your example, so fetch everything quickly now.

WT1: The price you set is here. Now you'll die! Are you dying or not? [i.e. are you satisfied].

(More bantering. Then a male voice scolds the women: 'You women only like to eat pigs, look after them now that the sun is scorching them!' But other men protest that they also eat pigs, they can't just blame the women.)

WT5: I am fed up with this endless discussion. Just tell us if the payment is adequate; if not we'll send the newlyweds to pick coffee.

(A chorus of *Bania! Pu! Pira! Mena alano. Mena meano* (Let's go! Go! Sit down! I give pigs, I receive pigs.))

WT1: Let's finish now. We've talked a lot, and our mouths ache. If there is some pay yet to be given the parents of the couple will settle it themselves later. Let's finish now.

The foregoing account requires some commentary. First, the marriage was between a Mapopidipia girl and a Tiarepa boy, both of Yala *ruru*. This is why the impropriety of the match is alluded to by WG2, who upbraids the wife takers for marrying their sisters instead of thinking of them as suppliers of wealth.[12] The men designated as wife givers in the *rekele* transactions were of Paripa clan (3) and Ausparipa (1). They were certainly not the girl's close agnates, but they were from clans which do not intermarry. All but one of those involved on the wife takers' side were of Tiarepa clan, the same as the groom.[13] Of those featuring in the transcript, only WT3 participated in the *rekele*, and he was a Tiarepa man from a clan section living very far away. A possible reason for his participation was his close relationship to the Tiarepa big man Mapi, who although a main speaker on this occasion (WT1) made no exchanges. On the other hand, two younger Tiarepa men participated in the *rekele* but not in the discussion. Two pigs, one from either side, were withdrawn because they could not be matched.

LeRoy discusses how south Kewa villagers recruit pig killers through existing marriage ties, and says that 'the act of recruitment is likened to marriage' (1979b: 181). The above transcript highlights how in this case marriage transactions are likened to warfare by participating males. However, it may be misleading to lay too much emphasis on the idiom used on these occasions. It would be difficult to argue that Kewa men are really thinking of war when they conduct marriages. What is far more likely is that they have a stock of idioms out of which they choose one on occasions requiring the use of metaphoric speech (*siapi*). What is important for the men is that the idiom exclude women; and what better idiom than warfare, which stresses male solidarity at the core of the group transacting women. Therefore marriage, ideologically, also stresses the group and not personal relations of exchange (cf. Lederman 1982). Women play no part in the discussions or transactions, merely tending to the pigs who are wilting in the hot sun. The bride herself has no part in the *rekele* transactions; when two men have matched their pigs she is simply given the pig ropes by her father to hand to the new owners.

A distinction must be made, however, between these transactions accompanying *rekele* and the other payments made directly to the girl's father. In this case they were two pigs and three shells, with K800 pledged. On the third day of the exchanges (that is, the day after *rekele*), the boy's father's brother gave a further K40 to the girl's father, while another Tiarepa agnate gave K10 to the girl, asking her to give it to her father. On the day of the *rekele* the boy's father had also given K20 to the girl to pass on to her father. Her father kept half and returned the other half, saying 'K10 I shall eat, K10 you must return in exchange' (*Ten kina ni nalo ten kinare mapu*). At the same time he sent his daughter to take pearlshells to the men who had participated in *rekele*. These men, since they had 'eaten bridewealth' (*yapa nala*), returned pearlshells of their own in exchange (*roponali*).

In none of these exchanges was the girl involved in any decision making, although she was commissioned to carry the wealth items from one man to another. Her father kept the initial pigs given him by the groom's father but gave the shells in *roponali*. How he will distribute the K800 when he receives it is not known, but both men and women said he would not consult the girl. Though the girl is seen to share out bridewealth, its destination is either predetermined as a result of previous exchanges, or largely decided by her father.

Following Barnes' (1962: 9) initial suggestion that in the Highlands 'matrimonial alliances are either concentrated or deliberately dispersed', some writers have tried to correlate this pattern with the absence or presence of large-scale exchange systems in the societies concerned. The argument, put succinctly by Meggit (1965: 95) in the case of the Mae Enga, is that since all sub-clans want to expand their exchange networks (which are exercised through affinal ties), 'it would . . . be foolish . . . to expend further brideprice in reaffirming these ties'. However Feil (1980: 288–93), citing this formulation by Meggitt, goes on to show that in spite of their participation in *tee* (a very large-scale exchange system), the Tombema Enga tend to concentrate their marriages in adjacent clans. In fact this concentration is regulated by the *tee*, whose sequences determine marriage frequencies. This is because 'Brides are taken from the direction the *tee* is coming, that is, from clans that will give *tee* to one's own.' Thus bridewealth is fed into *tee* exchanges. Since a man 'tries to take a wife from the opposite directions in the *tee* sequence from where his mother came', this tends to concentrate (but also alternate) marriages, at least in one-sequence intervals. Feil has a sample of 569 marriages, two-thirds of which were conducted with just six adjacent clans, establishing beyond doubt the actual concentration of marriages for the Tombema Enga. What may remain open to question is what determines that concentration.

Feil entitles his 1980 article 'A group of women takes a wife' and, as a sideline to the main contention of *tee*'s major role, argues briefly that 'there is another, more immediate factor constantly at work, which strengthens the concentration of marriages in near clans' (Feil 1980: 295). This is lobbying by in-married women who try to 'pull' sisters and brothers' daughters into the clans where they have themselves married. The idea of clanswomen seeking to 'take wives' is attractive, but perhaps not systematically demonstrated. It suggests that Tombema women have more solidarity as a sex than do other Highland women (such as the Melpa and Kewa for instance), and that in fact they are more integrated into the group and ideologically more a part of it than I argue is the case with Kewa women.

The Kewa have no positive marriage rule and marriages are contracted randomly. No pattern emerges and no concentration exists, so the converse of Meggitt's argument is not proven here (that is, that in societies without major exchange cycles marriages tend to be concentrated). Kewa tend to marry neighbours because they tend to marry people they know. When brides come from afar there is usually a reason for it. In the old days this may have been because one spouse was a refugee in the other's area, while in post-pacification days distant clans were brought together to work on 'community projects' such as road building. In more recent times spouses may be found during periods of migrant labour. However, to say that Kewa do or do not 'marry their enemies' (Meggitt 1964; Cook 1969) is not an informative statement, since in a situation of constant warfare and changing alliances everyone was a potential enemy, and marriages between groups did not change this situation. Marriage did not (and does not) signal a special relationship between two clans, since no formal exchanges were instituted between them as a result of such unions. Clans have never exchanged as clans, in the manner of Melpa and Enga clans in *moka* and *tee*. As a consequence, individual marriages had limited implications for relations between groups, so that it cannot be said that women linked groups in any way;[14] they linked only individuals, or at most family units. Conversely, groups did not interfere with individual marriages, and therefore no positive marriage rules existed of the sort described by Feil for the Tombema Enga.

When Kewa women are married their husband's clan does not view them with suspicion as being possible spies for their natal clan, but accepts them, as far as sisters are accepted, as clan members. Little distinction is made between the loyalty of a sister and the loyalty of a wife; the presence of both in the group is considered by male clan members to be contingent. This is not to say that individual in-married women are treated as outsiders or are thought of as casual sojourners who may move out at any time. Many women, once married, spend the rest of their lives with their husbands' clan and it would occur to no-one to say that their clan membership was ephemeral or unstable. What men can say generally, however, is that women's membership of any group is reversible, since it undergoes at least one change in their lives, and this gives men a powerful weapon to use against women in particular instances. This was clearly illustrated in the case of a recently-widowed woman who asked me to take a photograph of the mourning party around her husband's grave. When later I presented her with the photograph my host commented that it was a waste giving it to the widow; she would marry again and forget her dead husband and his settlement. But his brothers would always remain his brothers, so they should have had the photograph.

At different stages in their lives women have access to their natal land and their husbands' clan land. Women who marry close to home continue to garden on their natal land but this represents only a small percentage of their total gardening. Nevertheless they do retain links with their natal clan and will return there on divorce, although old widows tend to stay on in their husband's settlements. When married, women's rights to land are a direct result of that marriage and can therefore be revoked on divorce. This was vividly demonstrated on one occasion when a woman who had been divorced by her husband argued that she had a right to stay on in his settlement in spite of his rejection of her. She considered herself a co-founder of the settlement since she had helped in the building of the longhouse, and believed that her interests in the place should accrue as a result of her residence there over a number of years. Her claim did not even receive serious consideration however, for the group that determines access to land is the male core group which does not admit wives as full members with rights in perpetuity. The fact that men may also change their clan affiliation (though this is rare) is overlooked; as mentioned in the previous chapter, the idiom of brotherhood may include non-agnates, but it excludes women.

The position of uxorilocally resident men is not the exact converse of virilocally resident women, so the two cannot be contrasted. Especially in the past, men living uxorilocally were resident with the woman's clan before marriage, usually as war refugees, and had already been assimilated as 'brothers' before becoming affines (subsequently their lineage would assume full agnatic status). Women, on the other hand, could only be recruited as wives. Sisters, the one category of 'automatic' clan members, were those who would definitely marry out and leave their natal group.

Another example of the position of wives concerns the plight of a young widow. Before her period of mourning was over, her late husband's elderly brother began making sexual advances; these she repulsed. Although there is no levirate rule in this area, it became impossible for the widow to remain, unmarried, in her husband's place. Eventually the brother raped her and she fled to her natal clan, discarding her widow's weeds before the time was up. For this impropriety her guardian had to offer conciliatory compensation to the husband's clan, but at the same time the village court awarded the widow damages for assault. It was clear that although the brother's action was generally condemned as indecently untimely, a young widow with no protector had no place in her husband's settlement. If her husband had been alive the assault might have led to murder, but then the brother would not have raped her while his brother lived. He did in fact want to marry her, but she thought him too old.

Other examples could be cited illustrating wives' dependent position in their husbands' clan. In less serious but more frequent cases a woman may be evicted from her husband's settlement when a quarrel erupts between her and her husband or his brothers. She may sometimes decide to leave herself, and stay away in her natal place while the matter is *sub judice*. The husband would never be the one to go (except if he quarrels with his brothers), for he is the owner of the ground, she the permissive resident.

Women and marriage: peripheral sojourners

That women are exchanged by groups of men much like items of wealth is a well-established idea in anthropological discussions of marriage (see Lévi-Strauss 1969). Yet how far does this accord with indigenous subjective perceptions of what happens when two people marry? I believe that it is important to consider these because they often offer justifications for social practices. Do Kewa men and women think that men exchange women? Clearly men think that women are to be exchanged against valuables (see transcript of bridewealth exchanges above), but there is little indication that they think that 'a woman merits a woman'. In specific terms and concerning their own wives, men say that women come to them because they are sexually attracted. For their part, women say that they go to a man that they want. The verb 'to marry' is different woman-speaking from man-speaking. While women say simply that they 'go to a man', men use the word *lamula* which includes ideas both of sexual intercourse and the payment of bridewealth. This is not the same as the verb used for 'to exchange' or 'to distribute' objects (*roponali, moke pea*).

What happens in marriage is that women move while men remain stationary. So in this sense women *are* exchanged among men against objects of wealth, but are not exchanged *like* objects because they are persons who influence the choice of those between whom they are exchanged, and who may take their own leave from their 'possessors'. As well as running away they could commit suicide; an act for which their current clan of residence would have to compensate their natal clan.

But the fact that women move among groups of men who appear constant, rather than the fact that they are exchanged for wealth, colours the way women's status in groups is perceived. Because they move, they have a less stable relationship to land and therefore to the name of the land-owning group; so their rights to the land and the name become tenuous. This leads me to the discussion of the two self-referential concepts of 'sojourner' and 'peripheral'. Because as part of normal social practice (marriage, divorce, widowhood) women are expected to move at least once in their lives, men talk of them in general as being sojourners in respect of any one group. This status then informs their position *vis-à-vis* group ideologies, and physical sojourners become ideologically peripheral.

However, what is not acknowledged in this equation is that most women as wives are not in fact sojourners in their husband's group, but make it their own and stay for life. Thus the factual validation on which the ideological bias rests is itself largely an ideological bias, and not a true reflection of social reality. This is why I call these two concepts[15] self-referential: they offer a classically circular argument. The justification for women being peripheral in group ideologies is offered with reference to their status as sojourners, while the fact that many women are stable residents in one group is attenuated by the general claim that being ideologically peripheral rests on a reality regarding actual residence. As we shall see, ideological statements in general offer powerful validation for, or sometimes denial of, inequalities engendered within social relations.

In this discussion, women and men were shown to relate quite differently to social groups. Whereas men were the base-people of the place, women were sojourners who could not accrue rights in their husbands' settlements in the way that in-settled males could, but enjoyed only those rights contingent on their marriage and the good-will of their husbands. The twin concepts of 'sojourner' and 'peripheral' were developed to explain how this situation was validated. This inability of women to accrue independent rights to land is crucial, for it is the fact that men control land, and the resultant ideology that land ownership is by definition male, which lays the foundations for the sexual inequality discussed in later chapters.

Notes

1 'Platform house', so called because the bodies of big men, especially those who died in battle, were exposed on high platforms outside it until the flesh had decomposed.

2 So called because they were meant primarily for cooking food in. People said that they were 'feast houses', not 'sleep houses', although they did sleep in them.

3 Ideally, the *neada* should be inhabited only during the pig kill for which it was constructed and must be dismantled afterwards. This does eventually happen, but in my experience not before it has started to fall apart, at least these days. It is used as a half-way house for those whose own houses have fallen into disrepair and must be repaired or replaced.

4 Nor is there in the case of national elections a block *ruru* vote. In the 1982 elections, Yakopaita, Puliminia and Aka each voted for a different candidate (Aka's candidate won).

5 They supported their claim by showing the sites of their fathers' graves on the land. This evidence was often accepted by land courts

as constituting a very strong claim. The Koiari, who had returned to this land since pacification, could not produce their fathers' graves there; however, they produced those of their grandfathers.

6　This is why often in such cases although much wealth is collected together it does not become capital which is reinvested in some profitable venture. Instead it is broken down and 'eaten'.

7　Trying to patch up a quarrel, a Paripa Yala (Rimbu) said to a Tiarepa Yala (Mapi): 'We will build one *neada* and one church and become one belly.'

8　I discount those few sisters, in between marriages, who floated in and out of the settlement throughout my stay there.

9　One young Yala girl has run away from two marriages so far, always a day or two after the exchange of bridewealth. Her father has never appeared particularly angry with her.

10　This is not to say that Kewa pay bridewealth in instalments as a rule; but in special cases when the groom is facing difficulties a percentage of the sum already agreed upon may be accepted as a down payment. Often this leads to disputes and wrangling later.

11　That is, your rights in claiming bridewealth are questionable.

12　This reproof also implies that it is more dignified and befitting for a man to transact wealth than to lust after a woman.

13　WT4 was the Paripa man who had joined the Tiarepa years ago. However, although he took some part in the discussion he did not participate in *rekele*.

14　Yet a note must be made here of the occasions when women do link groups. These are quasi-mythical women such as the Paripa woman who married Riesi and gave birth to the Tiarepa clan. It was by virtue of this marriage that the latter became part of Yala, but its relations with Paripa remain ambiguous. In spite of the overarching agnatic ideology linking the clans, and the marriage rule prohibiting marriage with one's mother's clan, Tiarepa and Paripa continue to marry.

15　While 'sojourner' and 'peripheral' are not words used by the Kewa themselves, the ideas they express certainly inhere in statements men make about women's relationship to groups. I introduce them here for analytical purposes, as Marilyn Strathern (1972) introduced the expression 'women in between' to describe a different relation that Melpa women have to groups.

3
Change and continuity: Colonial and post-colonial developments

We saw in the description and analysis of the social context within which relations of domination and subordination become possible in the case of the Kewa, how the group, in a situation of constant warfare, gained political and physical strength from an open process of recruitment but a closed ideology of male agnatic solidarity. This had important implications for the relations of inequality: it limited men's ability to wield power over other men, and relegated women to a peripheral position within the group. The picture presented so far, though in many ways diachronic, does not take into account in an explicit way social changes attendant on contact. I will consider the effect of this very powerful cultural imposition by alien agents on gender relations and on relations of inequality as a whole. At the outset, however, some general background is necessary.

First contact: transitions

In 1922 Assistant Resident Magistrate Leo Flint visited Samberigi Valley, crossed into Kerabi Valley and reached the Erave river. There he stopped. In 1929 Champion crossed the suspension bridge over the Erave and looked over the ridge to the northern side at grasslands and smoke which suggested habitation, but ventured no further (Souter 1963: 166). Then in 1935 the famous Hides and O'Malley patrol described in Hides' *Papuan Wonderland* (1936; reprinted 1973) was mounted. Unfortunately Hides was no cartographer and his work was largely discredited when in 1937 Champion released a report of a patrol he had conducted the previous year which exposed many of Hides' inaccuracies

(Sinclair 1969: 214). Nonetheless, Hides was the first European to skirt the area described in this book (it is impossible to establish exactly how close he came) and write about its people prior to contact. He set out from Daru to ascend the Fly and Strickland rivers, travelling along the Rentoul until from Landslide Mountain he saw the huge and beautiful valley system of the Huli south of Tari (he called them the Tarifuroro). He wrote:

'I had never seen anything more beautiful. Beyond all stood the heights of some mighty mountain chain that sparkled in places with the colours of the setting sun. As I looked on these green cultivated squares of such mathematical exactness, I thought of wheatfields, or the industrious areas of a colony of Chinese.'

(Hides 1973: 77–78)

After a detour northwards Hides turned south-east again in pursuit of the Purari. At the Nembi plateau his party was involved in some killings which, it was said later, better judgment could have avoided. Then the party travelled down the Nembi river until it joined the Erave (probably at present-day Poroma) and proceeded down the 'broken-bottle country'. They made a raft, perhaps where the Sugu joins the Erave, and floated down the Erave for three days until they came to the home of the 'Iumburave', described as 'black Papuans'. Accurate placing of these people is not possible, but it is likely that Hides touched on Kewa territory on the west and south. These people knew steel, and were able to tell Hides of a huge river system which he guessed to be the Purari. The following year (1936) Champion bypassed the Sugu on the west, travelled as far as Mt Giluwe and ascended again via Pangia to the Erave and Purari rivers. Kewa country proper was not to be explored and systematically patrolled for more than decade.

In the late 1940s and early 1950s the Sugu River Valley was sporadically patrolled, until in 1957 Kagua became established as a Patrol Post under Erave in the then Lake Kutubu sub-District.[1] A compilation of an initial census was commenced in 1958, and in 1961 the sub-District headquarters were transferred from Erave to Kagua. The upper section of the Sugu Valley was the first area to come under full administrative control, in 1961, while areas located further down the valley took another year, according to Patrol Reports because the people were more aggressive, and ill-feeling still persisted in 1969. Kagua Council was set up in 1964 and Erave Council in 1967, although it took until the turn of the decade for all areas to send representatives. In 1974 some areas were still changing affiliations between Erave, Kagua and Pangia Councils.

Australian Administration moves at this time must be seen against the backdrop of international political tendencies. The trend was to decolonize, and Australia was feeling pressures to pull out of a situation damaging to her image abroad. At the same time Patrol Officers were exhorted not to press local populations necessarily to fit themselves into the neat administrative units, such as Local Councils, arranged for them. In the late 1950s the Administration launched a concerted campaign with the aim of pacifying the area and instilling an understanding of government, democracy, parliamentary representation and political self-reliance in general. Economic development, at this stage allocated a secondary role, advanced to a more prominent position in the late 1960s and 1970s.

Pacification appears to have been achieved swiftly, so that by 1957 no major fighting was under way. In the same year the first serious attempt to approach the people of the lower Sugu Valley failed miserably when Roga villagers tricked the patrol and ran into the bush with their valuables. The previously appointed Village Constable tried to intercede, but returned to tell the patrol that the people wanted to have nothing to do with the government. Lower down, in the village of Sumbura, patrols met a similar unwillingness to co-operate. In the following year the residents of Agema gave the same message to the patrol by withdrawing their pigs and other valuables. Bewilderment and apprehension motivated this response, especially as the patrol followed the arrest of a number of men in Batri for not working on a road, a move later condemned by more highly-placed Administration Officers (Erave Patrol Report (EPR) 5, 1958). Nevertheless in this year many groups, including some of those returning to their tribal territories following pacification, were willing to give the new power a chance. According to Patrol Reports, 'people realized that the Administration brought peace to their lives'. Many men whom Patrol Officers hoped were traditional headmen were appointed Village Constables. In 1961 the area was derestricted, and the first recruits were taken for the Highlands Labour Scheme to work in plantations in the Western Highlands. But locally a reluctance to offer for work persisted, especially as people realized they would be getting only a token 'self-help' wage for work on roads. When government officials told them that the road itself was their reward villagers were not convinced that it would serve only their interests.

New political structures were beginning to develop in response to the Administration presence which were not necessarily sanctioned by the Administration. Although there was no official designation of 'boss boy' in the area (the government appointed only Village Constables) in 1958 the first boss boy, apparently appointed by the Lutheran Mission, came to officials' notice (Kagua Patrol Report (KPR) 1, 1958). He had no standing in the village and people found it difficult to recognize his authority, but were also confused, not yet understanding the difference between mission and government: they thought him invested with government power. The Patrol Officer commented at the time that missions were not always scrupulous in correcting this impression when they became aware of it.

Soon many boss boys not connected with missions began to emerge in groups which had no established headmen. They were usually young men (mainly from Kuare and North-east Kagua) who had been to Ialibu and noticed that leaders in that area who discharged duties for the Administration held walking canes as a sign of authority. This was not common practice in Kagua, but as the Patrol Officer reported,

'Once they had visited Ialibu, or on no grounds other than ambition, these aspiring leaders acquired canes, . . . and let it be known that they had been given them by the Government as a sign of authority in their clan. They also adopted the title "boss-boy" which is now common usage in the Kagua dialect.

As rivalry among the young men became keener, more acquired canes until at the time of the patrol it was common to see five "boss-boys" each claiming full authority over the group, as at Ida. Each regards himself as having been recognized by the Administration and the rivalry among them makes for greater confusion in dealing with a group having no outstanding leader.'

(KPR 1, 1958)

In the Kuare valley officials solved this problem by appointing as official Village Constables the most likely boss boys, after ascertaining that no established headman existed. By 1963, however, many government-appointed Village Constables (whose general standard seems to have fallen from average to mediocre, with, one would suspect, a corresponding fall in their standing among the people) began to lose their authority to the self-styled boss boys. Patrols made efforts to discourage the boss boys from undermining the position of the official 'without destroying any natural powers of leadership' (KPR 3, 1963). Confusion was to be expected, for by 1964 there existed three sorts of 'headmen': the Village Constables, government-appointed; the Councillors, elected by the people; and the boss boys, self-made leaders claiming official backing. Patrol Officers lamented that the boss boys were too numerous and often used their influence to evade work and gain privileges. Moreover the functions of the two sorts of officials, although apparently distinct, were never really understood by the people.

Meanwhile Patrol Officers continued with political education leading to the House of Assembly elections in 1964. In the same year the Kagua Local Council was inaugurated, and Patrol Officers reported that voting for the Council received more enthusiastic support than voting for the Assembly in the areas which offered Council candidates. Work on the Kagua-Erave road started in 1968, with each village spending two weeks every two months on this work. In 1969 each Councillor had to provide five labourers, required to work from 8 a.m. to 5 p.m., four days a week for four weeks, for a 'self-help' wage of 20c per day, i.e. $3.20 per month. Absenteeism for some villages in that year was around 50 per cent. By 1970 there were still areas which had not joined the Council and populations could therefore not be taxed or recruited for work. Administrators from Port Moresby warned Patrol Officers that no pressure was to be put on these people to join the Council. At the same time the officers were complaining that co-operation with the Administration was falling off, and that by 1973 the attitude of local people was simply 'to get as much money [as possible] out of the Government without really working' (KPR 8, 1973). Patrol Officers were puzzled by what seemed to them an entirely changed attitude towards the government by the Highlanders, who, as self-government approached, expressed a 'growing, sullen non-acceptance of [its] inevitability' (KPR 25, 1973). They feared that such handing over of power would simply mean that all whites would withdraw, taking their wealth with them, while the coastals would move in to reap the benefits.

Nonetheless the Kewa and other Highland people could not stem the tide of the times. Self-government led to Independence in 1975, followed by the beginning of the establishment of Provincial Governments in 1977. In the same year there was pressure from the local people for the establishment of Village Courts, which were duly set up with elected Village Magistrates. Boss boys were no longer seen, and the position of Village Constable became obsolete. All people's representatives were now elected: Village Magistrates,[2] Councillors, Provincial Assembly Members and Members of Parliament.

What was the reason for the Patrol Officers' lament regarding the people's change in attitude toward government officials? A sensitive superior officer in his accompanying comments to his officer's report counsels a more self-critical and patient approach, while suggesting a reason for this change of heart:

> 'We too must adapt to changing times and conditions (or get out) just as we have, over the years, been demanding that the people with whom we have worked desire and accept changes which we have tried to force in too short a time, by methods not always acceptable and often at too great a cost to their accepted values . . .
>
> Advancement as we see it and want it for this country requires two vital factors of the people – self-reliance and a desire for progress . . . These people have lost a lot of their self-reliance through over-anxious desire of officers and politicians for quick and visible results and to avoid short-term difficulties for the people. They are now about to find it again, but at their own pace. Traditional society changes slowly and there is no active search for progress other than on the terms of the society – by accepting methods, at not too high a cost to their accepted values.'

(KPR 8, 1973)

What were these changes forced on the people in too short a time and sometimes by unacceptable methods?

Missions and traditional cults

From the time of the very early patrols in 1957, Patrol Officers were repeatedly exhorted by their superiors to use a more sensitive approach with the local people. The tactics of one Patrol

Officer in particular, who wrote in his report of 'sending men to find women', 'searching the houses for women' and 'dismissing' people he has finished with (he was carrying out a census) were likened by his superior to those of 'a Nazi village sacking party' (EPR 3, 1957). These officers at the same time kept a wary eye on the activities of the many missions which were beginning to crowd into the newly-opened region. The Administration's first objective was to dispel any confusion in people's minds about the status of the missions, which were sometimes suspected of trading on people's assumption that they were an arm of the government and therefore commanded obedience. Such disabusing proved a difficult task, however, for all Europeans seemed to local people to have the same provenance and therefore similar status. Moreover missionaries shared the same outward signs of affluence as Administration officials, so that even when people had somehow assimilated the difference they thought of missions as second-best but still able to provide any assistance and 'development' which they failed to get from the government. In those early days some missionaries showed little sensitivity towards local cultural and religious values, and their boldness seems to have convinced the people that they were the custodians of a more powerful cult which it might be in their interests to espouse.

Three missions were active in the area in 1959: The Unevangelized Fields Mission (UFM, which later became the Evangelical Church of Papua (ECP)), the Catholic Capuchin mission, and the Lutherans. The Capuchins had the most favourable report from Patrol Officers concerning their relations with the people, while the Lutherans (who employed many 'evangelists' from Lae and Madang) seem to have been treated by the people in a very cavalier fashion. They, as well as the Capuchins, conducted literary classes. Other Evangelical and Wesleyan groups, referred to by the people collectively as 'Bible Mission', arrived a little later. The Seventh Day Adventists (SDA) arrived much later (in 1970) and are still not very strong in the area.

Patrol Officers often commented on the over-zealousness of missions in getting people to destroy cults and discontinue traditional practices. The requirement that converts extricate themselves from polygynous marriages also caused some social disruption. Traditional dress, and especially decorations on special occasions, were discouraged by the missions, as were 'lewd' singing and courting parties. In later years the Capuchins employed a much more liberal approach, to the extent of having the resident American priest dress up in traditional garb during pig kills at Christmas.

In 1975, one cult outbreak in particular alarmed the Administration. In Kuare, Kuali Lombo and Katiloma the evangelical missions encouraged the sort of worship that led to trance-like states and paroxysms of hysteria. In some villages people abandoned their gardens and other work and gathered very early outside the church building, where they sang hymns until some of them began yelling out that they were possessed by the Holy Spirit and could fly. According to the Patrol Report, 'the missionaries of this church see nothing ominous in these antics and in fact regard them with favour as a vindication of their teaching explaining it all as a visitation by the Holy Ghost' (KPR 17, 1975). In one village, gardens, pigs and property were destroyed and the people crowded into the church singing hosannas. This was in response to a call by a pastor from Pangia-Ialibu, who belonged to the same mission as the Kuali Lombo missionaries. The expatriate Kuali Lombo missionary was very alarmed by the events and said that the pastor had 'misinterpreted the message'; the pastor finished by apologizing, and that was the end of the cult (KPR 18, 1975).

Yet in spite of the Administration's wariness, the people themselves were keen to have missions settle on their land. There are strict rules about land purchase in the area. Only the government is legally entitled to buy land from the people, and such land may then be leased to outsiders. In the case of the missions a free 99-year lease is normally given, on the understanding that certain improvements will be made by the lessee. When in 1969 a lease for 43 acres was refused to the Evangelical Bible Mission in Kari Tiburu Census Division because the Administration was not convinced that the people would benefit, the people themselves were happy to allow the missionaries to squat on their land. They reasoned that the mission would then be obligated to help them. As the Patrol Officer put it,

'The village leaders state that they have cried at Pangia, Kagua and Erave to try and find a European to sit down in their village and bring some business for them, so that now although they would prefer an Agricultural Officer, or a businessman, they are happy that the mission has decided to sit down in their village.'

(KPR 1, 1969)

In the Sugu Valley a Catholic priest visited Roga in 1961 and according to one informant told them that their dead were dwelling in a dark place but that one day they would be with them again. By way of explaining the reason for their conversion the same informant added that there had been many debilitating sicknesses in the days when they kept their 'satanic' cults, while they were now healthy. Another informant, from Agema, explained how they became converted there. The 'little Father' (*ogepara* 'because he was not the one in charge of the mission') first had them build a church in Aliwi, for which he paid with axes, shells and bushknives. Then in 1964 the *ogepara* came to Agema and commissioned another church, paying them with money as well this time. The informant insisted that he did not come with presents to 'grease' them into adopting Christianity; he came with a book, and told them they would rise again after death. He sprinkled holy water on the spirit houses which he said they must pull down and never touch again. A young catechist came with him, and acted as interpreter.

In order to gain a better understanding of people's readiness to convert it is necessary to know something about traditional cults and how they operated. The Kewa had a number of ancestral cults, the most pervasive being Ribu. They also had other deities, such as Yaki, who was not an ancestral spirit but an autochthonous sky creature who could be appealed to for garden fertility. According to one writer,

'"Ribu" stands for a collectivity of male ancestors not individually honoured, or a collection of ancestor-chiefs whose memory of heroic achievements in tribal war and leadership should be remembered by future generations.'

(Apea 1975)

There were several Ribu cults in the Sugu area; *Adalu* (long) Ribu, *Salu* or *Mae* (short) Ribu, *Koi* (bad) Ribu. The ritual practice in all cases was similar and followed a cycle lasting five to seven years. In the beginning, after some major disaster, a clan might feel that its established Ribu cult was not a powerful one and decide to purchase another from a neighbouring clan. The cult house would be built in two to three days, and the cult owners would hand over power in the form of painted sacred stones which with due ceremony and sacrifice were buried in the house. During the following years small numbers of pigs would be killed from time to time while large numbers were bred for the final celebrations, at which time as many as a hundred might be killed. All but three were killed outside the spirit house and eaten by everyone; these three were sacrificed inside and eaten only by cult participants. The cult would then be phased out, to be revived, or perhaps replaced, when another disaster occurred.

In this general context the acceptance of another Ribu, Christianity, did not perhaps involve much initial deviation. While at first sight it appears quite extraordinary that Christianity was embraced so easily and the traditional cults allowed to disappear almost without a trace in such a short space of time, some general features of these cults make this phenomenon more comprehensible. The first concerns their structure: they were cyclical and peripatetic, new cults being easily received as old ones were abandoned. Since they were transitory in nature, they were not rooted in groups as part of group structure and identity. They were supposedly efficacious in establishing good relations with ancestors in general, but were not connected with any one ancestor in particular. This meant that the fact that one's grandfather had adopted a certain cult did not oblige one to adhere to it on pain of facing ancestral wrath. Thus no particular cult had a special relationship to one group or was owned by it in such a way that it could not also be acquired by another.

A second feature concerns the peripheral role of the cults in beliefs to do with production and reproduction. While Ribu received sacrifices when major disasters befell crops and people, his blessing was not a daily requirement for garden fertility. Yaki, the sky creature, was more frequently called upon in this connection. Nor in the case of the reproduction of people did the Ribu cult have a central role. There were no initiation rites,[3] so that the ritual cycle was not inextricably part of the life of an individual in the sense that without it he would not achieve manhood or she womanhood. People reached adulthood, married and had children without necessarily being received into a cult. Women in any case were forbidden cult membership. Although most men would be initiated into some cult or another before their life was over, they could marry and become fully-fledged adult members of the community before this happened.

As with cults, cleavages in mission adherence followed political cleavages. One big man, though originally proselytized by the Catholics, showed his political independence from other clans by summoning the ECP to his newly established settlement.[4] Another used the anthropologist in the same way by allowing the rumour that in inviting her he was branching out politically, she being another 'mission' representative for the people at the time. Nonetheless the hopes and fears of Christianity in a very crude way have made inroads into people's thinking. Many converts will say, for instance, that they want eternal life and are afraid of Hell. Hope and fear are inextricably bound together, as the following conversation with an informant shows:

> *Informant:* Some special circumstances led to the killing of children in the past, but the missions have now outlawed infanticide.
>
> *Me:* Missions can't 'outlaw' anything; they have no power to gaol. Only the government can do that.
>
> *Informant:* (with a knowing smile) Yes, it is true that missions cannot gaol in this life. But they can gaol you in the next for all eternity.

In concluding this discussion on religion it must be said that the most popular missions in the area (ECP and Catholic) have in some ways been indigenized and built into people's daily lives. Local pastors have reinterpreted some canons and instituted new 'laws'. For instance, although pigs are no longer killed for Ribu, at the time of the Kewa *yawe*, which still persists, pastors and catechists were seen busily collecting a 'tax' of K2 for every pig killed. They explained that this was for the church. At the same time the people considered that the church provided a social and cultural service, and they would protest if the pastor failed to come and preach in their settlement. They saw their support of the church as paying for a service, so they expected to get that service. In many ways, by operating through local pastors and catechists who are available to the people, churches are far better organized at grassroots level than the government. Like the old cults, Christianity works through fear, but it also offers hope, far more than the cults did, because it claims total supremacy and the monopoly of all power, earthly and otherworldly. But the other side of this is that the Christian God is a jealous one, who will not tolerate other gods beside himself, whereas Ribu did not mind

the competition. This means that the many denominations sometimes confuse people. They acknowledge that many cults existed
before, but point out that they were not mutually exclusive; on
the contrary, many existed concurrently in the same settlement.
Yet Christianity, although it has eradicated cults, does coexist
with a number of traditional powers which existed independently
of Ribu and other ancestral spirits. These are various forms of
magic, both benevolent and malevolent, divinations, and dreaming. Malevolent magic is naturally considered 'satanic' by missions and condemned, but church adherents openly use white
magic, such as the sort that helps in the making of tree houses to
catch birds, and other magic connected with hunting. Divinations
may still sometimes be carried out; missions have allowed them
again, but they forbid action to be taken following their results.
Dreaming is the ability to see the future or discover some secret in
sleep, in a set of symbolic images. This is in no way disapproved
of, except if it leads to any violent action or reprisal. Pigs are still
killed when people are ill, although this is no longer openly
rationalized as an offering to appease ancestral spirits. Pigs are also
killed after the death of an important man. The symbolic meaning
of this is winked at by church officials, who offer prayers at the
event and treat it as a Christian custom. They will object,
however, to a gift of a pig made on such an occasion by an outside
group, interpreting this as *mena kiri*, a placatory payment linked
to war reparations. The objections are not always consistent and
justifications vary, but the point is that they are the people's own
response to culture contact.

Christianity, then, has been selectively appropriated. A certain
ecumenism may exist, but it is in embryo stages and not normally
resident in the village.

Development projects

Coffee seed was first received in Erave in 1955, and the earliest
gardens were made in Samberigi in 1958. In 1961 coffee was
introduced into the Sugu, when a Patrol Officer planted 20,000
seeds in nurseries. He enthusiastically stated his plan at the time:
that the whole community should work on the nurseries, with a
roster programme of weeding and cleaning by the women
('whole community' here means women). Then they would help

plant some coffee on the land of the man who had it ready first; this would be for demonstration purposes, and it would be fitting if such blocks were first established by Patrol Officers for the Village Constables. When ready, other men could plant their coffee on an individual basis, with advice from a team of Agricultural Officers and Administration staff.

There were some problems with this strategy. According to village informants, as soon as the Patrol Officers turned their backs, community labour fell off, and plot owners had to resort to traditional methods of working parties with pork payments at the end, in order to attract labour. Other men, who had by their personal labour cleared a garden, were finding it difficult in 1962 to acquire seeds (KPR 1, 62). In the same year, 64 per cent of seeds were lost in Kuare because of neglect and poor extension work. By 1966 coffee had quite soured on some people. Not only was marketing a problem – sometimes an insurmountable one – but in some cases when the grower did manage to get his beans to a buyer he found that they were unacceptable. One case illustrates this:

> 'One man at Sawmili even refused an offer by the Agricultural Officer to clean, prune and attempt to re-establish his small plot. The man explained that he had done everything the *kiap*[5] had told him to do a few years back but when he took his beans to Erave the kiap told him to burn them. "So I burnt all my coffee beans and will never grow it again." Naturally it was explained to the poor gent that there is more to processing coffee than just "washing" it and although this might not have been explained to him in the past, this was why the Agricultural Officer was not patrolling his area. The man still refused assistance, having like so many people in the area lost faith in the Administration.'
>
> (Letter from the Erave Assistant District Officer to the Kagua Assistant District Commissioner, 7 October 1966, Kagua and Erave Official Papers (KEOP), 1966)

In West Kagua, where the establishment of coffee blocks was on a 'community' basis with the Village Constable in charge, the projects ran into difficulties when the Village Constable system was replaced by the Local Government Council and the former no longer had any official authority. Unless an individual decided to take responsibility, the whole block was allowed to become overgrown with bush. Not many individuals could take responsibility, for their experience was limited and expert help not forthcoming (KPR 3, 66).

By 1968 there were only a few small coffee blocks in the Sugu area and most of them had completely failed through lack of specialized advice. There were no other cash crops. Forestry workers had planted 2,300 pine and eucalyptus trees in Agema (KPR 3, 1968), but nobody by 1981 had been back to tell the people what to do with them. Chillis, vanilla and cardamon were planted in Erave and some parts of Kagua in 1969 and 1970, but never provided significant revenue. In 1970 a Patrol Officer assessed the situation as follows:

> 'The present attitude of the people towards economic development is one of mild disappointment over the fact that after twelve years of contact there are still no cash crops in the area which they are able to utilize to earn an adequate income.'
> (Area Study, East and West Sugu DC 1970, KEOP, 1970)

The writer goes on to say that in spite of the interest shown by the people coffee planting was held back by the Department of Agriculture, Stock and Fisheries (now the Department of Primary Industry) because of shortage of agricultural staff, while cattle projects were held back because of shortage of stock. As many as twenty-nine cattle project areas were prepared by prospective ranchers who also had collected the money to buy the stock, but none was available. Many people then turned to migration to earn the cash which they now needed. The same study found that out of a population of 5,384, 43 per cent of East Sugu and 22 per cent of West Sugu potential male labour was absent from the village. Yet this migration hardly benefited them on their return, for they learnt skills (rubber tapping, copra preparation, tea maintenance) which were irrelevant to the village. According to one Patrol Report, the mainstay of the Kuare Valley economy in 1969 was still the wages of repatriated labourers, each of whom brought back an average of $36, i.e. $7,920 for 220 absentees in that year.

In 1972 there were 80 acres of bearing coffee in the whole of Kagua and it was not doing too well. Tradestores were multiplying – up to four in each village, but were sparsely stocked and generally not viable commercially. By 1979, when my fieldwork commenced, each settlement had a litter of defunct stores and a

few cattle, soon to be consumed. But world coffee prices had
soared, so more efforts were concentrated on coffee growing.

Effects of the imposition of the state and
the cessation of warfare

Physical, political, social and economic changes were ushered in
by the new centralized power which had subdued warfare. The
opposite of a state of war is not simply 'peace', a residual and
neutral category, but a total reorganization and restructuring of
all aspects of human existence. People moved to settlements
down the valley and close to the roads, placing themselves under
the protection of the new law. They began to participate in local
and national elections and developed an increasing dependence on
a market and an economic system shaped by events thousands of
miles away. They lost their self-reliance (as the Administration
officer cited earlier commented) to the extent that they lost their
self-sufficiency; an inevitable consequence of participation in a
world market economy.

On a more local level, a number of new political differentiations have taken place as a result of this restructuring. In the old
days wars shaped groups and to a large extent defined manhood,
prestige, glory: the fighting (although not the killing) concerned
men only and a hierarchization based on prowess in war was
created. The big man of exchanges and wealth (*amo*) may not have
been the war general (*mudu*), but he was very important during
the fighting nevertheless. He was the politician, the propagandist,
the maker of heroes and the winner of wars through sheer verbal
charisma. Now new categories of important men sprang up,
whose power still emanated from the group but who were
invested in addition with power which the group did not control.
The fact that these men were and are usually locally elected means
that the new state sponsors a 'traditional' big man, and by
sponsoring him confers on him a power that is not traditional,
because he may no longer be displaced or kept in check in
traditional ways. It also encourages him to act in untraditional
ways. The Village Magistrate, the Councillor, the Member of
Parliament, once ensconced may not be easily dislodged. In any
case, their constituents are not always able to judge their mis-
demeanours since they may appeal to an authority and a 'law'
outside the village. This could explain why some men, originally

designated traditional headmen and therefore appointed Village Constables by the Administration, in due course appeared to lose their standing in the village and were overtaken by the more influential, self-styled boss boys. Possibly the people lost respect and had only fear for men who appeared to be mere mouthpieces of the 'white-skins', forcing them to do things which, according to custom, were abhorrent. The Melpa big man, Ongka, in his self-account illustrates well the psychological effects that this had on such men, who could carry out their duties only by exaggerating them and announcing that they were creatures possessed:

'Some of these appointees went off and said "The white man has turned our stomachs around and put them in again backwards, don't dare to speak in front of us, we're not in our proper minds, we'll kill you!" If anybody looked boldly at them they said "The *Kiap* has made me a boss boy, why are you staring at me like that?" The other would reply "My sister's son, I wasn't staring at you, I was just looking normally." "No you weren't, you were staring insolently," they said. Then they would take the man and bind him to the central post in a house and build up a fire nearby until he choked in the smoke.

'The man would agree then to let go of his pigs as a "fine" to the boss boy. "I'm dying," they would say. "No you are not, I'm a *Kiap* and I'm watching over you," was the reply, and so they continued until the pigs were promised. When one particular man who was a boss boy went visiting he would say to the people "My stomach has turned round, the sun is high in the sky, don't come near me or touch me, I'll kill you!" and all the people fled like pigs in the woods. People used to shake with fear when they saw the boss boys coming with big cassowary plumes nodding on their heads.'

(A. Strathern 1979: 12)

Several incongruities emerge from this account. The response of the boss boy's victim, deliberately prefaced by the kinship term 'my sister's son', appeals to a relationship which the boss boy refuses to acknowledge and in fact violates by his actions. Not only the kinship relationship, but the rules of seniority and common decency are flouted by the boss boy, who exceeds his authority in an apparent bid to gain something to his advantage; at the same time, he resembles a man driven by a mad, blind fury.

The Kewa case is in many particulars not comparable with the Melpa one,[6] the former being the product of an altogether milder and more moderate culture contact. The terminology is different to begin with: officials in the Kewa case were Village Constables, while boss boys were self-styled, modelling themselves on the Imbonggu and Melpa example, and some perhaps receiving official recognition by being made into Village Constables. Also, the power of these officials never got out of hand to the extent just described for the Melpa. On the contrary, the Village Constables were often torn between new laws and the observance of customary duties towards the people they were appointed to keep in check. They frequently experienced difficulties in subduing recalcitrant elements in the community who preferred to support the boss boys, considering their attitude (of attempting to gain privileges for themselves while getting out of work) admirable.

Notwithstanding these local variations, state interference undoubtedly transformed leadership and leaders in important ways. Apart from the elected officers mentioned above, other officials of import in the village were appointed by the state or the church. These included the pastor, the catechist, the interpreter, the Agricultural Officer, and the District Officer. Most of these derived their standing solely from their official position, having no charisma aside from this. Accordingly, relations between local leaders and their clan-mates have changed subtly as patterns of dependence and expectations of support have changed. The resultant relationship between young men and older, established men, will be discussed below.

The cessation of warfare and the emergence of state power clearly affected the dynamics of group formation and the ideology of group solidarity. While the power of destruction bound people together and necessitated alliances, rules of recruitment to groups were fluid and agnatic ideologies glossed over many irregularities. Constant wars kept groups and their names going, though their composition changed. With peace and a changing economy rules of descent took on a more uncompromising aspect. Tribes and clans registered their members in the District Office and now have official, legal rights to fixed tribal territories. Land now defines the group more rigidly, and encroachment on tribal territory keeps members together. Patrilocality has become more strictly observed. As one man said,

'Why should I leave my father's land and live with my wife's or mother's people? In the old days when war harried us we did this, but now we prefer to stay on our father's land, where our rights are supreme.'

What of the role of the ceremonial pig kill in this connection? In *The Rope of Moka* Andrew Strathern reports how the relationship between war and *moka* is described by the Melpa, then assesses the description himself:

'"Before we fought and killed each other, and this was bad; now a good time has come, and we can pay for killings and make *moka.*" Although such statements are *post hoc* evaluations, they do reflect the fact that *moka* and warfare are seen as two different ways of asserting group and individual prowess.'

(Strathern 1971: 54)

For the Kewa there is no such contrast, for the ceremonial pig kill (which is the nearest equivalent they have to the *moka*) is not a recent innovation but was always closely tied in with warfare in the past, as a mechanism uniting diverse elements following dispersion attendant on war. Nonetheless, the cessation of warfare has meant that pig kills have acquired more ideological significance as group events and occasions 'of asserting group and individual prowess'. Although the warrior is no longer, the transactor can still transact and build up a reputation that way. In fact the 'businessman', as I shall discuss later, is often sacrificed to the traditional transactor.

Even before land had become fully exploited commercially, its potential commercial value was being felt in the Sugu Valley. Even when lying idle it began to be thought of as a potential commercial commodity, its usufruct no longer being granted so casually. No cash crops existed in the valley apart from coffee and some commercial vegetables. Cattle were bought now and then and used as 'large pigs' in exchanges and pig kills; there was no local cattle breeding.[7] A number of tradestores still functioned desultorily and intermittently in 1980, but reaped no significant profits; travel costs to bulk stores were far too high. Trucks were bought from time to time, but had short lives. Some local entrepreneurs ran passenger buses which they failed to license and were therefore always getting caught and being fined. They might at the same time do some business in coffee buying, but their operating capital was usually small, and fluctuating coffee prices (from 1980, constantly falling) made buying difficult from local growers who would not accept the dictates of the world market. Coffee buyers were no less in the dark regarding world markets; they knew only that sometimes the price was high and sometimes low. Moreover, they often bought blind because they were intimidated by villagers who objected to their wares being examined, and because they did not have the experience to know how the big companies would sort and grade the coffee. On top of this they had truck operating costs and on the frequent occasions when trucks were out of action and they could not afford to hold on to coffee bought, they had to shoulder the huge costs of hiring a truck and driver to transport them into the urban markets.

In the West Sugu area there was only one coffee buyer, and he tried to do business by undercutting other buyers who came to Sumbura market from East Sugu, Kuare, Kuali Lombo and Mt Hagen. This man started in business some years ago by planting peanuts which he sold, and opened a tradestore with the proceeds of K100. Eventually he managed to save K1,600 to which his wife's people contributed another K1,200 and they bought a truck. However there were disagreements over this truck; according to the West Sugu informant (who is a staunch and fearful supporter of the 'Bible Mission') these arose because his partners wanted the truck used every day for business, while he thought that Sundays were sacred. Eventually he sold his share to them for K1,000. With K200 of this he 'helped' another man from his village (Puri) to buy a truck, and this was the vehicle that my informant now used. However, use of it was not free; he had to pay a hire fee of K80 for the day every time he used it.

Coffee was the single most important source of cash for the Sugu Kewa. Out of a total Agema Yala tribal territory of 1,500 hectares, 25.5 (i.e. 1.7 per cent) was under cultivation. 3.3 of these hectares were given to coffee. There are 36 individually-owned coffee gardens, with a total of 21,050 bearing coffee trees, i.e. an average of 584.7 trees per owner. This was unequally divided, some having only 30–100 trees and others as many as 800 to 900. The number of trees was no indication of yield or revenue, however, since cherries were sometimes not picked but allowed to rot on the ground. For 11 months, between 20 February 1980 and 21 January 1981, full accounts were kept of the coffee sold by the owners of these gardens and their representatives. A total of

K4,508 was earned by them for that period, i.e. an average of K125.22 for each garden, or K11.38 per garden per month. This means that each tree brought in 21 toea for that period, i.e. 2 toea per month.

Very little time was given to cleaning and pruning the coffee. Some trees had grown so high that owners used ladders to pick the cherries. Picking was done haphazardly when owners needed some immediate ready cash, although there are definite coffee flush seasons (September–January) when most of the coffee was picked. Many coffee owners who did not have the time or inclination to pick and wash their own coffee gave picking rights to relatives who sold what they picked and kept the proceeds. The owners said that they were 'helping' these relatives and this was chalked up as a favour.

Access to coffee and to revenue from it was therefore open to everyone – old people, children, men and women. Whoever prepared the coffee had a right to the proceeds from its sale. However, where it concerned the household, the practice was not as egalitarian as it appeared at first sight. Apart from the small amounts that they cleaned for themselves and in their names, women and children also provided labour for the preparation of the larger bags of coffee, the revenue from which had a more complicated destination. Whereas the small amounts were 'pocket money' or 'for eating', these larger amounts were channelled into ventures controlled by men, such as tradestores, truck buying, or ceremonial pig kills. Occasionally they might simply be frittered away in gambling.

Early fears that villagers were putting all their eggs in one development basket by growing coffee almost to the exclusion of any other cash crop were shown to have some foundation in 1980 when world prices slumped and quotas were given for the total amount a country could export. Sugu villagers responded for a long time by withholding their coffee from buyers altogether, some for as long as four months. They reasoned that prices would go up again eventually, if they waited long enough. As the need arose they would sell a few Kina's worth, but hold on to the bulk of their pickings. Eventually hoarding became impracticable, and as prices were still falling, many growers sold. However they began at this time to neglect their coffee even more than before, for they argued that the measly returns did not justify the work that had to be put into cleaning and preparing. In this opinion they differed widely from the Administration officer who in the previous decade had tried to drum into them that however low the returns, 'one cent was better than no cent', since he judged that given the alternatives offered to them villagers would either accept low returns or cease to be productive altogether. For their part, villagers thought that their time could more fruitfully be spent on other activities which were not necessarily commercially productive. These included socializing and organizing large-scale exchange events.

In response to encouragement from Extension Officers from the Department of Business Development (DBD), a few villagers planted large gardens with market vegetables such as cabbages, which were to be transported with the help of the DBD to urban markets in Mt Hagen in the Western Highlands. Although the gardens did well, the Extension Officers failed at the last moment to provide transport and help with marketing, so the would-be entrepreneurs were forced to give away most of the cabbages, while the rest rotted. They did hope, however, that by their gifts they encouraged local people to develop a taste for the new vegetables which would create a small domestic market for them in the future.

The other major avenue for cash earning was wage labour. In the village, opportunities for wage labour were virtually non-existent. Apart from the pastor and the interpreter (a public servant who still drew a salary though the position had become obsolete), a few men worked as drivers for local entrepreneurs. From time to time a road maintenance contract was offered by the local Council providing limited opportunities for cash earning. However these contracts were thought to pay very little and were as a result unpopular, attracting only very young people and especially girls, whose prospects for migrant labour were very restricted.

Migrant labour on plantations was therefore the only significant opening for young men to earn a cash income. The pattern and intensity of outmigration from the area has been discussed elsewhere (Josephides and Schiltz 1981); here I want to examine only how it affects the position of the younger, unestablished men in the village. Most of these young men have had no schooling at all, although a few might have completed some classes at primary school. They start migrating in a very casual way to the Western Highlands plantations from the ages of sixteen or seventeen, returning home frequently to spend the little money that they have earned. When they are a little older they attempt to save some money so that they can marry and establish their own coffee gardens in the village. This is not an easy task, for little can be saved on the plantations. Also, because of their frequent absences the young men are not able to build up a patron-client relationship with an established man who will come to their aid. This partly reflects a larger problem, that of the market economy's general infiltration of the village community, which by offering alternative avenues for raising wealth has made people less dependent on each other.

While a more generalized access to wealth has made young men more independent and at the same time more mobile, established men at home respond with a marked reluctance to invest in those on whose reciprocity they cannot depend. In addition, they may not feel the same need for the support of these young men as in the days when threatening war made extra warriors welcome. This is not to say that all young men were sponsored by older ones in those days, or that none is now. But what is clear is that it is extremely difficult nowadays for a young man to 'make good' on a plantation and as a result establish himself at home. While in the early 1970s it was still possible to obtain reasonably cheap labour on a communal basis to start one's coffee garden, this facility is now disappearing and the hire of labour in the village can cost more than the migrant labourer is himself paid on the plantation. What does the young man do in these circumstances? He returns to the plantation and passes a few more years. Some may eventually drift into towns and live the chancy life of the peripheral vagabond. Most, however, do return home and try to shift for themselves, probably 'pulling' a woman and bringing about a situation in which their clan brothers are forced to assist with bridewealth.[8]

I have mentioned the infiltration of the market economy into the village community. This refers mainly to the fact that villagers have become producers and consumers of commodities which circulate within this economy. While they produce coffee, chillis and cardamon (and on plantations also tea, copra and rubber) for a world market, villagers earn cash with which they buy imported clothes, imported food and imported technology. Yet this participation in the international capitalist economy does not make them into capitalists, for it is the social relations within which commodities are produced and consumed that determine the economic system, and not the commodities themselves.[9] The social relations within the village are still characterized by a gift economy; a situation which becomes clear in the discussion of pig kill exchanges. While much of people's cash returns goes into the buying of imported food, the pig kill exchange tabulations offer an important checklist which shows just how much money and wealth is still circulating in this gift economy in which men make their names.[10]

In the last two decades Kewa country and Kewa society have undoubtedly been transformed on a revolutionary scale, far outstripping the speed of transitions previously experienced. Rugged footpaths have given way to motorable roads and air-strips; valley floor family vegetable gardens have been transformed into coffee gardens, while introduced vegetables are beginning to be planted on a commercial scale for urban markets. Large plantations stretch further than any of the gardens Hides came upon in 1935. Villagers ride about in motor cars to work hundreds of miles away, or to attend court proceedings or council meetings. They vote for their representatives in the provincial and national elections and may stand for Parliament themselves. They send their children to school, and themselves attend churches of the various denominations which proliferate daily, while the old cults have disappeared from the face of the land. They eat more and more imported food which they buy from the many local tradestores with money earned in coffee selling or migrant labour on plantations.

However, while the ordinary villagers have become sucked into a world capitalist system as petty commodity producers (see Kahn 1978), they cannot be described as budding capitalists as Epstein (1968) and Finney (1973) have argued for the Tolai and the Eastern Highlanders. Although the Kewa social system also has *'significant inbuilt inequalities'* (Good 1979: 103, emphasis in original), this feature by no means facilitates the establishment of a capitalist system of production. The concepts of 'mode of production' and 'relations of production' have so far been avoided here, because the controversy surrounding them is not central to my thesis. However, it is necessary to stress at this stage that neither people's behaviour (e.g. self-seeking or business-like), nor the levels of technological development or the mere fact of participating in a cash economy, define the 'mode of production' of villagers. What is crucial is the total social relations within which they produce, and these are not within the cash economy. The separation of the producers from the means of production, in this case land, is a prerequisite for the emergence of capitalist social relations. At the moment Kewa social relations of production exhibit the characteristics of an incipient peasant economy (see Frankenberg 1967; Shanin 1976; Kahn 1978). Inequalities do exist, especially on gender lines. Yet this has not predisposed people to behave in a 'capitalistic' way. It has not encouraged 'good business sense', capitalist accumulation or investment in the area. This is because the indigenous gift economy remains the dominant mode of interaction, as the following chapters will further illustrate.

Corollaries for gender relations

The various developments discussed have naturally affected the position of women in society. In the old days constant war waging was men's activity, and it made women dependent on them for protection. At Independence the new state pledged itself in its Constitution to a social restructuring which would treat women as equals to men, to be involved equally in nation building (National Planning Office 1975). However, ever since the early days of contact and economic development officialdom has addressed only the men as heads of families; they were expected to control their women and involve them only in the sort of activities they deemed proper. It is true that young people are now jointly educated and no formal discrimination operates in enrolment procedures, although as a result of parental prejudice female intake is much lower than male. But such girls as do receive education move out of the community (as indeed do the boys), so that there is no feedback in the rural community of this sort of equality.

In general, then, how have changes in the economy affected male domination in respect of relations of production? So far, not much. While women are now able to earn and keep wealth in the form of cash, avenues for investing this wealth usually lead to its loss for them. Tradestores in which they hold shares go out of business, trucks are smashed. Women may also use their earnings to pay school fees, buy clothes and food, or finance card playing, or they may circulate them in exchanges. Although women may enjoy revenue from coffee and tradestore sales, they can never own the coffee garden or the tradestore, because they do not own land. Although their rights over their crops are undisputed, and they nowadays sell these in the market for cash, they may not operate the large commercial market vegetable projects because, first, they do not own land; second, they cannot call up the working parties necessary for the clearing of large tracts of land; and third, extension officers do not approach women offering encouragement and assistance for such enterprises. Thus old distinctions still operate to stop women from prospering in new ways. While traditional land holding persists women will not be able to overcome these restrictions, except by leaving the rural community and participating in the urban economy. Not many women are likely to be able to do this.

Though still in its initial stages, the argument developed concerning gender relations draws much on the importance of virilocality and the ownership of land. These are ethnographic variables. An argument concerning the subordination of women built around these variables may therefore seem to be ethnographically contingent. It may be further argued that women cannot overcome traditional restrictions on their economic activities, not only because they do not own land, but because local conditions in general are not conducive to profit-making. This affects both men and women, and is therefore no longer a question simply of gender relations. Men also will invest in exchanges, trucks and tradestores, businesses which frequently founder. But the subject of discussion here is the edge that men have over women within those relations of production, which are predicated on specific, empirical variables such as ownership of land or patrivirilocal residence.

This undoubtedly raises further questions, some of which are discussed by Modjeska in his comparison of African and PNG Highlands patterns of gender domination. In his discussion he cites an African example where 'the structural practices of exogamy, patrilineality and virilocal residence, made possible by male-controlled bridewealth . . . together construct the conditions for male appropriation of the surplus' (1982: 59–60). However, he notes that this explanation works only with local exogamy, so that 'one is here confronted with either an empirical difference or an analytical error'. Further, 'if the former, then the specific circumstances upon which domination ultimately rests may vary substantially in different cases'. I believe that there is little doubt that in any society it is on the specific cultural circumstances that domination rests. Exogamy and patrivirilocality, although specific and variable, are fundamental, and determinant of actual gender relations in the case discussed. This does not mean that we have to bow to a cultural relativism, for the model of domination and subordination which may be constructed in the process will be applicable to a whole range of societies, and make sense of a whole range of ethnographic facts.

Notes

1   This historical account is gleaned from Kagua and Erave Patrol Reports covering the period 1956 to 1980. Reference to these will be given as KPR or EPR followed by the number of the report and the year.
2   Strictly speaking, Village Magistrates are appointed, not elected. However, local groups usually choose their candidates, whose appointment is merely rubber-stamped by the official in charge.
3   Most Highlands societies do have initiation rites; see for instance Poole 1982 and Herdt 1982. For a survey of initiations in Melanesia, see Allen 1967.
4   This man explained his move by the argument that the Catholics were too lax and liberal: 'They don't ban enough traditional customs.'
5   *Kiap* is a pidgin word originally used for Patrol Officers. In Kagua nowadays this is extended to refer to all those in positions of authority.
6   A comment here from Andrew Strathern: 'Don't discount Ongka's humour and exaggeration!' (Personal communication).
7   There is one large cattle project in the Sugu area, but it is expatriate-managed on land alienated from the local people. The history of this land acquisition provides interesting reading. In spite of the ADC's opinion that the 6,600 acres involved 'could hardly be utilized to its full potential if offered to developers as cattle country', and that it should be used for tea and mixed farming (KPR 12, 1970), the land was in fact purchased for a cattle project. Local administration and the Australian businessmen involved in the project hoped that the land owners would invest some of the money they had received for the land (a total of $34,000) in the business enterprise which wanted to develop the area, and were given a number of talks on the desirability of this:
'It was explained that the company insisted that the ex-owners have a 10 per cent interest which would involve the investment

by the natives of \$20,000 in the project. This money must be obtained from the owners as quickly as possible, not only so that the projects can proceed, but also the money the former owners received for the Sugu lands is fast disappearing.'

(KPR 7, 1970)

However, although people expressed interest no money was forthcoming, and Patrol Officers were struck at how so much money could be 'so well hidden' (KPR 14, 1971). In the event there was no immediate investment by the former owners, although job opportunities on the site were welcomed. The business was later acquired by Kagua Council.

8   Young men may do this by being caught in compromising circumstances with the girl. Their agnates, who may have been reluctant earlier to contribute towards bridewealth, are now forced to pay either compensation or bridewealth. The marriage described in Chapter 2 was the result of such *flagrante delicto*, when the girl's father refused to accept compensation (he was the local pastor) but demanded 'full pay', i.e. proper bridewealth.

9   The term 'commodity' refers to objects of exchange in a way that 'goods' does not. Discussing the different approaches of Political Economy and Economics, Gregory mentions their use of these terms as denoting their theoretical interests and antecedents. While Political Economy talks of commodities, Economics settles for goods. While the former stresses an objective relation between things exchanged, the latter stresses a subjective relation between an individual and a desired object (Gregory 1982b: 7).

10 Speaking of the more commercially advanced Melpa, Andrew Strathern described similar motives in the case of one big man who, although he may be spurred on by the same 'spirit of competitive risk-taking and achievement' as the leaders of the new development corporations, presents his objective practices nevertheless as

'entirely different from those of plantation acquisition and profit-making. Thus, his whole aim is to maintain exchange partnerships, to keep wealth flowing and to make generous distributions to his kin and neighbours. If others are envious of him, it is not envy of a more comfortable life-style, or a larger bank balance, or of ownership of more land, it is envy simply of his personal capacities to speak and act, and thus to justify his name as a true big man in the Hagen style.'

(Strathern 1982a: 157)

In an economic sense, then, the aim of the big man seems to be the opposite of the capitalist's. Gregory characterizes this difference as the former's attempt to gain prestige by 'maximizing net outgoings', and the latter's goal of gaining wealth, power and influence by 'maximizing net incomings' (Gregory 1980: 636). The explanation of this paradox requires an examination of economic practice; see my critique of Gregory's formulation in Chapter 8.

Part Two
The production of inequality

4
Concepts and models

The ethnographic exposition so far has used a number of key concepts which must now be explored in the context of existing literature. These concepts are gender, exchange, power and inequality.

Gender and sex in New Guinea

I do not propose to give a fully documented survey of anthropological interests and biases in the study of sex and gender in New Guinea: Herdt and Poole (1982) have already done this admirably, and their essay[1] provides some of the background material for this section. What I plan to do here is, first, to define the term 'gender'; second, to discuss how far anthropological writings about sex and gender have reflected the researcher's bias rather than the true social conditions in the society under study; and third, to make some suggestions concerning the fruitful employment of the concept of gender in analyses of social relations.

The term 'gender' has come to be used to distinguish socially ascribed sex-linked attributes from physiological sex (Rubin 1975; Molyneux 1977; M. Strathern 1976, 1978). According to this distinction gender is a socially imposed division of the sexes which denies many similarities between the physical make-up, abilities and aspirations of men and women. The sexual division of labour is an example of this sex/gender system. While it is found in all known societies, the variety of forms it takes demonstrates that it has little to do with biology. Gender, then, is not a 'natural' (i.e. physiological) category, but a social one. Further, the division of labour anchored in the social category of gender does not only divide the sexes and their work, but also ranks them. Moreover, this ranking is invariably to the detriment of women, whose being, attributes and achievements are culturally less valued than men's.[2] In sum, I shall use the term 'gender' to denote a social tool for the validation and perpetuation of a set of unequal relations.

The next question must be that of the anthropologist's bias. This discussion requires first a brief survey of the literature in order to demonstrate the sort of biases referred to. Right from the beginning anthropological writings on male/female relations in the New Guinea Highlands have stressed sexual antagonism (Read 1951, 1954; Reay 1959; Meggitt 1964, 1965, 1976; Langness 1967). In all cases this antagonism was accompanied by residential separation, varying degrees of pollution fear, and, above all, the domination of women by men. Meggitt coined the phrases that divided Highlands men into two categories: they were either lechers aggressively determined to assert control over recalcitrant women, or else they were prudes anxious to protect themselves from contamination by women (1964: 221). These statements express the fears and aspirations of men, and present women not as subjects but as objects, obstacles in men's way, to be quelled. A later crop of anthropologists has tried to break through this bias and view women as persons, seen not only through male ideology, but as reported extensively through women's own statements, aspirations and activities (e.g. M. Strathern 1972, 1981b, 1983; Faithorn 1976; Gillison 1980). But even in the present theoretical climate, when these issues can no longer be ignored with impunity, must one assume that studies which present women as politically dominated by men are necessarily suffering from male bias? A brief comparative discussion of Gahuku-Gama, Hagen and Kewa will inform my view.

In 1982, Read was unrepentant about his assessment of male–female relations among the Gahuku-Gama. While in 1950 Gahuku-Gama women were 'beyond question' dominated by men (even though this was 'an uneasy domination requiring vigilance and ritual reinforcements'), in 1981 'political control and the control of primary resources [remained] in the hands of men', women having made 'almost no inroads on their political power and authority' (Read 1982: 76–77). He narrates the story of one Gahuku-Gama girl who had broken away from male control, refused to marry, and ran her own life in the village; but points out that 'one or even several swallows do not make a summer'.

In this book, I will make a similar assessment of changes in male–female relations among the Kewa, where by 1981 not even one swallow had come to roost in the village. As reported for the Gahuku-Gama, men still owned the basic resources of production and women still did not occupy any significant political position, but remained peripheral to group ideologies. In the 1950s Read had emphasized 'ideological oppositions, anxieties and antagonisms rather than simple reciprocity' as the most salient aspect of male–female relations. Although in many roles and spheres of interest men and women were complementary, this complementarity 'does not necessarily entail mutuality'; nor had mutuality been achieved by 1981 (Read 1982: 77). I will describe male–female relations as being characterized by 'dominance and subordination' rather than mutuality, because in spite of the milder form of male–female antagonism among the Kewa there is little doubt that in any confrontation of interests the men's political muscle, which gains its strength from their control of productive resources as well as the exchange sphere, will prevail against the women. Politically, women are indeed dominated by men, and it would be taking great liberties with the data to present the case as being otherwise.

But although we as 'aware' anthropologists may report extensively on women's activities and give much space to their verbatim statements and cultural assessments, are we still falling into the 'male trap' of labelling, a priori, only male activities as being 'political'? Weiner (1982: 55) laments that we need to understand more about women than that they are 'secondary to men in status and power'. If we are to respond to this call we must go beyond the study of gender, and beware that we do not raise it to the status of a sub-discipline. But as a starting point we need to have a true and lucid representation of the respective statuses of men and women in the societies studied. A rosy lens, or one green with hope and wishful thinking, can distort as much as an androcentric one. In order to understand these statuses we must tackle, head-on, the questions of politics and social power.

In this book, I define political power as the ability to control events within the group. Power comes from the group; it cannot be wielded by any individual in isolation. Further, I describe Kewa women as peripheral to group ideologies because they are considered to be sojourners in respect of any group. This structural position means that they do not represent the group and its name, and since the group legitimizes political authority, women are in no position to build on personal advantage and gain influence.

This characterization of women as 'sojourners' and 'peripheral' invites comparison with Marilyn Strathern's 'women in between' (1972). Hagen women are 'in between' symbolically, culturally, and politically; while they carry messages between their natal group and their husband's group, and while they link those groups politically and economically in a complex of exchange relations, they themselves are never permanently or completely identified with a group. In consequence, just as in the case of Kewa women, political decisions do not rest with them. The individual's relationship to the group, then, is of the utmost importance when discussing questions of political power.

Strathern describes women as political minors, but says that, jurally, they are considered responsible for their actions. The result of this is that in day-to-day affairs women end up with more duties than rights, since the extent to which 'rights' can be claimed is a function of political power and influence (M. Strathern 1972: 260). In Hagen, transaction is a culturally more prestigious activity than production, so women, being primarily producers behind the scenes rather than transactors, gain less prestige, and therefore less political influence. Sometimes women do come to the foreground on ceremonial occasions, and attired in splendid dress take part in the dancing. But M. and A. Strathern (1971) describe this as an expression of the prestige and power of the husband, which the wife merely personifies on this occasion. This interpretation of the event has received criticism from Weiner (1976), who argued that there was no reason to assume that women were not expressing their own power in their own right, rather than vicariously.[3]

Although Kewa wives do not decorate, there is one occasion in their lives which can be compared to the Hagen event. At the time of the pig kill husbands set aside large cuts of uncooked pork for their wives to distribute to their kin. While the wife is doing this it may look as if she is really transacting exchanges; however, in point of fact she is presiding over a distribution, as her husband's agent. She is not free to dispose of the pork as she chooses, but must give it to her kin. In her role as distributor she discharges her husband's obligations; she does not create any towards herself. It is this creation of obligations to oneself that really distinguishes exchange prestations from mere distributions. Thus although Weiner's (1976) point is taken concerning the pitfalls of accepting at face value men's statements about women and their power, we must also guard against instant characterizations of social relations from the direct observation of social practices.

My conclusion is, quite simply, that although we are not always rigorous in our reporting and analysing of social practices, are often neglectful, biased, or plain confused, and that we must at all times be vigilant in order to improve these shortcomings, there is, nonetheless, little doubt that in the societies discussed (and in many more besides) women occupy a politically weaker position than men. To recognize that the politically weak are just that is not to misrepresent their situation or prejudice their case when we point out that their condition is neither terminal nor congenital, nor anchored in their ontological status as persons, but that it is a function of social relations, which are transformable.

The 'gender concept' revised: models for analysis

How can the concept of gender be usefully employed in analyses of social relations? This question requires an appraisal of the theoretical uses of the concept, rather than its ethnographic content. I shall outline some problems surrounding its use, then examine two models for the analysis of gender.

I have already pointed to the sort of biases found in discussions of women in anthropological writings. The most important of these is insufficient time and attention given to the statements of women themselves, with the result that they and their actions are always viewed relationally, through men's needs and statements, which become central to the research and subsequent analysis. Right from the beginning there is a feedback effect between fieldwork and theory, so that biased ethnographic data (themselves partly determined by pre-fieldwork theoretical predilections) then inform the theoretical framework of the analysis. Sometimes anthropologists deny that neglect of a substantial category of people in the field area permeates their global statements, but imagine that they can make objective generalizations from the observation of just one category, albeit the most vociferous one. The plea on these occasions may be that the other category was inaccessible to them,[4] and that in any case it was peripheral to the subject studied. Sillitoe (1979) makes such a plea; which, given the centrality of this question, is perhaps worth quoting in full:

> 'Perhaps I can plead that the concern of this book with men is the result of this separation between the sexes made by the Wola, who rarely permit women to handle wealth except under the guidance of men, and not, as some people in our women's lib conscious society have suggested, the result of my own male chauvinism.'
>
> (Sillitoe 1979: 21ff)

The first thing to note is that 'the Wola' clearly refers here only to Wola men. Or does the author mean that *both* men and women 'rarely permit women to handle wealth'? It is not clear, either, whether he is simply reporting men's statements about women and wealth, or his own observations of women's actual social positions. Perhaps the most serious criticism is that the author seems to believe that since Wola men make these claims (irrespective of their truth value) this excuses him as a social scientist from the necessity of discussing women's roles and locating them in his analysis. It may be that the author is unaware of the dismissive connotations of the expression 'women's lib', and is not intending to belittle feminist views. However, the suggestion that any criticism from this quarter would be misplaced, ethnocentric and irrelevant, requires, I think, more explanation than his footnote can offer.

Perhaps partly in response to this kind of attitude, a spate of feminist works have made their counterclaims. Reviewing some of these, M. Strathern (1981a) sums up their claims in three propositions, which she assesses in the following manner:

> 'These three propositions – "women" are a category suitable for study; women anthropologists obviate customary male bias in a self-conscious focus on women, and women anthropologists are likely to have a sensitive insight into the condition of women elsewhere – are tantamount to the manufacture of a sub-discipline.'
>
> (M. Strathern 1981a: 669)

Strathern presents a superb discussion of these points, bringing out the full implications of manufacturing a sub-discipline for the study of women. At the risk of impoverishing her argument I shall condense it here, and then mention some ways in which my interests and therefore formulations diverge.

The most stimulating part of the discussion concentrates on the notion of bias as the critic's tool, described by her as a 'powerful ingredient'. If the presence of 'bias' can be identified in any generalization, this is sufficient for it to be discredited and there-fore discounted, and its critics are not obliged to disprove it in any other way. But critics of 'male bias' suffer from their own biases, and bias itself, as the straw man of universalizations, is a marker of paradigmatic shifts. Some women's studies employ the straw man when they posit the universal woman as object of study, and reveal their bias when they claim that women researchers in that field have an empathy and sensitivity which should result in 'holistic, accurate, and objective studies' (M. Strathern 1981a: 667). There is here a claim and a denial: while it is claimed that, cross-culturally, a woman researcher with her 'double conscious-ness' (of bias and of womanness) has greater facility in under-standing a woman researched, it is denied that one sex can know the other, even in the same culture. In other words, the existence of universal womanness is the a priori, original premiss of this view. But there is no such thing as 'woman', Strathern argues, and the way in which certain cultures value women tells us more about those cultures than 'womanness'. The belief that particular studies can yield human universals leads to biased assessments of writings on cultures which exhibit different variables, and there-fore different valuations of women from the paradigmatic case. In constructing a model for the analysis of gender we can start from the débris of universal woman. While I agree that different cultures construct gender categories differently and symbolize male, female and their relations differently, there is little doubt that distinctions on gender lines are universally made. The par-ticular cultural instances of gender ideology may indeed diverge, but the function of this ideology universally is to distinguish and rank the sexes. Universal woman is a straw woman, but gener-alizations about gender and the position of women are the creative outcome of comparison and theoretical model-building.

The notion of 'paradigmatic shift', accompanied each time by a straw man, may suggest that the development of anthropology is not in the long run methodologically and theoretically cumulative but always reflects the biases of the times. Yet if it were not cumulative, the comparative method would achieve little beyond establishing cultural diversity. But the acknowledgment of cultural diversity must not, and need not, lead to cultural relativism. While Strathern quite rightly warns of the danger of universalizing from one instance, she may be too lenient if she is suggesting that it is only this activity which creates fakes. To elaborate: discussing Malinowski's writings, Strathern describes how the 'universalizing mode' substitutes Trobriand Man for Straw Man, 'real for fake' (p. 666). Yet Trobriand Man is himself the anthropologist's creation and may be, if not actually a fake, then a biased, inaccurate misrepresentation. When Strathern (discussing Weiner 1976) points out that Trobriand and Hagen cultures value their women differently, she allows that Weiner has drawn the right conclusions from Trobriand cultural usages, and criticizes only the universalizing of these. Clearly, it was not Strathern's intention to reinterpret Weiner's material. But in our activity of model-building we cannot take for granted that each anthropologist can best interpret her or his own material; further, the material must be presented in such a way that it could be re-analysed for a variety of purposes. Here I am interested in gender models, and ultimately in the reproduction of relations of inequality. For the construction of these we must look beyond cultural representations of women to gender relations; these relations are the stuff that models are made of.

I will suggest two models for the study of gender, encompassing the sort of 'universalizing' which is possible when analysing male–female relations. The starting point for both is that analyses of gender must be rooted in analyses of social wholes, and to this end they employ wide-ranging, though distinctive, approaches. While the first uses an analytic method within one society but a comparative one in relation to others, the second concentrates on an internally comparative method.

Collier and Rosaldo (1981) elaborate an analytic model constructed from ethnographic variables drawn from simple, brideservice societies. While they believe that a gender model must show connections 'between productive relationships, political processes, and folk conceptions of human nature' (p. 277), they also see cultural conceptions of gender as being systematically linked to the organization of social inequality. For these reasons they would expect the model to be equally informative when applied to diverse social groups. Their comparative discussion of three brideservice societies encompasses sexual, productive, economic, and ritual life. Formal statements made in each of these domains are shown to be altrocentric, symbolic representations which can be understood only with reference to the content of one of the other domains. Thus none of these can be separately analysed or understood. Though in ritual women's sexuality is stressed, married women are not allowed to forge political links using their sexuality. Though hunting for game and headhunting are valued behaviours, performance of these does not necessarily result in public rewards: 'It is not hunters who receive wives, but husbands who hunt' (p. 313). In other words, success in hunting does not of itself gain a man a wife, but a man who is already a husband nourishes this cultural idiom by the repeated perform-ance of this valued behaviour. Culturally and ritually claims are made which are not a picture of social reality but a description of ways that people defend what they claim to be the case. In this manufacture of a fake reality the elders are able to mystify the basis of their privilege, which rests in their access to, and control of, women. While all adult men, when married, appear as the forgers of social relations, wives become more domesticated and their relationships are restricted. This has to do with the pro-ductive base of each sex: men's product (meat) is a social product distributed widely within the group, while women merely feed the family. Male and female products are not equally exchanged because they are not equally valued; and this valuation is deter-mined by social obligations preceding the exchange.

At the same time women do not need husbands for meat, while men need a wife to provide their daily fare. For a woman, marriage means obligations, but no additional social rewards, so women are often reluctant to marry. Men, on the other hand, need wives in order to become independent and achieve equal status with other men. This need shapes men's relations with other men and with women. While the fact that men do not need to appropriate a woman's surplus, but only to be fed by her, leads to fewer restrictions on women than those in bridewealth societies, because the marital state is desired far less by women than by men, the latter must constrain women to marry them and stay married to them. In these circumstances rape, and especially gang rape, appears as a weapon which affirms male solidarity against recalcitrant women. This suggests a picture of a harmonious world of men opposed to a conflict-ridden world of heterosexual relations (Collier and Rosaldo 1981: 299). However, this harmony is often a deliberate decision by men to assert their status and manhood by engaging in violence against women rather than against each other, in situations where they fear that violence between men may lead to more social disruption than they desire.

While Collier and Rosaldo's analysis locates the gender system within the social whole, their methodology uncovers social connections found in diverse societies. For instance among the Kewa, a society in which marriage is by bridewealth payment, we see also how harmonious relations among men are punctuated and affirmed by expressions of uncompromising dominance, if not violence, in relations with women. Men can only be equal while women are constrained; this is one simplified message from the examination of the gender systems of brideservice and bridewealth societies.

The second model for the analysis of gender is applied more systematically to Kewa material in the following chapter, so will be reviewed only briefly here. In their introduction to the collection on *Sexual Meanings*, Ortner and Whitehead (1981) suggest that the gender system of a society is one structure among many, whose full social connotation can be understood only in its contextualization. Accordingly, they first describe the general features of gender ideologies before outlining their interesting and rather creative formulation of gender as a prestige structure. They then contrast and compare it with other prestige structures in the society, and by this method learn something about prestige structures in general rather than merely about gender systems. This model tends to look at social relations through ideologies, whereas the previous model looked at ideologies through social relations; two complementary rather than mutually exclusive methods.

In this book I try to employ both methodologies; that is, I combine throughout examinations of idioms and ideologies with analyses of practical social relations. In this way the study of gender relations is not isolated as part of a sub-discipline dubbed 'women's studies', but becomes merged with the analysis of social relations as a whole. The concept of exchange will now be considered as a more encompassing description of these relations.

Exchange as economy

Highlands' ceremonial exchange systems have been extensively documented (e.g., in Bus 1951; A. Strathern 1971; Meggitt 1974; Feil 1978; LeRoy 1979b; Sillitoe 1979; Lederman 1982). The appeal of these descriptions has tended to encourage the assumption that these exchange systems are more widespread, or homogeneous, than is the case. A handful of comparative attempts (e.g. Healey 1978; Modjeska 1982; Godelier 1982b) has pointed to the diversity in Highland cultures, but the popular picture of the Highlands as an ethnographic area typified by big men conducting magnificent, far-reaching exchanges still prevails. For the Kewa I describe lesser big men than those appearing in Hagen. The Kewa exchange complex is accordingly more spatially restricted, and their ceremonial exchange less socially encompassing. It is not a single system of total prestations into which all exchanges are fed, as is the case with Enga *tee* and Hagen *moka*. Nevertheless, exchange is a central organizing principle of Kewa social life. Accordingly, I shall be concerned here with exchange at a very basic level, not only as it climaxes in periodic group events but also as it shapes the humbler day-to-day aspects of life, linking them to those larger events. I shall take as a starting point Mauss' essay on the gift, and review the literature as it relates to the theme of exchange as reciprocity and/or competition.

That exchanges in social systems characterized by a gift economy are somehow 'equal' is implicit in an analysis which posits an obligation to make gifts, to accept them and to return them (Mauss 1974). For Mauss the obligation to return gifts arose out of the powerful relationship between gift and donor, such that the recipient could not enjoy the fruit of the gift without making a return to the donor. Highland exchange systems have often been described in terms of the system of 'total prestations' delineated by Mauss in his essay on the gift. Yet the competitive aspect is usually also stressed. How are these two aspects to be reconciled? I shall suggest an answer to this puzzle from insights gained in Kewa ethnography. But first the problem must be stated more precisely and located ethnographically.

Andrew Strathern (1971) stresses competitiveness and the creation of inequalities in his analysis of *moka*. While 'alternating disequilibrium' operates in respect of groups – that is, each group gets the chance, the following time round, to beat their exchange partners by making them a larger return gift – within the group men do not take turns at outdoing each other, although a few men do consistently better than others. Women, being producers rather than transactors (M. Strathern 1972), take no direct part in the competition. Tombema Enga women, on the other hand, are reported by Feil (1978) to be active in *tee* exchanges. Feil further describes those exchanges as having social organizational functions, but considerably plays down their competitive aspects (but see Meggitt 1974). Sillitoe (1979), writing on the Wola, describes their exchange system as a basic organizing principle which individuals choose to abide by because they see that it is effective in ordering social life. No coercive element exists because no man has power over another; however, women are dominated by the men, who do not allow them to handle wealth. In her analysis of Mendi exchange, Lederman (1982) also gives this activity prominence in social ordering and re-ordering, but contrasts it with important group events. These group events (*sem*) always take precedence over personal exchange networks (*twem*), so that excellence in *twem* does not lead to ascendancy in *sem*. *Twem* is egalitarian – women freely engage in *twem* relationships, controlling the circulation of their products in these networks – but social power, ultimately, is with *sem* and not *twem*. And in this the basis of social inequality is to be found.

Lederman has stressed an aspect of exchange not brought out so clearly by other writers, that is, she has distinguished between group events and personal everyday events, and shown that there is a difference and a hierarchy between the two. Further, she has shown that this discontinuity hides a continuity: while *sem* events are presented as entirely different from *twem* ones, they are similar in that they use the same objects of exchange that circulate in *twem* networks, and in that they also create debts and obligations. The difference is that women whose products are drawn off in *sem* events may not look for a return. While they may choose to help men in these, they have no part in shaping them, so they lose control over the products of their labour (p. 253). Although for the Kewa I do not characterize exchanges in exactly the same way that Lederman does for the Mendi, and certainly Kewa women do not appear to have the multiple personal networks described here, nevertheless the analysis of what happens at *sem* events is reminiscent of happenings at Kewa ceremonial pig kills.

I return now to the puzzle posed earlier: how is the fact that exchanges are often competitive, leading to social inequalities, to be reconciled with the claim that in gift economies gifts must always be reciprocated? Put more simply, how can reciprocity create inequality? Lederman's work suggested an answer, which I will now try to formulate from my Kewa material. Gift exchange, as well as delineating ceremonial systems which 'rank clans and men', or acting as a political mechanism for creating peace out of a state of war, is actually the basis of the local economy. Even within the small group co-operation is minimal at the domestic level, but exchange is a necessary part of everyday life. The periodic group events are part of this gift economy, but because of their political function in group formation and identification, as well as their importance as arenas in which groups and men distinguish themselves in impressive exhibitions and distributions of wealth, their economically extractive functions are misrecognized. Yet even prior to the big event, a number of exchanges towards it creates smokescreens in which the provenance of items circulating in them is dissipated; therefore the link between product and labour is cut. This is the crucial point. Gift exchange rests on domestic production, whose goods it alienates by converting them into values in a separate domain. At the time of the big event these goods are presented as disappearing up, supposedly for the glory of the group. Prestige does indeed accrue to the group, but it accrues also to individuals unequally: those whose personal exhibitions and distributions were more munificent gain greater prestige, and, in due course, receive material returns. I characterize this as 'maximizing net outgoings' of other people's products while 'maximizing net incomings' to oneself. The specific relations that make this possible are contingent on a gift economy in which structures of exchange are, first, dominated by men in so-called agnatic lineages, and, second, harbour 'unlike for unlike' exchanges and pass extraction off as a group offering benefiting all members equally. What sustains these relations of inequality?

Inequality and power

These are two sides of the same coin. While 'power' is the ability to influence social decisions and control group events, 'inequality' is the unequal share in this power, as a result of unequal access to the goods and statuses to which it relates. I am interested only in political power because I believe that other sorts – cosmic, or mystical, say – become socially relevant only as they express themselves politically. In other words, whatever its pedigree, power must become politicized before it can have any influence on social life. It cannot exist outside the social group and independently of it.

Early accounts of Highland societies, notably those of Vicedom and Tischner (1943–48), stressed a social differentiation, and a rigid social structure which has since been much modified. It may be that the accounts have become modified as the structure has, but for Andrew Strathern, the main critic of these early writers, the rigidity was from the beginning overstated.

Strathern simplifies the class model elaborated by Vicedom and Tischner, stressing enormous mobility within the three social categories which he retains, and playing down the importance of heredity. While Vicedom and Tischner have a self-perpetuating class of big men at one end of the social scale and a class of 'slaves' on the other (who could not be self-reproducing since they did not marry), Strathern limits the effects of heredity to 'a matter of emulation' (A. Strathern 1971: 211), the advantages of having a good example and a head start. From there a man must be able to pull it off on his own merits. *Moka* transactions were the enterprises in which men demonstrated their ability to 'pull it off'. Accordingly, Strathern stresses the function of exchange in the creation of social inequalities. Inequalities were created between men and women because women did not transact, and among men because some were better able than others to control and regulate *moka* events – an advantage traced back to a man's personal charisma, and especially to his persuasive 'talk'.

This sort of analysis, which ascribed to exchange productive and creative powers (see A. Strathern 1969), he later modified in acknowledgement of the fact that wealth must come ultimately from production, not transaction (see A. Strathern 1982a: 158). Recently, the study of social inequality has concerned itself more directly with production, and its links with exchange. This approach brings women, as producers of wealth transacted, to the foreground of the analysis. It also escapes the tendency of talking about the big man as if that is all there is to say about inequality in the Highlands. This tendency has in the past prejudged, to a certain extent, the issue of power and inequality by fixing it to statuses assumed to exist all over the Highlands. Yet there is wide-ranging variation, as writers such as Godelier (1982a, 1982b) have shown. Such variations have been tied to productive levels, and to different cultural and social practices. But how exactly have these new methodologies and their insights enriched our understanding of the issues? Let us probe this a little with reference to two essays, by Modjeska and Godelier.

Modjeska (1982) correlates intensification of production with the development of inequalities among men. The causality posited is not linear, but the argument suggests that (in a dynamic way) two sets of causalities, social and ecological, constantly bring about spiralling changes in their own and each other's contexts. Depleted natural stocks lead to a shift to horticulture; populations grow as a result of better diet; higher population densities lead to increased inter-group contact, and therefore a higher incidence of conflict. At a certain stage, a 'cross-over' of values results in the pig's being accepted as indemnity for human lives, so that it mediates between the social and the economic. This 'mediation' is in the form of exchange. The intensification of production, coupled with the growing importance of exchange as an alternative to violent forms of retaliation, opens the way for some men to gain more control over the means of production than others. Exchange, especially in elaborate, ceremonial forms, is the moment and mechanism of appropriation. Because men appropriate not to consume but to redistribute and create debts towards themselves, this control and manipulation of exchanges leads to inequalities. When he applied this model to the Duna people of the Southern Highlands, Modjeska found that while intensification of production is a social precondition for exploitation, in respect of individual men their domestic pig production did not determine their status. Persuasive 'talk' appears as the final determinant here; those who can talk others into giving them pigs are big men among the Duna.

Concerning male-female relations, women's dependent position was achieved in two steps. First, with the shift to horticulture their labour was moved to the domestic site and men's labour (in garden clearing) was made a prerequisite for women's production. Second, as exchange gained in importance as mediating between groups and allocating goods and resources within groups, it became defined as a male pursuit because it perpetuated male-based groups. The social relations in which both production and exchange take place are thus relations of inequality, discriminating against the activities of women in terms of personal freedom, prestige and social power.

However, here I must interpose that the placing of women within a domestic production site is not a necessary precondition for the domination of women. In general, gender inequality is not the result of the sexual division of labour, but is presupposed by it (cf. Godelier 1982a: 38): an unequal division of labour is built on a pre-existing hierarchy. In the brideservice societies looked at earlier, women's production was not dependent on men's; but although in these societies women are less constrained and subordinated, in important matters men still dominate them. As was pointed out, this is because they engage in unequal exchange of goods and services. While women's products are consumed domestically and therefore not widely valued, men nevertheless need wives for status and subsistence. Men's product (meat) is widely distributed and hunting prowess is part of a prestige structure, but women do not need husbands for meat. Women are reluctant to marry because this means added responsibilities not matched by rewards, but men must marry to attain the status of manhood and become independent of other men. Though women produce in 'nature' (that is, as gatherers), their produce is nevertheless controlled by men who are the forgers of social relations, into which they can force women. Thus women's labour power is controlled because its products are controlled, in a system which designates these products as fit for domestic consumption only, not for exchange. Control of labour, then, is possible even in hunter-gatherer societies where there has been no shift to horticulture, or where planting is minimal.

Analysing Baruya social practices, Godelier (1982b) accounts for the absence of big men in this society with reference to the practice of sister exchange. He describes the warrior-category of *aoulatta* as 'great men', whose prestigious position offers them no possibility for personal or material gain. Because no man is dependent on another for a wife or for the achievement of full adulthood, economic exploitation and political coercion among men is not realizable. Sister exchange is the structural factor which precludes the growth of inequalities among men; but at the same time it demands the subordination of women.

For Modjeska, the major precondition for inequality to develop is intensification of production, while what decides which particular men will exploit is 'persuasive talk', by which a few men claim pigs at distributions following exchanges. Women as a group are dominated by men as a group, both at the point of production, and at the point of exchange and distribution. For Godelier, the absence of brideprice obviates both the need and the desire to accumulate; therefore exploitation and control of other men's productive or political activities cannot be successfully carried out in sister exchange societies. However, women as a group are again dominated by men as a group. As with brideservice, the same cultural variable which ensures relative equality among men enforces the subordination of women.

How has this discussion come to grips with inequality and with power? By stressing production, it has highlighted the big man's dependence on other people's wealth products, which in exchanges he appropriates and reallocates; therefore it has demonstrated that the exercise of social power depends on the control of labour. However, in societies with no elaborate wealth exchange systems, where men do not depend on the products of women's labour for their social position, inequalities among men are less pronounced. But women are not accordingly more independent, and their labour power is controlled for other reasons than the need to appropriate its products for circulation in exchanges. Whatever the specific cultural usages, the following becomes clear: power differentials among men are differently expressed and have a different base than power differentials between men and women. While inequalities among men are created in political arenas (though their effects may be economic) where individual men compete for status and prestige, the position of women is economically dependent from the outset. No individual woman can overcome this dependence or rise above it and remain in the community.

Notes

1 The essay is entitled ' "Sexual Antagonism": The Intellectual history of a Concept in New Guinea Anthropology'. Herdt and Poole characterize sexual antagonism as a 'pseudo concept', subsuming too great a variety of cultural phenomena and therefore providing an 'awkward and unwieldy lens' for the study of sex and gender. In their programmatic conclusion the authors suggest areas of vigilance and

further work: First, that while men and women be allowed to 'speak' in our ethnographies, we must be aware of the full complexities of the background of this discourse, and the 'informal tenor' of inter-sexual relations must be fully documented. Second, cultural diversity must be taken into account by comparative approaches. Third, the historical dimension of social change must no longer be ignored. In my analysis I have tried to apply the first and last principles; the comparative perspective is by necessity a little under-represented.

2   This statement may invite an accusation of androcentrism: whose 'culture' values men's things more than women's? Does this way of putting things already present a male view? In defence I reproduce the words with which Ortner and Whitehead (1981) tried to forestall criticism for not including an analysis of gender culture from the 'female point of view' in their edited collection *Sexual Meanings* (though they add that this viewpoint is discussed within the analysis of the 'hegemonic', i.e. male-biased, ideology):

> 'We consider this approach to be theoretically justified, in that some form of asymmetry favoring men is present in all cultures, and that women's perspectives are to a great extent constrained and conditioned by the dominant ideology. The analysis of the dominant ideology must thus precede, or at least encompass, the analysis of the perspective of women.'

(Ortner and Whitehead 1981: x)

The 'dominant ideology' values women below men in my discussion; and since this is so, the ranking becomes a social reality.

3   A detailed discussion of this appears in Josephides 1982b.

4   Yet note that Maurice Godelier who worked among the Baruya in the Eastern Highlands managed to gain access to women, and even attended their initiation ceremonies, though he had to undergo a purification rite before being allowed back into the company of men (Godelier 1982a: 76–77).

5
The construction of gender categories

This chapter will describe the sexual division of labour and forms of co-operation, the separation of males and females, and the interaction of their 'domains'. In order to investigate the function of gender structure I shall use the 'prestige structures' model elaborated by Ortner and Whitehead (1981). Seen as an emic intellectual activity, the construction of gender categories provides the ideological rationale for inequalities at the base of society. Although in this analysis gender structure as a prestige structure will be found to be decidedly male-oriented, it will be suggested that male prestige needs are, in some measure at least, a male defensive response to the imputed (and feared) powers of women. However, this view will not claim that women were originally, or are now in some mystical way, more powerful than men and above men's paltry power games. Rather, it will uncover the underlying feelings of insecurity at the core of men's attempts at total domination. This of course does not explain the origins of domination and inequality, but simply records one type of socio-psychological response to a perceived imbalance. Another strand will pursue the legitimacy (and therefore successful exercise) of power within a society. If men want to gain power (that is, control over people and events), they must claim a certain efficiency superior to others. That this efficiency is claimed by men over women as a sex opens the possibility of the same idiom being used in relations among men. Gender becomes the idiom of domination/subordination.

Division of labour

There is a sexual division of labour among the Kewa which has both ideological and practical aspects. Women tend gardens, pigs, and children. They usually cook for the household and keep the house clean. Nowadays they do the washing, most market selling, a lot of coffee picking, and cleaning. Men prepare garden sites from bush (very infrequently; subsequent grass burning of a plot is normally the work of women), hunt, transact exchanges, arrange pig kills, fight wars, and lead religions.

Modjeska (1982: 62) refers to the social division of labour as effectively defining men as potentially independent, and women as necessarily dependent. This followed from the shift to horticulture, when there was 'a strategic male technological intervention in women's condition of production . . . Instead of nature as the subject of their labour, garden work places women within a domesticated production site' (p. 69). Since men are the producers of garden plots, their labour is a prerequisite for female production. In the Kewa case, that women are in general dependent in this way is, ideologically, a very powerful concept, which incapacitates a woman practically. While it is generally true that men's initial labour is needed before women may produce, it is not the case that each individual Kewa woman must wait for a man to prepare a site for her before she can garden. There are many available disused sites, needing only female labour to resuscitate them. Fresh gardens rarely encroach into the bush nowadays, since Kewa use sites without fallow for upward of twenty years. Yet because women do not own land, but hold it only by virtue of their connection with a man, their position and therefore their labour is considered dependent.

The same trend is continued in the modern sector. Although women put a lot of hard work into coffee gardens and their rights are recognized when they are allowed to sell their pickings, the gardens themselves can never belong to them.[1] 'Pickers keepers' is a common trend. Some men whose coffee gardens are extensive may 'help' less well-endowed relatives or friends by allowing them to pick their coffee and sell it for themselves. The question of a wife's pickings is a little more complicated. Although usually she may keep the proceeds, this is not a well-established right which can always be enforced. If the husband insists on keeping them there is little she can do about it, either in the Village Court or the Local Court, or by appealing to 'tradition'.

But even with a lenient husband who allows his wife to keep her earnings a woman may not do so well. First, she is likely to find herself working much longer hours in the coffee garden than her husband, while the coffee bags designated as 'his' will invariably be larger and more numerous. One informant described how the whole family worked together filling each other's coffee bags, but concluded that 'although we say that we all put labour into the filling of all the bags, I contribute little to my wife's and children's bags'. When it comes to coffee processing, then, women's labour is disproportionate to their portions. In the original garden clearing and planting, it is true, mostly men are active, although women help, something usually unacknowledged by the men, who say that only they can plant coffee. Second, the uses to which these proceeds are put even when women are allowed to keep them, effectively channel them out of their control. They may be spent on tradestore food or other European goods, put into exchanges, or invested in businesses run by men. Tradestores are owned by men, and although women often contribute towards stock buying, they do not usually act as store keepers.

Wage labour on plantations is not the exclusive domain of men, but women's participation in this sector is restricted and often unacknowledged. When the Highlands Labour Scheme first got under way only men were recruited; nowadays it is still mainly men who go off on casual, recurrent wage labour trips. Women go only where they have male kin, and their labour is often unofficial. Usually they travel no further than to plantations in the Western Highlands where their pickings are included in the bags of male relatives whose names actually appear on the payroll.[2]

The same trend appears in the sphere of religion. Modern religious offices, like the traditional cults, are closed to women. Men are catechists, pastors, deacons, and the like. In the lay sector this trend again prevails: men are magistrates, councillors, members of provincial and national governments. In the Kagua area no woman has to my knowledge ever stood for these positions. In spite of the national Constitution's call for 'equal participation', both men and women seem to take it for granted that this is men's domain.

The sex domains also extend to items which are thought to belong to males or females. Land belongs to men; bananas, yams, and pandanus are men's, while sweet potato and many greens and grasses are women's. Pigs may be owned by either sex, although those belonging to the household are usually claimed by men. Axes belong to and are used by men only, but bushknives and spades are used by both sexes.

Separation and co-operation

Although in the past men and women had separate houses, married couples now share a family home which is usually built in the new style with a raised floor, woven pitpit walls and is rectangularly shaped – the so-called 'station house'. This trend may be one of the factors discouraging polygyny: in the old days co-wives had separate quarters, but now that spouses live in the same house much acrimony results from the cohabitation of wives.

When new gardens are made husband and wife often go out together to work in them, and sometimes also go together to harvest. Pig care may be shared between men and women, although men tend to be away a lot visiting, at meetings or at the Village Court, so a heavier share falls to the women. In addition, the sweet potato fed to pigs is also the product of female labour. Men help with looking after children, but again their assistance is erratic. Housebuilding is men's work, but women help with some stages, especially with fetching *kunai* grass for the roof. Large trees are felled only by men, who are the owners of axes, and so house posts are cut only by them. Women may collect firewood but men also perform this task. Everyday cooking is done by the women; I never saw a married man peel a sweet potato, although I have seen them clean traditional taro and yams, which are occasional foods. Ceremonial meals – *mumu* in pidgin and *yawe* in Kewa – require the labour of both sexes, but men usually heat the stones, arrange the food in the earth oven and remove it when it is ready (women, again, prepare the vegetables). Undoubtedly in everyday production there is much mixing of female and male labour, although many tasks are 'sexed'.

Some of Modjeska's (1982) findings concerning the work patterns of three Highland groups are of interest here. In a comparative table of woman/man hours spent on 'subsistence' activities, Modjeska demonstrates that the proportionate work put in by men and women is not as unequal as men sometimes claim when they say that gardening is women's work. Out of the total hours spent on this work, Kapauku men (Wissel Lakes) contribute 54.5 per cent while women contribute 45.59 per cent; Duna men (Southern Highlands) contribute 44.3 per cent, women 55.7 per cent; and Raiapu Enga men contribute 41 per cent while women contribute 59 per cent (Modjeska 1982: 73). Often the main difference between male and female labour lies in the fact that women's chores are regular while men work in outbursts. Although I never did a time and motion study of Kewa activities there is little doubt that women spent consistently more time in the garden than men. But another point made by Modjeska in the same work must be conceded, though it is not discussed here: that the time men spend discussing politics, pig kills and exchanges may also be thought of as (re)productive labour.

Husbands and wives co-operate in business, exchanges, pig kills, and compensation payments. Women refer to this as 'helping the husband' and 'lifting his worry'. His worry they do not think of as their worry, but they feel it is their duty to help him. One woman who contributed a large sum of money towards a purchase that her husband was making explained her reasons to me. 'I am sorry for him, and want to help him. If I don't help him, who will? You see that his brothers don't lift a finger.' This particular case concerned the purchase of my motor car. The woman's husband had been my host, and wanted the vehicle to stay on in the settlement for a number of reasons which could be bracketed together as 'male prestige needs'. He cited two of these: that the car had to stay because it had carried his dying father, and that if the car left with me, people of the neighbouring clans would taunt him with his demotion. 'They would say, "You had white people living with you who brought many goods but now they have left and taken their goods with them, and you are again an ordinary bush *kanaka* just like the rest of us." They would say this with malicious pleasure and I would be shamed because it would be true.'

Often Kewa women's decisions to help their husbands are their own, and in this respect they are 'affective acts'. It is true on the other hand that if wives do not readily help their husbands they are likely to face reprisals, coercion, or at best unpleasant home conditions. They will certainly suffer loss of reputation, and this is something that they are truly concerned about. Although they often (but not always) say they want to help their husbands, they also say that if they do not they will look like rubbish women and will be ashamed. It is expected of women to help their husbands and women accept this duty. It is also prestigious for a woman to be known as a hard worker, the owner of many gardens, and producer of a surfeit of vegetables. Pigs are not thought to result from her efforts in the same way, so if a woman has no pigs her husband is more likely to be blamed.

Unlike many other Highland societies (as, e.g. in Herdt 1982; Poole 1982), the Kewa appear to have had no formal, obligatory initiation rites for either sex. Some usages were recorded, such as ear and nose piercing for children of both sexes, but this was casually undergone (if at all) and led to no change in status. Fears of pollution were accordingly weak (cf. Meggitt 1964; Allen 1967). There were no rituals for cleansing young boys of their mother's milk, nor of protecting young husbands from their wives' supposedly harmful secretions. Following Meggitt's (1964: 221) famous distinction, the Kewa were probably more lecherous than prudish, although 'mischievous modesty' may better characterize their sexual behaviour. Apart from the *post partum* taboo there were few taboos on sexual intercourse. Prior to battle, for instance, warriors were not required to desist from sleeping with their wives. Questioned about this, two elderly men (in their fifties and sixties) responded amid outbreaks of hilarity: 'Not sleep with our wives the night before a battle? On the contrary, we made sure we did, for if we were injured we would be kept in isolation for a couple of months and *then* we wouldn't be able to sleep with our wives!' Although men may say that a man who spends most of his time with women cannot be much of a man, this is not taken too seriously and men do not appear worried about any specific evil befalling them as a result of associating too closely with women. On the whole, they do not appear unduly concerned about women's menstrual fluids posing a threat to their well-being. There were menstrual huts in the past, but these have long since been abandoned.

Childbirth is another matter about which Kewa men do not appear openly hysterical. Women have told me that their husbands help them on this occasion by planting a post in the back of the house for them to hold on to as they crouch to give birth (though most births take place in gardens). Some may even assist at the birth itself by crouching behind the woman and holding her breasts from the back. Women said this relieved them, and helped them to push. On one occasion when a woman had given birth but did not pass the placenta, I was asked to take her in the car to the hospital in Kagua. She was doubled up, holding the baby attached to the placenta and was almost carried in by her husband and mother, both of whom accompanied her. On the way there (on a very bumpy road), she passed the placenta. Her husband sitting beside her did not seem concerned about the blood, which he then helped to mop up. It is possible that in the old days when there was more separation, unfamiliarity with the other sex's physical functions bred awe or fear of pollution; but from the accounts of elderly people such fears do not seem to have been prevalent.

Power of women

Although men say of women that they are weak, inconsistent, impressionable, gullible, easily led, and intimidated, they still accord to them powers that can ruin or heal men. While men are the operators of lethal magic (*romo*), women are the owners of strong potions (*ali rakia*) which make men besotted, or, in the case of spurned love, inflict a painful punishment on them. *Ali rakia* is a plant grown by women which they mix into the food of the man they want to attract. Some old women told me that they rubbed the bodies of their young children with it, so that when their husbands held them they felt drawn to their wives and disinclined to make further marriages. One form of vengeful magic punishes the inconstant lover with painful cuts to his feet. The woman follows the man, and in a piece of tree bark picks up some clots of earth on which he has stepped. When she puts the bark with its contents on a fire, deep gashes appear on the man's feet.

Women sometimes have the power to neutralize the deadly magic of men. *Nu yapara* (literally 'string bag cloak', usually referring to the placenta) is directed by men at other men. The operator rubs a stone with special leaves and pig's blood, and from a hiding place points the stone like a gun at the victim. If the magic takes, the victim loses his senses, and can only be saved by a woman. If his sister, mother or other close female relative finds him she will put his hand on her vulva; if his wife finds him she will make him have intercourse with her. This will flush out the magic and the man will be well again. Women's 'strong things', then, are thought to be only for personal and domestic use. In accordance with this, women's interests are considered predominantly domestic, and their powers unsuitable for the public domain.

Gender domains

In all contexts of Kewa social life a dichotomy between the sexes is maintained, both in terms of their imputed potentialities and the social roles expected of them, women, as shown, being identified with the domestic domain and men ideally with the public. People say that women belong in the house and the men abroad. However it can readily be seen that in practice these distinctions are not so clear-cut: women are well represented at gatherings, and most men certainly spend a lot of time at home, and on domestic tasks. In marriage the domains meet, as shown by the discussion on co-operation between husband and wife. Moreover, 'the domestic domain, where goods are produced and people reproduced, services the public domain, where leadership struggles to control group resources depend on success in controlling domestic resources' (Josephides 1983: 291). The 'domains model', then, is not constructed from clear-cut distinctions in social practices. It is used here as a heuristic device only, because its idioms are important in the construction of gender categories.

Definite dispositions also go with the domains. Women usually concur with what men say of them, averring that they are not strong, own no wealth, have no 'talk', know no stories, have no judgment, and are ignorant. They are afraid of men, who are 'strong'. In pidgin this word means forceful, persistent, determined, obstinate, and harsh. Men are 'strong' in sexual matters and women succumb even though they may be uncomfortable. Not that all women are afraid of sexual union, even for the first time, or that men are always brutal. One old woman described what she felt on her first sexual encounter with her husband: 'He looked into my eyes and I looked into his, and I was not afraid.' A younger woman's experience was a little more conventional. 'I was ashamed, so he covered my head with my *laplap*. I was afraid

Yago settlement prior to pig kill. The settlement is built on a ridge overlooking the valley. There are two longhouses, pigs lined up, an earth oven dug out, stacks of firewood at the ready. This is a fine example of an old type settlement.

Lari with steel spade working in garden, with young daughter Payanu.

Women, children and an old man husking coffee.

Women selling vegetables at Sumbura market.

Rimbu reviewing his shells prior to major pig kill.

Rimbu and his mother Payanu prior to pig kill. Payanu is stroking a pig she has raised which her son will kill.

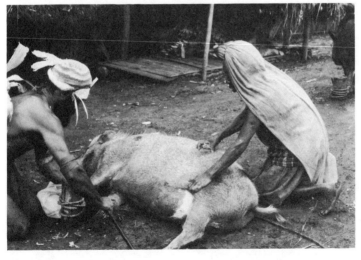

E.K.C.C. LIBRARY

Neada *under construction.*

Pisa making a speech and presenting kepa.

the first time, but he insisted ['strong'] and afterwards it was all right.' While I was in the field there was one case of a young bride who died after her husband had had intercourse with her. The medical details were unclear, but I was told that she haemorrhaged badly. Some men muttered that she was probably too young to be married, and the general opinion was that her husband was 'a pig who did not know the proper behaviour of men'.

From my fieldnotes I culled recurrent statements made by men about themselves and about women, and by women about themselves and about men, made by people of all ages and varying importance. I reproduce some of them here because they give a good general impression of relations between and within the sexes. Men say of women:

'Women cannot talk sensibly. They cannot settle any dispute, but only make trouble. Women bicker, they talk about small, unimportant things, they argue about trivial things among themselves until men have to intervene to put an end to the matter. Women don't help their husbands, they only make trouble for them. Most of the time they don't appreciate a man's position or understand the exigencies of the various obligations that he is bound to discharge. This is because they themselves are not subject to such obligations and are not constantly in the public eye, being women. [These obligations invariably involve the alienation of goods and money.] Women are just women, *meri tasol*. They just want to consume all the time, they don't care for politics or the name. Women do not own wealth, they are weak, and cannot fight. They cannot make a fire by traditional means because their backs would hurt. They can't climb bananas and bind the fruit. They have no ritual power. They can only 'grease' men, but they also have strong sexual powers and potions to turn men's heads. Some are good workers, however, and know the proper role of women.'

It is invariably wives who men talk about in these terms, for it is wives they live with, and not sisters. Old mothers may sometimes feel disgruntled but usually with their daughters-in-law, not their sons. The sons play a conciliatory part in such cases, normally taking their mother's side. Rimbu did this when at the pig kill Lari claimed some pork which his mother thought was coming to her so that she could discharge her obligations. The mother was reduced to tears, when her son intervened, giving her the pork. 'We can't have the old woman being shamed because she can't pay back her debts. It is not right.' This reinforces the idea that it is the wives who are intractable. Throughout the men's mutterings and complaints cited above, women are described *relationally*, in terms of their compliance or otherwise with male concerns.

At the same time it must be made clear that these recurrent statements describe a stereotype, and are made routinely by men in a *quasi*-formal manner. When men talk of particular women they do not normally use such denigrating terms. Usually they seem to appreciate the worth of their own wives and accord them due respect and consideration. However, the stereotype described is ideologically a very powerful tool when men on specific occasions want to get the upper hand over women. It is also the general rationale for women's dependent position.

Men say of men:

> 'Men only decide about important things. We try to follow in our fathers' footsteps, and kill pigs and display wealth as they did. We are strong-headed, we get angry easily and are violent. We do evil things all the time, and are ignorant compared to Europeans. Probably we will go to hell like our fathers. Perhaps our children will know better how to live, having been to school.'

Women say of women:

> 'We are just women. We do not know any stories, or myths. We don't talk in public places. We don't arrange pig feasts and kill pigs ourselves. Our mothers didn't used to do this, how should we? (Or: "We didn't learn to do this from our mothers.") We are ignorant, we really know nothing at all. You are wasting your time with us. We can't tell you anything; just women's things. In the old days we just knew how to work in the garden and have children, but that's all. We don't know what men used to do. But we did have love magic, and magic to make pigs grow fat.'

This self-effacement and denigration must be taken with a grain of salt. Men also humble themselves *vis-à-vis* Europeans, as their statements above illustrate. Women simply do it more consistently and to a greater degree. Although I cannot know how women talk to each other when I am not present about their positions and capabilities, I have observed that they are by no means docile or servile in their behaviour. And the fact that they sang to us old love songs belies their claim that they 'really know nothing at all'. On the whole, women do not talk as much as men do about women's status.

Women say of men:

> 'Men talk much, they do little productive work. They don't help women much in the gardens. Men are lazy, women do all the work. Men are concerned with talking in public places, filling public positions. Women would be afraid (*pala*) or ashamed (*yala*) to do this. Men will decide whether a child goes to school, or what children to give a women when they divorce her. Men are "strong" when it comes to sex; women are frightened and ashamed. Men like to marry many women; they are always flirting with girls. That's their way. They take their wife's produce and use it for bridewealth negotiations. Men are violent, they fight easily, and they beat their women to get their way.'

There is no doubt that almost invariably women protest vociferously when their husbands attempt to take additional wives. Sometimes all three end up in hospital, and often wives manage to block negotiations before they get very far. In one recent example the wife sat sulkily by while her husband discussed the terms of the bridewealth settlement with his intended bride's brothers. When he attempted to lead one pig to them, however, his wife sprinted across and pulled the pig away. The brothers were much embarrassed and sat around for a while while husband and wife shouted insults at each other from opposite ends of the settlement. In between, the husband tried swaggeringly but with little conviction to reassure the brothers. They eventually left, explaining that they could not bring their sister into a household where she would be resented. 'There will be trouble,' they said to him. 'If you manage to get the old woman to agree let us know, otherwise it is not possible.'

Women say women want:

> 'Women want to have fun when they are girls, but when they are over twenty they want to be married (so do men). They want to have good gardens, a helpful husband, children, some

(but not too many) pigs. They don't want co-wives. They want to have enough food for themselves and their children, and money for clothes. They want to be able to give presents to their own natal group and discharge their debts so that no blame attaches to them – they want to be irreproachable. They want to have some money of their own, and pigs to appease the ancestors when their children fall sick. They want their husband to be above reproach and ridicule when distributing. They want their husband to honour them by giving to their clan, and they want to be consulted about any prestation. They want their husband to help with pig raising, gardening and other household duties. They don't want him to gallivant too much, or play around with other women. If he does have another wife he must be generous and scrupulous when dividing his services and gifts. For their part, they like to be able to help their husband "lift any worry".'

Though gender ideologies may downgrade women and allocate them to a position subservient to men, women themselves make use of them when expedient. Many are the occasions on which a woman will upbraid another for speaking out of turn at a meeting concerned with some public event; more numerous the occasions when women have taunted men for being unmanly. A prominent occasion concerns one of the major wars in the area. One couple fell into an argument while returning from a pig feast. To avoid a thrashing, the wife goaded her husband into attacking two men from an enemy clan. 'If you were a man you would kill them, not beat your wife. But you are a woman yourself.'

Yet although women also make use of gender categories, the rules for the 'gender game' are not the same for both sexes. Gender ideology delineates men's ideal domain as the public, but women welcome their participation in the domestic. By contrast, men jealously guard the public domain from female incursions. In other words, a man may cross the gender line with little trouble, whereas a woman will be blocked by a hostile, united male front.

Prestige structures

In their introduction to the book *Sexual Meanings* (1981: 12–17), Ortner and Whitehead elaborate their methodology for investigating gender relations in any society. They designate gender systems as 'prestige structures' in order to 'bring into fuller articulation what it is about the political-economic organization of a society that most immediately and intelligibly affects that society's formal understanding of sex and gender'. What are these prestige structures? They relate to positions or levels 'that result from a particular line of social evaluation' and are '*culturally salient*' – that is, actors are aware of them. Moreover, prestige structures (of which the gender system is only one) 'in any society tend toward symbolic consistency with one another'. Thus one prestige structure may be metaphorically invoked with regard to another, and values or yardsticks may be transposed from one to the other; or, 'two or more dimensions of prestige may appear conceptually fused into a single system'. As one example of this they cite the harmonization in many societies of gender with age status or with caste.

That gender systems are prestige structures can be demonstrated by many ethnographic examples. As the authors say, it can be noted cross-culturally

> 'that the concepts used to differentiate men from women in terms of social worth are often identical to the concepts used to distinguish other differentially valued social types, and identical as well to the concepts used to grade individuals of the same gender.'
>
> (Ortner and Whitehead 1981: 16–17)

They are, in fact, 'common axes of social evaluation'. In the Kewa case it is derogatory to call a man a woman but to call a woman a woman is also a kind of reproof. It calls attention to her limitations and is in fact a check to a woman who aspires too highly. To call a woman a man is simply withering sarcasm, the ultimate ridicule for a woman's impertinence. This relates to another point Ortner and Whitehead make: that 'gender concepts are functions of the ways in which male prestige oriented action articulates with structures of cross-sex relations' (p. 18).

That prestige structures are concerned with male prestige is axiomatic, since the most prestigious categories (warrior, hunter, elder) are by definition male. The authors pre-empt any criticism that they are analysing gender culture from the 'hegemonic' – in this case male-biased – point of view by stating clearly in their Preface that since in all cultures women's perspectives are constrained and conditioned by the dominant (male) ideology, analysis of this ideology must precede any other. The very terms that apply to males and females are already part of the status hierarchy. As the authors point out,

> 'To be a warrior or an elder in societies in which these are primary categories of manhood is not simply to perform a certain role in the public domain, but to be located at a certain point in a hierarchical scheme of culturally ordered prestige.'
>
> (p. 19)

Women, on the other hand, are defined cross-sexually and re-lationally as wives, mothers, sisters and so on. Whichever of these labels predominates will depend on the relevance of the roles to male prestige. Since the public domain or 'sphere of wider social co-ordination' is dominated by men, and it is in this domain that larger prestige structures take their shape, Ortner and Whitehead conclude that 'the other-than-gender prestige hierarchies of most societies are, by and large, male games'. While they stress that their viewpoint is not opposed to that of Collier and Rosaldo in the same volume, seeing the organization of social relations (including gender) as a 'dynamic interdependence between trans-actions of an economic-materialist nature and those . . . more ideologically constituted' (Collier and Rosaldo 1981: 12), they do claim an encompassing cultural salience for gender-based con-structs. In the case of the Kewa, can all their cultural usages be accounted for with reference to gender categories? I shall probe this question by discussing three major points made by Ortner and Whitehead in support of their argument. (1) That gender is a prestige structure, in which the most valued terms are male; (2) that female positions/activities are defined and valued in terms of male prestige needs; and (3) that prestige structures may be fused, or one used to invoke the other (and in case of gender structure, that its concepts are extended to intra-sex relations).

GENDER IS A PRESTIGE STRUCTURE, IN WHICH THE MOST VALUED TERMS ARE MALE

What is meant by this proposition? Generally, that within the social organization and cultural beliefs of a society the gender complex is made up of propositions which when applied to individuals may bestow on them social approval and power, dignity and prestige; or they may have the opposite effect and imply that a person is unworthy or second rate. The idioms of gender can be used cross-sexually, so that a man may be said to be womanish or a woman mannish. Thus 'man' and 'woman' are not only value-laden terms but are also ideal categories which are not abstracted as an average from a number of instances; they are 'given'. Each person is then measured up against a category and scores minuses and pluses. For a man to be described as a hunter or warrior is at the same time to be placed on a certain scale along a continuum of valued qualities. There are degrees of manliness in a way that there are not degrees of womanliness. A woman is a woman, no more no less (which does not imply that in practice men do not distinguish between women and prefer some to others). But a man can span the whole range of valued terms. Women will say that they are 'mere women', implying a certain shortcoming. Whereas *ni ali* (I'm a man) has a ring of pride. While it is an insult for a man to be told he is not a man, for a woman to be told she is not a woman is a retort with little cultural content (except if the implication is that she is a spirit). For a man to be called womanly denotes regression and deterioration. When a woman is accused of trying to be like a man she is ridiculed for aspiring so high. This is because women are born, whereas to a certain extent (even in this society with no pronounced rites of passage) men are made. Men are born biologically male, but the degree of manhood they achieve depends on their efforts.

So far I have been talking about value 'inhering' in terms. This may imply static classifications, but social reality is far from reflecting such fixed evaluations. The fact is that men first *create* the values to which they then aspire. That is, they create a separate domain (of exchange, warfare, hunting etc.) in which only they are active, and make this the political centre of group activities. (I return to this question in Chapter 8). To the extent that the dominant ideology pervades a society, women also share these values; they can thus be described as the society's values. In itself a term has no value, but only in its social use. When I talk about valued terms, then, I do have in mind this activity of value-creating behind them.

The term 'man' (*ali*), then, is more valued than the term 'woman' (*wena*), precisely because it is men, by and large, who create these values. For the same reason, 'valued statuses' are not really separable from 'valued activities' among the Kewa. With this understanding, what other valued terms can be bestowed on individuals in Kewa? *Ada ali, amo ali, mudu ali, kalu ali,* and now *kadipi* or *kiapo. Amo* is the wealthy politician, the transactor, the leader of the ceremonies, war maker and peace maker, the mediator of disputes within the group. *Mudu* is the war general who leads the warriors into battle. The *mudu* and *amo* may be one and the same, but this was not usually the case. *Ada* simply means 'big', and is often used as a term of courtesy for visitors and elderly men. The *kaluali* was a cult elder in the old days. *Kadipi* is the word used for Europeans, and *kiapo* is a District Officer (from the pidgin *kiap*). These two words are now used to refer to anyone with an official position (such as Village Magistrate or Local Councillor), or more generally to anyone who has been educated and is working outside the village.

Only in old tales does hunting appear high on the lists of valued activities; now it is more of a sport than productive labour, and certainly very little protein has its source there. But men will refer to it approvingly as a manly activity (I have not heard women mention prowess in hunting or fighting with approval, though they admire wealthy men and compose love songs on their manliness and beauty). There is no single Kewa word for 'hunter'; one would have to say 'the man who kills cassowaries' (*yaari li ali*), 'the man who kills possums' (*yapa li ali*), or 'the man who kills pigs' (*mena li ali*). Only men hunt with bow and arrow, spear, and now shotgun. Women may catch bush rats and other small game but they do not handle weapons. They do use traps for small possums and also for fish. Women do not normally go into the bush for hours or even days, as the men do, on 'hunting' trips. When women do make such trips they are considered rather eccentric. One woman went off in a huff after a fight with her husband, saying she would spend the night in the bush. When the men on the settlement teased her and asked what she would eat there, she retorted that she would catch possums. She returned in the small hours, quite pleased with her evening's meal and the point that she had made.

While the term *ada* may be extended to industrious women who have many pigs and gardens, women may never become *amo* or *mudu.* Although in this society status is achieved for men, it is ascribed for women, who may enhance their reputation by their achievements but not change their status. One middle-aged woman elaborated on the sort of importance men and women could achieve:

'Pisa was the big man before, because all the men of his generation died and Pisa was left. Now it is Mapi, because he is the Village Magistrate and has 'talk'. A woman could be important (*ada*) too. When a woman gives wealth to her husband's line when he is sick or depressed she is truly a strong woman and acknowledged as such. But to discuss pig kills is not women's work, although when it comes to distributing the pigs my husband and I decide together how it should be done. Only men discuss pig kills; women eat the pigs and enjoy themselves. Women look after the pigs and the men kill them. Men are interested in celebrating the group name in these pig kills, but women are only interested in eating pork.'

A woman is 'strong' when she helps her husband initiate or participate in public events; she does not initiate any herself. This was true even in the case of the above informant who was generally more outspoken and alert than her husband (and certainly more so than many other women). Thus women often describe their own worth relationally to men's needs and expectations of them.

Kinship terms also have value, especially when honorary. Women will routinely address as 'sister' (*aki*) any woman with whom they do not have a specific, close kinship relationship. Among men, *ame* (brother) is a most valued term, and close friends often say that they have 'put their bellies together', and are therefore like brothers. But this is a different sort of value from that achieved by the *amo* or *mudu*. Whereas the word *ame* denotes acceptance as a kinsman and an equal, *amo* and *mudu* clearly imply superiority and distinction.

Industry is valued in both men and women; it does neither any good to acquire the reputation of being lazy. When Kewa refer to a hard-working man or woman, 'work' (*kogono*) usually denotes productive labour in the garden, pig care, housebuilding and other activities concerned with feeding and sheltering people. Nowadays men often use the pidgin word *wok* to refer to time and energy expended in negotiating sessions concerning marriage, compensation and dispute settlements, pig exchanges and other redistributive occasions. The Kewa expression for such activities has a much more prestigious ring: it is *yapisi* or *mudu agele*, 'talk of top priority'. Men talk as if this type of activity in which mostly they are involved has more social value than the first (that is, productive labour). Further, when women are present on these sorts of occasions they are thought to be observers (except when they are litigants), so their participation is not counted as 'work' and is therefore dispensable. Yet it is in this type of 'work' that major decisions concerning production and its allocation are made. The most valued activities, then, are concerned with social and political power; and they are the business of men.

FEMALE POSITIONS/ACTIVITIES ARE DEFINED AND VALUED IN TERMS OF MALE PRESTIGE NEEDS

It has already been mentioned that approved female industry supplies the wealth items necessary for male prestige activities. Women are praised if they help their husbands in their exchanges; they themselves desire to do this and judge other women's worth by this yardstick. I have also mentioned how the term 'woman' may be informed by qualities inherent in 'wife', 'sister', or 'mother', depending on which is culturally most salient; this can again be traced to male needs. Kewa wives can more effectively be controlled and dominated than sisters, whom exogamy and patrivirilocality put beyond a brother's reach. The same two practices make a woman dependent on her husband, the official owner of the land on which she works. While his sister and her husband may become important exchange partners, his wife's product will be entirely his to control.

But perhaps it is not the whole story to say that women are defined and valued in terms of male prestige needs. For there is a recalcitrant quality which may not be so defined, and is in fact a source of fear for men. Eric Schwimmer (1983) in his reinterpretation of a Baruya myth characterizes this fear as the reason why men need to become warriors – because only in this way can they liberate themselves from women. The myth (narrated in Godelier 1982a: 243–45) concerns a woman who conceives without male intervention. She is the apical ancestress of the human race. But though the woman conceives a number of times, her companion, a dog, twice enters into her vagina and eats part of the foetus. She manages to give birth to a well-formed child only after she has trapped the dog in a hole, from which he eventually escapes by turning into an eagle and flying skyward. Though the dog/eagle/ man is not successful in robbing the original woman of her procreative powers, his ferocity becomes the power which enters into men at times of war; it is therefore the origin of war. Schwimmer concludes that at the symbolic level everything happens as if Baruya war is waged against women, but that women always end up by conceiving. Thus war as a socio-psychological institution is closely linked with male/female relations: 'L'homme ne réussirait jamais sa lutte contre la femme sans être guerrier' (Man never succeeds in this struggle against woman without being a warrior.) (Schwimmer 1983: 192)

Men's prestigious activities in the Baruya case may be seen on one level as a response to a primordial fear of women and their powers. Although Baruya men own all weapons and tools (the means of destruction and the means of production), myths exist of women being the real, original owners of these things which they lost through negligence or inefficiency. In waging war with weapons originally belonging to women men liberate themselves from incarceration by women (according to the myth) and at the same time make themselves indispensable to them as protectors and defenders of hearth and home. Thus men make women dependent on them for protection against an evil of their own making.

Although I have not collected similar myths of origin in Kagua, this insight from a society with more overt male/female separation and antagonism than the Kewa is very suggestive. Kewa men's highest prestige needs are also in spheres where women may not participate, so that men and women never compete directly and openly. In myths Kewa women remain in the background, even when they are exceptional and indispensable to their husband's reputation and achievements. But instead of their reproductive powers being given prominence as in the Baruya case, the central role of their labour power in determining their husband's reputation is brought out. A recurrent myth (see Josephides 1982a: 18–20) is one of a spirit-woman who is content to be out of the limelight and help her husband with miraculous labour and the production of wealth items which add glory to his name. However, she eventually vanishes after a single crass act of disobedience on the husband's part, and all the goods created by her are reclaimed by a luxuriant but overpowering nature.

In real life Kewa women do not put themselves forward on festive occasions but work diligently in the background to swell their husband's display. Men do not always acknowledge the full extent of women's contribution to these events except in these old myths where their fears of female withdrawal and non-co-operation are given expression. A full acknowledgment would strip these events of their mystique and disclose their function as mechanisms for extraction and domination. The suggestion that women's activities are defined and valued in terms of male prestige needs, while these are themselves partly a response to male fears of a power in women which they cannot completely subdue, highlights a situation in which women's powers are turned against them and their own products become the vehicles for their domination.

PRESTIGE STRUCTURES MAY BE FUSED OR ONE USED TO INVOKE THE OTHER; IN THE CASE OF GENDER STRUCTURE, ITS CONCEPTS BEING EXTENDED TO INTRA-SEX RELATIONS

Age structure as a prestige structure is the one that can most readily be compared to gender structure in Kewa. Thus young men may be likened to women, women to children. Qualities that women are said to have may be childish: they are illogical, weak, uninformed, easily led, gullible. What can we gather from the fact that in present day Papua New Guinea there is a Ministry for Women, Religion, Youth and Recreation, the incumbent Minister being a man?

The fact that gender concepts can be used in intra-sex relations reveals the function of gender as a mechanism legitimating inequality and domination. Men who are politically weak, who put on a poor show in major displays and exchanges and are inefficient in the management of their affairs and especially their women, may be likened to women themselves and fail to accumulate much prestige. Although such men will kill their own pigs at the pig kill, for outsiders the additional numbers will enhance the reputation of the big men involved in the event while the actual owners of the pigs will go unnoticed. In the following chapter this sort of symbolic exploitation will be discussed more fully.

Although unimportant men are conceptually thought to partake of the same dispositions as women, and although it may be asked rhetorically of such men whether they are really men or women, lexically the word for 'rubbish man' is *tieboali*[3] – that is, suffixed always by the word for 'man', *ali*. It is important to note that in the Kewa case the worst insult for a man is not necessarily to be called a woman; it really depends for what he is accused. If it is cowardice and indecision he will be called a woman; but if it is failure to display wealth or to honour obligations in the proper manner he is more likely to be called *tieboali*.

The systematic application of Ortner and Whitehead's 'prestige structures' model to Kewa material has yielded a number of insights, though it has often been necessary to go beyond it for a fuller analysis. Perhaps I have refined the model in the process. Though the enquiry has established that most valued terms are indeed male, it has also pointed to the activity of creating these values, and hinted at how men do this. While it demonstrated that women, their positions and activities are defined and valued relationally to male prestige needs, it went further into the provenance of those needs themselves, and uncovered women's power in the fear of men. I would conclude however, that gender constructs, though powerful cultural symbols, did not in fact describe the total social reality. While women's position and evaluation as persons could be explained with reference to these constructs, evaluation of male qualities sometimes employed concepts not borrowed from gender constructs and not applied to women. It is therefore necessary to look at the total social relations, of which gender is an important part, to understand fully Kewa cultural usages. In the following chapters this will be done, when the bases of inequality between sexes and within each sex will be investigated.

Notes

1   Here I am referring to traditional land ownership, and discounting land purchases that some sophisticated women make. Such purchases are unheard of in the village.
2   This 'ghost' workforce also includes many children; for details see Josephides and Schiltz 1980.
3   The literal meaning of *tieboali* is 'man of short stature'.

6
The ideology of equality and the politics of power

I shall start by picking up an earlier theme, that of the ethic of egalitarianism among the Kewa. I shall then look at how inequalities are engendered in practice, not only between men and women but also among men. Following a discussion of Kewa social categories the careers of three men, each of whom had achieved some degree of prominence, will be briefly examined. Then I shall attempt to draw some conclusions concerning the social significance of the role of the big man.

The egalitarian ethic

The absence of formal structures ranking individuals along a social scale in societies such as the one under study has encouraged the view that these societies are in fact 'egalitarian' in their practices. This view is misleading, because it assumes that a social system can be deduced from structures; in this case, that the absence of ranked order implies the absence of positions of power and political coercion. But it is the *practice* of social life which sets up and perpetuates inequalities in these cases; for this reason I have tried to concentrate in this analysis on relations of dependence and the economics of exchange.

Nothwithstanding the inequalities engendered within social practice, there is a strong egalitarian ethic in Kewa society which commands at least lip service. A widely held belief is that all persons have intrinsic value and must be accorded a degree of respect and consideration. This is the sort of thinking behind pay-back killings and the payment of wergild; nobody can be killed with impunity. All deaths must be mourned with the proper decorum, although some deaths call for much more ceremony and expense than others. Nevertheless, some minimum requirements must always be met, even at the deaths of small babies. The following example will illustrate how one such death, because it legitimates some claims, can become the occasion for many resentments and antagonism to come to the fore.

Rimbu was preparing to 'cook the food' of his three-year-old daughter. This is a small feast given for a child who is considered to have overcome the dangers of infant mortality. The child was named after me, so I was a sponsor to the feast. A day before the event Kabenu, the wife of Rimbu's older brother Nasupeli (at the time doing a spell of migrant labour in a plantation in the Western Highlands), gave birth to twins. One of these died on the morning of the feast, when all preparations were ready. Rimbu asked Kabenu if it was all right for the feast to go ahead, since otherwise the food would spoil. She nodded dispiritedly, and we carried on. Kiru, Rimbu's FBS, did not attend the feast but sat with Kabenu instead, having first made a coffin for the baby.

Some days later Nasupeli returned from the plantation, but did not come to visit me. When I ran into him in the market I asked if anything was bothering him; later he came to see me with the following story:

'When I went to work for money I thought that my wife and children would be cared for by my brothers, but this wasn't so. As soon as I returned Kabenu told me that our child died and while you cooked food only Kiru sat with her and held the child, and made a box for it. If you had buried the child first before cooking food it would have been all right. Now I have to sell my pig in order to make a gift to my wife, who is very upset over her treatment. Other men would take this very ill, but I am easy-going. When Wapanu [Rimbu's daughter] was a child I used to look after her, and washed her face when she ate her own faeces, because this is the sort of man I am. And when Rimbu was away I planted and tended his coffee garden for him, for which I was never compensated. He should have buried my child before cooking food for his.'

This incident makes a number of points concerning the accepted ethic of 'egalitarianism'. Nasupeli, taking advantage of an occasion when Rimbu was obviously in the wrong and could not defend his actions, brought up a grievance which he had been nursing for some years: Rimbu's failure to compensate him for helping to plant his coffee. Rimbu's actions on this occasion had also offended Kabenu, whom Nasupeli had to compensate for his brother's lack of delicacy. (Nasupeli would have had to compensate her anyway because she bore him the child that died, and because he was away when it happened.) While Rimbu offended Nasupeli by not showing due respect for his wife and child, he also offended Kiru, who thought his FSBW deserved better treatment. (But Kiru had other grievances and was looking for a peg to hang them on.) All three – Kabenu, Nasupeli and Kiru – had to be compensated because their feelings of what was the right and decent thing to do were violated.

When I asked Nasupeli how things could be set right he said his erring brothers must make a gift to him. He conceded my admission to some responsibility (since I had participated in the feast) but pointed out that we were not the children of the same father and therefore I was not to blame as his brothers were. Eventually we all made some exchanges and the situation, at least for the time being, returned to normal.

So even a newborn baby has 'value', and his/her death cannot be ignored. Apart from upsetting the living, failure to observe the right procedures when a person dies angers the ghost (*remo*), which may attack the negligent relatives. Fear of the mother's ghost may lead to the extra careful handling of her young offspring. Many men said they would immediately grant a recently orphaned child all its requests, lest it cry and be heard by the mother's ghost who would then avenge itself on the child's caretakers.[1]

All people are allowed the right to feel affronted or neglected, and may take their complaints to court if they are not satisfied with unofficial procedures. Women are not jural minors, being considered responsible for their actions. We have already seen that they are not forced into marriage, and that bridewealth is not thought to buy their person outright.[2] Because so many people have rights in the same person, no person can belong to one individual or even to one group. This means that transgressing against one person could offend so many others that such action cannot be taken lightly. If a man's own child falls ill he may have to compensate his wife's people, to whom the child owes its physical body. This debt refers to the fact that the child's body is formed within its mother's, and is double-edged: while it gives the maternal kin the right to compensation when the body is sick, it also imputes to them the power to harm it. Often when a child is sick, the father thinks that it is the anger of the maternal kin that is the cause, and offers them compensation. This is why 'skin' payments are made to maternal kin. The state of the skin, as well as being the sign of beauty and health, is in another sense 'the mirror of the soul' for the Kewa: their transgressions, by omission or commission, are reflected on it.

Friends with whom one has lived for a number of years acquire rights so that they also have to be compensated when one is injured or killed. Since women move from group to group more than men (as a result of patrivirilocal residence), they distribute rights in their person wider afield. Their natal group always has rights, as has their mother's group. The husband's group acquires rights on marriage in a way that the wife's does not have in the husband. When a wife is wronged or injured, the husband's group can claim compensation from a third party; while in the case of a husband's being wronged or injured his wife's group would have no such claim, except in cases of uxorilocal residence.

We have seen that the notion that 'persons have value' and should be accorded respect and consideration plays a role in the kinds of reasons people give for their actions on certain occasions. So far, fear of offending other living persons and fear of provoking the ghosts of the departed have been cited as motives behind these actions. A third major motive is the fear of risking the security or sullying the name of the group. The last point is interesting, because it transforms an apparent concern with the individual to a concern with the group. When a payback killing was carried out in the past or when compensation for a death was demanded, the victim's clan presented its grievance as an affront to the notion of this personal value. Yet the matter concerned first and foremost the prestige and security of the group, as well as the glory of its living members. A group had to maintain an uncompromising and warlike appearance if it wanted its name respected and its territory impregnable. A group that never avenged its dead became the target of attacks. In this respect the status of the dead person was immaterial; the death simply had to be avenged. The man who carried out the payback killing also accrued prestige to his name as a fierce warrior.

I do not think it can be denied that Kewa believe that all persons have some power which could harm anyone who injures them.

Perhaps it is partly fear of this that sometimes becomes translated as 'appreciation of value'. A further explanation for this belief is the fact that social organization is based on a kinship ideology from which ranking is formally absent, and which presents its members as equivalent links in an inter-connecting chain. But while genealogies are presented as objective and value-free accounts, as Chapter 1 has shown, they are invariably skewed. For it is people in whom genealogies live on, and these people from time to time make a selection of what they consider to be important links and allow others to fade from memory. Thus even those links presented as equivalent are a distillation and a re-ordering by agents with political interests.

Nonetheless, in an abstract sense people seem to believe that a man is worth a man, and perhaps sometimes that a woman is worth a man. But this does not mean that in practice people are equal, or even that there exists such an emic notion of 'equality'. These concepts, however, may require some clarification.

The limits of ideology: claiming rights by traditional and modern means

The words 'equality' and 'inequality' have been used, but no definition of them has been offered, nor have any Kewa language equivalents been mentioned: this is because no such equivalents exist. When some injustice chokes them, men may protest that they too are men; a woman may also say that she too is a woman, but that is no argument against being put upon by a man. No word exists for 'human being'. 'People' is *wenali*, 'woman-man',[3] but an individual can never use this compound word to stress a claim to some abstract humanity. While English-speaking apologists for the usage of the term 'man' – as in 'mankind', they elaborate – insist that it refers to women also, Kewa will never say that *ali*, 'man', has the same extension. Women and men, then, are never linguistically referred to by the same term, so each cannot claim to have the same rights as the other because of being a member of the same class (cf. M. Strathern 1978). The force of this 'egalitarian ethic' is immediately reduced when men and women cannot even be compared.

A man's indignant retort 'I too am a man' (*ni page ali*), does not mean 'I am as good a man, or as deserving a man, as any other'; it may suggest that he has rights as a man, but not that he has exactly the same rights as another, or all men. It means that he is 'the same kind of thing' as other men, and that potentially he can achieve what they have achieved. But what Marilyn Strathern has said for Melpa women applies here: the degree to which rights may be claimed depends on one's political muscle (M. Strathern 1972: 260).

As far as my own usage of these key terms is concerned, I offer a preliminary definition here. When I use the word 'inequality' I shall refer to unequal access to power; and by 'power' I shall mean the ability to influence social decision, to speak for the group. This ability, in turn, can further be traced to key positions within the social relations which confer greater control of the pool of labour on some members of the community than on others. This will be discussed more fully in Chapter 8; here I will concentrate on the political, visible aspects of power: that is, the ability to influence social decisions and to speak for the group. No Kewa would dispute that this power is unevenly distributed, depending on a man's personal endowments and achievement. Women are not formally allowed such influence, although, as well as politically weak men, they have a certain threshold of rights, and the community will normally guard them against their infringement.

I want to discuss more specifically how the 'threshold of rights' fares as a result of the combined action of Village Court proceedings, traditional forms of mediation, and political muscle. This is designed to show that an abstract recognition and acknowledgement of rights does not necessarily imply that these will be granted in practice. As a background to the discussion I want to give a description of modes of dispute settlement in the past, and Village Court proceedings today.[4]

In the days before contact disputes between members of different political groupings were not usually resolved; they were either buried or led to war, depending on the strength of the groups concerned. There were no mechanisms for settling inter-tribal disputes, and no compensation was paid for enemies killed. However, as I demonstrated in the section on warfare in Chapter 1, the categories of friend and foe were transient, so when an erstwhile enemy became an ally debts were remembered and reparations made for manslaughter or unpaid bridewealth.

Within the group, disagreements between individuals and

divergent claims were thrashed out as fully as possible in open sessions. Sometimes they resembled therapeutic sessions in which resentments were alleviated merely by being externalized. Indeed, externalizing was a very important aspect; people attributed many ills to the fact that feelings of resentment were bottled up or facts concealed. I came across a number of instances in the field when people fell sick because somebody bore them a hidden grudge. Likewise, if wrong-doers do not own up to their misdeeds, trouble ensues. A woman's children will fall sick if she commits adultery and hides the fact from her husband. The same could happen when a sister fornicates and then gives food to her brother's children, without telling him. Whether this happens *mutatis mutandis* in a man's case was never indicated to me.

These open sessions were presided over by the big man, who invited all the disputants to voice their grievances in detail. (M. Strathern (1974: 41) refers to this as 'talking out'.) Everybody else who had a point of view contributed. The role of the big man was then to find a formula acceptable to all parties. What this meant in practice was a compromise in which one party did less well but acquiesced because she or he lacked the support to do better. But to put it like this may be to simplify matters, because although ostensibly it was between two people, a dispute often involved, directly or indirectly, many more. Disputes in any case were never finally settled but were simply put on ice, to surface again when some other event brought them into focus. This is why there was always so much background to each dispute. The ongoing discussions afforded a platform for those with grievances to give vent to their feelings and made them feel better because their rights were recognized in the abstract, even when practically they could not be claimed. The Village Courts established since Independence, though based on Western-type concepts of justice, do not offer very different solutions to disputes.

The Village Court system was described in Chapter 3. The West Sugu area is served by one court which is staffed by five Magistrates, one Clerk of Court and two Peace Officers. Technically, the positions of Magistrates are official appointments, but practically the people choose their own representatives. Although no formal voting takes place, some sort of consensus is reached by the groups concerned. The Magistrates are paid a small fortnightly salary and hold court twice a week. The justice dispensed

by the Village Court is an historical amalgam of traditional
mediation methods, the 'umpire' system of snappy judgment
provided by Patrol Officers prior to Independence, and Western
ideas of abstract justice contained in Australian law books.[5]
However much the Village Court owes to customary law, and
granted that village people in many areas were in favour of its
introduction, the fact remains that it was the child of the new
nation state, ultimately enforcing the sanctions the court imposes.
For this reason people look at it as a higher authority than village
modes of mediation.

This amalgam results in considerable confusion about the
powers and jurisdiction of the Village Court. The set of guidelines
given to Magistrates leaves much to their discretion, and this is
informed by customary practices and motivations. Thus it is
impossible to separate completely the 'new law' (*abi au*, now
fashion) in the form of the Village Court from 'traditional law'
(*abala au*, previous fashion), and this must be kept in mind when
considering the court's decisions, which often exceed the limits of
its jurisdiction, but are nevertheless accepted by the people where
questions of prestige are concerned.

As well as their official authority during court sessions, Magistrates also exercise unofficial power at informal sittings. Before
going to the Village Court many disputes may be heard in the
settlements with one Magistrate presiding, and attempts will be
made to settle them there. This is where the Magistrate's powers
of mediation, and the strength of his own base, in his village, may
be tested. His role, then, is in many ways an extension of the role
of the big man in another milieu; and the workings of the Village
Court, in spite of its imported justice in the form of 'law books',
by no means revolutionize the base of Kewa morals, and their
approach to conflict management; although of course in con-
junction with other political innovations they are beginning to
remould Kewa society.

Below I offer one example which illustrates a cluster of points
discussed or hinted at: that the court exceeds its official powers;
that its decisions are informed by local needs and customs; and
that it can be used in questions of prestige, almost to publicize a
group's largess and the wisdom of the Magistrate's judgment.
The first part of the following anecdote does not deal directly with
the court; but it shows the Magistrate giving an *ex officio* but also
very partisan opinion.

'When Wapa died in the Kagua Health Centre his body was brought to Yakopaita for burial, in a truck belonging to the local Councillor. The Councillor demanded K165 for this service, which Rimbu and other of Wapa's sons complained was quite exorbitant. I mentioned this to the Chairman of the Village Court (Rusa, a Kamarepa man), thinking that he might be able to take some action. Instead he said to me with pride: "We paid more than K500 to have *our* father transported from Mendi when he died." I told Rimbu and the others that they did not have to pay this amount to the Councillor, but they replied that they could not haggle over their dead father's body. They paid the sum immediately.

At Wapa's funeral some Yala from Wapia, where Wapa had spent a part of his youth, tried to claim Wapa's large pig as a consolation for their bereavement. When the claim was resisted very strongly by Wapa's sons, the Wapia guests made attempts to seize the coffin so that they could bury Wapa in Wapia. A scuffle ensued in which Pusa, an old Wapia Yala, was hurt. Tempers flared and the situation looked nasty, but the Wapia eventually withdrew. Within a month Pusa, on the advice of his sons, sued the Agema Yala for his injuries. The Village Court awarded damages of K600. Again Rimbu grumbled about this, and I consulted with Rusa again. Rusa said that he always endeavoured to settle disputes before they entered a really critical stage, when huge sums of money or payback killings could be involved. In this case he knew that if there was no settlement, or if compensation was too low, the Wapia would bear a grudge and were likely to attack the Agema. If and when Pusa died, of whatever disease, the death would be laid at the door of the Agema.

Rimbu was not satisfied and he called for the case to be heard again when the Village Courts Officer, a kinsman of his, was visiting the court. This man found that there was no case, because in order for responsibility to be established the injury must follow immediately upon the act that is judged to have inflicted it, not a month later. Thus it was illegal to award damages to Pusa. But the officer did not want to undermine the authority of the Village Magistrates by reversing their judgment. Instead he reduced the figure from K600 to K300. A collection was taken by the Agema Yala which totalled K512, including pearlshells and one pig. Rimbu said that they wanted to compensate the Wapia well, so that there would be no ill-feeling. In fact, after all the fuss and bother, they were now paying of their own largess almost the equivalent of the original amount awarded, which they had challenged in the beginning.'

The Village Court, then, has powers exceeding its official juris-diction where its judgments are in accordance with traditional mores, or at least where they seem to satisfy the needs of the community. In this case, 'traditional mores' dictated that where there was injury compensation had to be paid, and that therefore responsibility had to be allocated. Further, this responsibility was invariably collective. The two together – collective responsibility and the payment of compensation – act as a quasi-formal in-surance policy whose crucial role is acknowledged by the courts. The important questions of saving face, propitiating, and avoid-ing bloodshed also informed the Village Court's decision in this case. At the same time, the defendants turned the decision to their benefit by organizing a public compensation payment where their group's name was glorified. This was a case where both plaintiffs and defendants had got something out of the decision and were satisfied. But this was a dispute between two different residential groups (though both Yala) and involved questions of prestige. How do more domestic disputes fare?

For this discussion I return to the 'threshold of rights' men-tioned earlier. These 'rights' have to do mainly with abuse of another person's body, with flagrant alienation of another per-son's undisputed property, and with failure to compensate for labour and care. Offences in this connection include causing grievous bodily harm, verbally abusing in a manner likely to make a person ill, rape, adultery, stealing, failing to pay back a loan, and allowing animals or people to cause damage to gardens or homes. Blood, people say, must always be compensated; hand fights in which blood is not drawn are not taken very seriously. There are many cases of women taking their husbands to court for beating them, and damages are usually awarded. Men also often have damages awarded against women. Sometimes all the parties involved end up with short prison sentences. This happens especially in polygynous marriages, or in monogamous mar-riages when the husband proposes to take another wife. All three may become drawn into a fight and finish up in hospital. This experience has discouraged a number of men from taking second wives.

But although women sometimes seem successful in blocking their husbands' moves to take another wife, they fare less well when it comes to being awarded property on divorce. No matter what the reason for the divorce, they must leave their husbands' settlement and their gardens, which are on the husbands' land. Pigs are also considered to be the husband's property, except if they have been given specifically to the wife. Thus although it is a 'basic right' that one's undisputed property should not be alienated, in the case of women 'undisputed property' boils down to very little because they cannot own land. The example of Lapame below will illustrate a number of complex points regarding basic rights and how they can be claimed:

'Waliya married Karupiri when Lapame left him after he failed to allocate sufficient pork to her family at the time of the pig kill. When Lapame returned and wanted to live with him again he took her to court and divorced her. He had a clear case because of her original desertion. She was forced to leave his settlement although she considered herself co-founder of it, having helped in the building of the *neada*. She was awarded no pigs but took only a chicken with her. When his brothers began to grumble that Karupiri was not as industrious as his first wife, and when she also failed to become pregnant,[6] Waliya fetched Lapame back. Since then all three have had daily fights. Waliya's brothers now say that Lapame is always provoking him so that he will hit her, and then takes him to court and forces him to pay compensation. The last time this happened she was awarded a small pig, which she arranged to give to her brother. By the time this brother arrived she was involved in another suit with Waliya. To her embarrassment Waliya hid the pig and would not let her brother have it. There was support for him in the settlement (especially from the women, who were very hostile towards Lapame), and the dispute raged most of the day, with the Yala Village Magistrate mediating. Waliya's terms for returning the pig were that she should drop the present charges against him. While the men were adamant in their stand, their interactions with the brother had an embarrassed and apologetic air, and he in turn responded awkwardly and in subdued tones. Only Lapame had hysterics,

crying and laughing in frustration in the middle of the settlement, as if pilloried. Eventually she agreed to drop charges so
that she could give the pig to her disappointed brother.'

Although Lapame's predicament was a result of her own original
action[7] – she had chosen to leave Waliya because of what she
considered his poor treatment of her – what happened afterwards
was the result of a series of decisions made by other people, that is,
Waliya and his brothers in the settlement. While again it was
Lapame's decision to take him to court after a fight, its decision to
award her a pig was checked by the actions of the men in the
settlement who blackmailed her into dropping further charges
against Waliya. So the ability to claim rights, whether these are
acknowledged or not, is indeed a function of political power and
influence. On two occasions Lapame made decisions, and on both
occasions she failed to achieve her goal. When she left Waliya it
was to press him into giving her the pig she thought was her due
(this is a common ploy of women); instead he divorced her. When
next she made a decision and took Waliya to court, this decision
was challenged and her follow-up moves successfully blocked.

Men may also find themselves in positions of weakness when
claiming compensation for their goods or labour. Papola, a
married Yakopaita man, killed a cow on a public occasion on the
understanding that his brothers would compensate him. They
never did, and he has been to court many times, but the case
always seems unresolved and ambiguous. Papola is not a prominent man in the settlement, and nor is Nasupeli, although he is
Rimbu's older brother. Nasupeli has been complaining for years
that he planted Rimbu's coffee, for which he was never compensated; this case is also unresolved. This line of discussion shades
almost imperceptibly into another area, that of the control of
labour. It is nonetheless a continuation of the discussion of the
limits of ideology insofar as it shows how an abstract ethos of
'equal rights' does not imply equal opportunities in practice.
However, we are now no longer concerned specifically with
formal and informal modes of dispute settlement. I shall pursue
this question of equal opportunities with another example, which
adumbrates the situation of many young unmarried men:

'Rika, a young unmarried man recently returned from migrant
labour on plantations in the Western Highlands, bought some
seedlings from Erave in the hope that he could start a coffee

garden. He prepared a nursery of his own, then made various attempts to raise money in order to hire help to clear a garden and replant the seedlings. (This sort of work could not normally be undertaken by a single man.) This proved impossible in the village, or in Kagua and Erave, where Rika (who had a driving licence) attempted to get a job as a driver. At about this time Mapi, the Yala big man, together with Ipa, the local interpreter, held a *ki kogono* to clear extensive sites for their commercial vegetable gardens. These working parties (*ki* = hand, *kogono* = work) were often organized in the old days by big men, who then held a feast to recompense their assistants. It was difficult, especially in those days, for some men to refuse to respond to the call of the big man. Rika worked on Mapi's *ki kogono*, for which he got pork but no cash, which did not advance his own schemes. His seedlings withered before he could replant them, and he himself returned to the Western Highlands for more work on plantations.'

Since participants in *ki kogono* were paid with pork, was their labour exploited? The first point to be made is that it is difficult in a society not based on wage labour to decide what would constitute adequate and fair payment for work done. It could be said perhaps that while the hired men were working for big men for some immediate payment and the consumption of pork they were neglecting their own gardens or other business. However, in the Sugu area at least such big works are not performed sufficiently frequently to interfere with men's own work. The really significant point about these occasions is that only big men can afford to organize them. So although big men may not be controlling in a direct way the labour of other men, they do have the power to call it up when they need it. Big men can finance big schemes; little men cannot. This unequal access to the pool of labour in the community results in unequal exchange: while lesser men provide labour which enlarges the surplus of the big man, the big man merely provides food which sustains these men for a day or two. Different things were transacted, and the two sides benefited in different ways. This aspect of the transaction is of vital importance to my argument in this book because it means that the labour of certain categories of men, as well as the labour of women, is separated from its product through the mechanism/strategy of exchange. I shall come back to this in the following chapters.

Here, I want to pursue the question of Kewa social categories, and what makes a big man.

Social categories

The question of social differentiation is not easy to tackle in the Kewa case. No great inequalities were observed in the living styles of village people. So designated big men did not live in better houses, wear better clothes or eat better food. Some families did perhaps eat meat and fish more regularly than others, but I have no statistics on this. It is in any case unlikely that it bears any real relevance to the discussion. The level of nutrition in a man's family is no criterion of his status; some big men's children looked very neglected and sickly. Although people say that a big man works hard, this is not a true criterion either. I will argue later that the real criterion is the ability to *stretim ol samting*, as people say in pidgin: that is, to settle disputes and keep the community running smoothly.

Apart from these big men, were there and are there any hard and fast social categories among the Kewa? I shall discuss this question in a comparative way after a short review of social differentiation among the Melpa of Mt Hagen, this being historically the best documented case.

In his analysis of Melpa society, Andrew Strathern (1971) suggests that big men were more powerful before contact, at which time the influx of shells 'democratized' the system. Prior to this, big men monopolized the pearlshells which were necessary in many areas of social interaction, and made ordinary men dependent on them for their procurement.[8] Strathern reviews the material of Vicedom and Tischner (1943–48) and simplifies the social categories into which these writers had classified Melpa society, cutting them down from five to three: big men, ordinary men, and men of low status. Women are not mentioned in connection with any of these categories; they clearly belong in one of their own. Men of low status did not marry or make *moka*, the central mode of group interaction. Usually the big man assigned them to one of his wives, for whom they did men's work in return for their food. Ordinary men did marry, but did not normally have many wives. They could make *moka* individually with their agnates and affines but could not host group events with other clans. They did not head a *rapa* (men's house group) or control the labour of other men, although sometimes they might have had a few hangers-on.

The situation is much changed now, when erstwhile 'rubbish men' or servants (*kintmant*) can earn money in wage labour and obtain wives for themselves. Nevertheless, big men still find ways to set up relations of inequality with other men. In *moka* exchanges, the arena where big men distinguish themselves, the contributions of lesser men are sometimes swallowed up and the big man's debt to them is obliterated.

Kewa do not have a system of *moka*-like group prestations, for which eventually there is a return that must be distributed among the group; therefore the claims of unimportant men cannot be bypassed in exactly the same way. The only occasions on which the group makes a joint prestation are war reparation payments (*mena kiri*) and wergild payments (*ali yoto* or *ali abulalo*; 'man's body' and 'I pay for man'); but in these cases there is no return, so contributors cannot be cheated. Nevertheless big men do exist among the Kewa, although we would be hard put to discover the social categories described for the Melpa. No rich historical material exists in their case, apart from oral history and the memories of the elderly. These elderly informants usually claimed that in the old days there were fewer and more powerful big men than today, whom ordinary people obeyed because they were afraid of them. These men controlled long-distance trade. When shells, decorating oil and other items came from faraway places only the big man would go and barter for them, because he was the owner of all the wealth. Then he would redistribute the items to his own people (though 'retail' may be a better word; he did not do it for nothing).

The category of 'rubbish man', or unmarried servant working for a big man, does not seem to have existed for the Kewa. In the whole of my fieldwork area I found only one old man who had never been married, and he had an obvious handicap.[9] Among Kewa villagers nowadays there are hardly any single able-bodied men of over twenty-five years or so. The only one in our settlement was deaf and dumb, and his celibate status was explained with reference to the unavailability of his peer: 'You see, there are no deaf and dumb women in this area.' While some young bachelors may work in the gardens of their older agnates for food and other goods, mature, married men do not work for anyone else. The expression 'rubbish man' (*tieboali*) does have current usage, but it is a term of abuse rather than an established social category. People may use it to refer to men who are mean with their money and goods or who do not share or distribute properly, do not work hard or handle their affairs and domestic problems well, do not honour their debts, or keep their word. The term may also be used to refer to men of low stature and generally poor physical appearance.

In the Melpa case the main reason why some men did not marry appears to have been because their patrons failed to raise bridewealth for them. Kewa men insist that they raise their own bridewealth. In the words of one old man: 'My eldest brother did not marry my wife; I married her.'[10] He went on to describe how he made gardens and took vegetables to his married sisters, who in return gave him pearlshells and piglets. He raised the piglets and hoarded the shells until he had sufficient for bridewealth. Other old men confirmed that they provided most of their own bridewealth.[11]

Nowadays practice varies. From the marriage histories collected it seems that most men did raise their own bridewealth, often by working in plantations and breeding pigs at home. In these cases it was invariably the mother or other female kin who provided most support. One young man, recently returned from plantation work, negotiated his own marriage for which he proudly said he paid sixteen pigs. Other male kin were loth to help him because they were preparing for a pig kill. He himself killed only one pig on this occasion, saying in pidgin: '*Maski kaikai pik; kaikai kaukau pastaim*' (Never mind about eating pork; I must eat sweet potatoes first). By this he meant that it was more important for him at this stage to have a wife who would work in the gardens than to participate in a pig kill. What he failed to mention, however, was that the pigs were raised by his mother while he was away, and that in any case most were from a recent litter and very small.

This particular young man's father was dead. Other young men may get assistance from their fathers, especially if they force the issue by being caught in compromising circumstances with a girl. In such cases compensation demanded by the girl's people may be so high that the father will prefer to give bridewealth. However, the provenance of the pigs will still be the same, raised mainly by the mother. The difference is that when the father is alive he has control of those pigs which his son can only get through him. The son will then say that his father helped him. But his mother's help if his father is dead is taken for granted, so that the son can claim that he has raised his own bridewealth. A father will usually attempt to procure a bride for his son, although this does not necessarily mean that he will fork out the money for the bridewealth. This happened in the case of Rimbu, my Yakopaita host. His father had courted a girl for him while he was away working in a plantation, and when he returned with some of his earnings his father insisted that he use them on bridewealth for this girl. Dramatic and highly-charged events followed when the son resisted and distributed his money elsewhere. The father wept, fell sick, became violent and intimidating, and used every trick he could conceive of. He even got the money back from where Rimbu had distributed it, so that his son could not use the argument of poverty. Eventually Rimbu did marry the girl (Lari), because, he said, he did not want to be responsible for his father's falling sick. Both he and Lari protested that it was under duress (but they seemed to be enjoying a happy marriage nevertheless).

Other cases seem to fit better into the classical mould of patron–client, but they are unusual nowadays. Young men returning from migrant labour attach themselves to an older, married man who eventually helps them with bridewealth. This does not have to be a big man; in fact the cases observed involved ordinary men. There are, then, a number of ways to raise bridewealth and obtain a wife; moreover, big men's contributions are not necessarily required.[12]

In conclusion, I could find no clearly defined social categories among the Kewa. Apart from the periodic joint work on special gardens or *ki kogono* sessions, married men did not normally work for other men although unmarried men did. However, these men eventually married, with or without help from so-called big men. There was no social category of 'rubbish man' or bachelor. Women were the only category whose dependent status was not transitory. Nevertheless big men did and do exist among the Kewa. Although they do not always bind their followers personally to them in the way described for Hagen big men, they have indirect ways of controlling their political actions and their labour power. These are the areas of unequal exchange and unequal access to opportunities already discussed and to which I shall return, from a different perspective, in Chapter 8. This interested

aspect of the big man's power – absolutely crucial to the maintenance of his position – is not, as one can imagine in societies
sporting such an 'egalitarian ethic' as the Kewa, given prominence
as a recognized criterion of what makes a big man. It is to these
criteria, and to the personal and social demands put on a big man,
that I now turn.

The big man

As in Hagen, Kewa big men achieve their status through their
own efforts. Andrew Strathern (1971, 1972) describes how some
big men may give encouragement and a head start to their sons,
but that ultimately these sons have to pull it off on their own
merits. A man's ability to do this will depend to a large extent on
his 'oratorical talents, his persuasiveness, his capacity to make
people listen to his plans and follow his lead' (M. Strathern 1972:
136; see also A. Strathern 1975). He is the initiator of peace,
because through *moka* he offers a positive alternative to warfare
(A. Strathern 1971: 76). His rhetorical arts of persuasion must be
powerful indeed, for they are successful even though no physical
sanction reinforces them. A big man must shine at *moka*, and his
most powerful action is the control of the timing of this event so
that it takes place exactly when he is ready. In order to succeed in
this he must have the wealth items required, the networks and
contacts through which to pass the transactions, and the prestige
and influence to gather people to these events. He must have a
strong home base, for without the support of his own group he
will be unable to pull off such a major event.

Though oratorical skills are given much prominence, clearly
they are not decisive. At a *moka* prestation itself many formal
speeches are made by established speechmakers, but these are not
necessarily big men and the content of their speeches is irrelevant.
They fulfil a formal requirement and gain prestige accordingly, as
good artists. Although a big man usually is a good speaker, his
'gift of the gab' is different from this. His talent is not so much in
flashy oratory as in persuasive talk, which wins respect with its
reasoned credibility (see A. Strathern 1971: 173). Oratory then,
although it may be the hallmark of the big man, is not the decisive
factor to which his prestige may be traced;[13] this must come from
elsewhere.

For the Kewa, powerful oratory is a useful attribute, but the ability to settle disputes is crucial. Big men must have workable solutions that people will accept. It is not a question of abstract justice or of right and wrong, however defined; it is rather one of efficient dispute management and social organization. Village Magistrates are important because they have a power sanctioned by the state; however, their own power in their own right predates this, otherwise they would not have been put forward for the position. They are men who are well-versed in the social mores, are at home in their cultural milieu and can act in accordance with it. They can convince other people that their decisions are not only the best, but are acceptable to all parties concerned. In the final analysis, Kewa are pragmatists in their attitudes towards their leaders. Responding to my question as to why Mapi and not Rimbu made the major speech at the Yakopaita pig kill, Waliya, a quiet and unpretentious man, offered the following comments:

'Because Mapi is our big man. He is the big man of all Yala. He is the Village Magistrate. He is in that position, it is true, because we vote for him, but we vote for him because he is conversant with both traditional customs and the ways of modern government.[14] This is why when sometimes he makes mistakes we forgive him, because in the long run he does well. We listen to Mapi now, but we don't know if we will listen to him in the future. It all depends on how straight a path he steers. Perhaps we'll put forward a different candidate next time, I don't know. But right now I think we'll probably vote for Mapi again.'

Men make a cool assessment, then, in the case of each man, of how successful he is on average at finding acceptable and workable solutions to the various problems besetting the village. If he can represent their interests well *vis-à-vis* the outside world (that is, the provincial and national governments), so much the better. However, that is a more important requirement in the case of national politicians than of local big men/Village Magistrates. People do say that they will vote for the parliamentary candidate who will bring most 'development' into the area, but it is difficult to assess if this desire really informs voting patterns. Generally there is a trend for more educated politicians to be elected to Parliament; the long-standing MP for Kagua and Erave, who spoke no English, was replaced by a more literate person in the last elections. The strength of one's home group – sheer numbers – is also crucial for aspiring provincial and national politicians.

I now intend, after describing the phenomenon of the big man, to characterize its social significance. These are two different questions: what a big man is and how his status is achieved; and what this status means in the social context, that is, its socio-structural position. The first question will be discussed anec-dotally, using as examples the careers of three men: Rake, Mapi, and Rimbu.

When I arrived in the Sugu Valley the big man for the Council ward which included my fieldwork area was Rake, who was a Councillor and Village Magistrate at the same time. He was of the Perepe tribe, one of the largest and most dispersed in the area. Within the Yala tribe living in Agema, Mapi was the established big man. He was also Village Magistrate, and acknowledged by outsiders to be the overall Yala big man in the area. In Yakopaita, the Yala settlement where I settled, Rimbu was the most promi-nent man. Rake and Mapi were age-mates, while Rimbu was their junior. The prominence of these three men was not really distrib-uted over concentric circles, as this brief introduction may sug-gest. In many ways they had different influences in different spheres, but in other ways they competed. Nor was it always obvious who was more influential, or how one's power encom-passed the others'.

Perhaps because he was at the same time Councillor and Magistrate, Rake was spoken of by all as 'our big man'. He had been a cook for Patrol Officers in pre-Independence days, and was in his forties in 1979. He spoke pidgin but was illiterate. He did not appear to work hard in his gardens, but rather enjoyed dispensing justice and telling people what to do. He was fond of threatening people with imprisonment, and when I first arrived in Kagua offered to have my house built with convict labour (I did not take up the offer). He had two wives (a third had died) but only three children. The second wife, a Yala, was in constant conflict with him. She had had a child which died. The health of the two younger children was poor; they were covered in sores and suffered from frequent attacks of malaria. His house, in a bad state of disrepair, stood isolated on the main road near the courthouse. Rake had recently moved to this position. Earlier he had been living in a settlement with other members of his clan, when government officers started enquiring about gravel in the area. When they showed an interest in the quarry near the courthouse, Rake immediately put up a house there and went to live in it. In this way he hoped to establish rights to the quarry and to be paid compensation when the government began to exploit it. To his dismay, however, the quarry was abandoned for a better one down the road, on another tribe's land. But Rake remained in his isolated house on the road.

Although Rake liked to hold forth, people often grumbled that he did not offer satisfactory solutions to problems. To some extent he owed his position to the accident of being picked by a Patrol Officer some years before to act as cook, which had given him the opportunity to learn pidgin. It is unlikely that his paternity offered him an advantage; his father had not been a particularly prominent man, and Rake was in fact a younger brother (his older brother was still living but people said he had no 'talk'; indeed, he appeared most inarticulate and far from alert). When Kagua Council was set up this ability to speak pidgin, and the fact that he was considered to be well-versed in the ways of white people, made him an obvious candidate for the post of Councillor. Later, when the Village Court was established he was put forward as Magistrate, and in fact became the Chairman of the court.

The court was very rowdy during Rake's term as Chairman. While waiting for my house to be built in Yakopaita I lived in a hut, built as shelter for plaintiffs awaiting their hearings, next to the court, from which Rake's loud abuse and threats to litigants issued remorselessly forth. Eventually he lost the confidence of other Magistrates, who sacked him as Chairman and replaced him with Rusa, a Kamarepa man who conducted the court in an orderly and dignified fashion. Rake's prestige then became tarnished, and he lost some of his flamboyance. His image had always been flawed and he had never completely enjoyed people's trust. Probably in the old days he would have shone more as a *mudu* than an *amo*. He drank a lot of beer and attended 'six-to-six' socials,[15] which was not considered proper behaviour for a big man; perhaps some lip service to 'mission laws' was expected.

Rake left a lot of unpaid debts when he died, but no outstanding credit. He did not leave many pigs, cows or other items of wealth. His debts, I was told, died with him. Friends and relatives made contributions towards his funeral expenses, and the occasion was attended by one of the largest crowds I had seen. Undoubtedly he was known over the whole area, and his name had influence. Secret divination ceremonies were performed on his body, to discover the cause and agent of death.[16]

In questions concerning one's own home group Rake's power and influence did not interfere with Mapi's or Rimbu's, but Rake and Mapi did clash in many ways in the public sphere, especially where relations between their respective clans were concerned. As a result of one such clash it was feared that Rake's death would lead to a fight between the Perepe and Yala tribes. This concerned acrimony over a land dispute which had been simmering for some time, causing much bad feeling. On one occasion Mapi, who has a reputation as a dreamer (that is, he dreams of things which are to happen), told Rake that their dispute would soon be at an end, since he dreamt of Rake's death. Inevitably this led to accusations against Mapi when Rake did die, and the two groups stood poised for a fight for a few days. Eventually the situation was diffused, probably to surface again when another dispute brings it to the fore. Although he came into conflict with Mapi, Rake was never in conflict with Rimbu. The latter in fact sided with him against Mapi, but not too openly.

Mapi's and Rimbu's stories can be told together, because they are so interwoven. Their influence and fame did not extend outside their tribe. They came from different Yala clans, Tiarepa (Mapi) and Umba (Rimbu). Mapi was the older man by about ten years. He first asserted himself by organizing a pig kill some years ago, when members of the tribe moved from the ridges down to the road. Rimbu did not participate in this pig kill; their relations were already soured. The background to this souring was as follows.

When Mapi first began to organize for the pig kill, Rimbu made the counter-suggestion that they buy a truck. The reason why Rimbu suggested this was not because he wanted to advance any business interests; to him, as to many villagers, trucks were an alternative to pig kills as carriers of prestige. Mapi at first opposed the idea, saying that they had to kill pigs before starting on any other enterprise. Rimbu, who had already collected some money towards the truck, was quite dismayed and said he would use this money for something else. In the meantime, however, Mapi started looking for a truck himself, and having found a second-hand one turned to relatives for contributions. With ill grace,

Rimbu made a contribution, vowing not to participate in the coming pig kill. He addressed Mapi thus:

> 'You planted bananas first, you built a *neada* first, kept cows and bought a vehicle. I was small and watched you, thinking that I would do the same when I grew up. You are eating greens with *pitpit*, and I must watch and bide my time.'

Mapi had the truck registered in his name, and proceeded to organize the pig kill. Rimbu was furious; Mapi was the Village Magistrate and owner of the truck, and now the *neada* would exalt his name too. In addition, Mapi won the support of Roga, Rimbu's senior FBS, who was unsympathetic to Rimbu's complaints and told him he could go off and build his own *neada* and buy his own vehicle. So Rimbu and his supporters scraped together K1,300 and bought a truck of their own, while Mapi and his had their pig kill. Soon after, Rimbu's truck was involved in a fatal accident, and the compensation payments which followed put quite out of the question any possibility of an early pig kill.

Though the competitiveness and hostility between Rimbu and Mapi was sometimes expressed as group hostility between their clans (with Umba-Paripa fearing that Tiarepa were outnumbering them), the Umba-Paripa invited Mapi to mediate whenever there was a dispute in Yakopaita. It was on such occasions that Mapi was obviously more influential than Rimbu, because of his official position as Village Magistrate (not forgetting that, in Waliya's words quoted earlier, he was elected to this position because of his influence). During these informal hearings Mapi personified an authority to which Rimbu had to bow. In the case of one directly political dispute, openly to do with power and control, Mapi was called in to deliver a reprimand to Rimbu. The background to this was as follows.

For reasons of personal prestige, Rimbu wished to be in charge of my transactions in the village. On one occasion when I distributed gifts without consulting him he became sulky and angry for a number of days. Although he never said explicitly what was the matter, the other people in the settlement were well aware of what was bothering him and forced him to admit it. The trouble with Rimbu's position was that he could not externalize how he felt without laying himself open to criticism. He was angry with me but if he admitted to this his motives would become obvious, and he would be seen to be violating the egalitarian ethic that was thought to lie at the base of group solidarity, at least among his peers. So he had to pretend that nothing was really wrong, that he was not angry, and had no right to be, that he had simply got used to my consulting him, and so on. The outcome was that he was put through a sort of public degradation ceremony in which he had to disavow any claims to being more prominent or important than his brothers. This was mediated by Mapi, who delivered a homily to Rimbu. Rimbu, subdued and flushed, concluded his disavowal by thanking Mapi, 'our big man', for setting him on the right path again after he had gone off the rails so badly.

This incident illustrates the very sensitive position of any aspiring big man (cf. also A. Strathern 1971: 226–267). Because Rimbu's base was small, he had to be extremely careful not to alienate any of his supporters. This gave him a very narrow margin for any direct forms of control over their social and exchange relations. As well as being small, Rimbu's base consisted mainly of his peers. The population of Yakopaita fluctuated between thirty and forty people, including three brothers, their father, a FZS brought up as an agnate, and a number of FBSs, all classified as brothers. The brothers were of similar age, and there were no gross inequalities in their possessions and lifestyles. While Rimbu was generally accepted as the most prominent man in the settlement, he knew that he might not get sufficient support if he ran for public office. He would have liked to be Village Magistrate but he knew that if he put forward his candidature against Mapi's he might not be chosen, and it would be too direct a challenge. He did run for Councillor when Rake died, but lost by two votes, as a result of his own clan's prevarications. Many different elements voted for him, but Rimbu was aware that his chances of attaining public office were small because his own clan is not numerous and his personal pull insufficient to attract members of other clans within Yala.

How, then, does Rimbu merit the name of big man? He was not as diligent in garden work as Mapi and had no commercial vegetable gardens. In common with other village men (including Mapi) he ran a small tradestore which, unlike those of the former, was usually stocked, thanks mainly to the free transport which I could offer. He had only one wife to Mapi's three, but Mapi's wives were obtained before he became a Christian (he was a staunch supporter of the ECP), and one had since left him. Although he sometimes attended services, and paid lip service to 'mission laws', Rimbu's Christianity was not very exacting. Finally, Rimbu was no great orator; Mapi was, and usually took over this function on public occasions.

Yet throughout my stay in the field it was obvious that Rimbu was in charge in the settlement. He appeared to be making the decisions, although discussion usually preceded these. He was the first to approach me while I was on an exploratory trip and invite me to set up house in the village. In all clan events he played a leading role. The pig kill in Yakopaita was organized by him, and although he did not kill the highest number of pigs, he transacted many more. In questions concerning relations with other clans and tribes, he is always consulted before any action is taken. He speaks lucidly and soberly on such relations, and his judgment is fair and sound. On one occasion when I attended a neighbouring pig kill with another village man (Rimbu was unavailable) a very unpleasant incident arose which would have been avoided had Rimbu been there. The occasion was a *mena kiri* in Yago (a Tiarepa[17] village), to which the hosts had invited dancers from Ialibu.

A number of Yala wives come from Yago, so the Tiarepa invited us to attend their group displays. I went along with some villagers. My official protector was Agema, a young married man. As was my habit on these occasions, I took out my camera for some shots of the dancers. Immediately their leader, a man in a safari suit who really looked like a press manager, stepped in front of the dancing group and held up his hands. If I wanted to take photographs, he said, I must pay them first. Where was the payment? he continued threateningly. He became very abusive, and Agema fell into a violent argument with him which almost led to blows. I said I had taken no photographs and would take none, and pulled Agema away. The situation could have turned very nasty, and Agema was still fuming about it when we got home.

Rimbu was soon apprised of the incident, and immediately came to obtain full details. After I recounted what had happened he asked many searching questions, such as, 'Where was the Yago big man while this was going on? Was he within earshot? Did you talk to him about taking photographs?' Having reconstructed the situation Rimbu eventually said that no further action was necessary. If I had been insulted they would have had to demand satisfaction, but from my story Rimbu gave the following assessment of the incident:

'The Yago were not to blame for what happened. They did not insult you. The Ialibus behaved badly, but that's understandable. The only wealth they have is the gifts for their dancing; they have no coffee, no business. Dancing is their business. We wouldn't behave like this but then our situation is different. In any case they were hired people who are not our neighbours, so we can't get back at them. What should have happened if Agema had been more circumspect and cool instead of impetuous and irascible, and what I would have done had I been there, is the following: When this uncouth Ialibu challenged me I would have said: "Excuse me brother, but I am a guest here. The Yago big man, who is paying your fees, has invited me and wants me to take photographs. Let's go and ask him." Then we would have gone to the Yago big man and he would have confirmed our story. There was no point arguing with the Ialibus; this wasn't their place, they were just paid dancers and they had no say. Only those who paid for their services could have a say in who was and who was not to take pictures. As it was the Yago big man was not called, so we cannot blame him for anything. No, if there is any blame to be attached then I am afraid that it is our Agema who was wanting in judgment and *savoir-faire*.'

Thus Rimbu is one who has *savoir-faire*, who can judge a situation correctly and is well-versed in the social mores as well as in proper etiquette. He does not lose his temper and is not dismissive or openly scornful of anyone. He is patient, and listens to everyone's point of view and everyone's problems, which he discusses for hours on end. He is generous, hospitable, available and helpful. In the months preceding the pig kill Rimbu complained to me that it was very hard work arranging it. He could not turn anyone down, and had to entertain all the time. In every group prestation he had to make the largest contribution. In short, he had to keep everyone happy and splash his money about; but that money will not be lost, and all the wealth will come back, Rimbu usually finished off by saying.[18]

As well as *savoir-faire* and other qualities described above, an aspiring big man must be energetic and ambitious. He must have drive, he must *want* to be a big man and accept the obligations and responsibilities that go with it. Not all men want these. It is hard work, and many people prefer not to put themselves in a situation where others may come to them for advice, or with blame. The confrontations that Rimbu has had with members of his clan have not been over issues where bids for leadership clash, but rather when Rimbu's attempts to exert authority interfere with their autonomy and control over their own affairs. They were not vying with him for leadership because they had neither the ability nor the disposition; but they challenged him and sabotaged his schemes when their own autonomy was at stake. As long as Rimbu could demonstrate that his interests coincided with group interests he was successful as a leader; his organization of the pig kill and other ways in which he represented the group were seen by all to be beneficial for the group, even when his personal interests were also served and his personal prestige augmented. But when, as on the domestic occasion described earlier, he was unsuccessful in merging his interests with group interests, his moves were resisted. In most day-to-day affairs Rimbu's initiatives were tolerated or supported, because in his role he united the group and kept together disparate elements that might otherwise have drifted apart. The brothers themselves recognized this role of Rimbu's and deferred to him in many ways, though sometimes grudgingly. They themselves were certainly not ready to take on any responsibility for the group; but from time to time they felt the need to assert themselves or at least to show that they were not to be pushed about. Thus not all men want to be leaders, but few will succumb to being led. Above all, they protest that they are all equal.

But why then, given the exertions, demands and frustrations which accompany this social role, do some men pursue it? For it is true in this case that, in T. S. Eliot's words, 'uncertain the profit, certain the danger'. Big men do it first and foremost for the power and prestige, of which undoubtedly there is a lot. Even though their power is circumscribed, even though they have to move gingerly through group ideologies and accept disappointments with good grace and renewed strategies, even though it requires sacrifices, patience and some gambles; still it is possible to gain prestige, and power, and through these, advantage. The constant build-up of renown and prestige over a long period establishes the sort of capital which Bourdieu (1977) dubs 'symbolic', because its assets are primarily social recognition. The mere exhibition of this capital, once created, can call up material wealth in a process encapsulated by Bourdieu as 'capital [going] to capital' (Bourdieu 1977: 191; see also Josephides 1982b for an attempt to apply this model to the Highlands).

At the beginning of this section, I set out to do two things: to describe the phenomenon of the big man, and to characterize his social significance. What a big man is and how his status is achieved was discussed, using the careers of three men. In this discussion heredity was hardly mentioned, as it seemed irrelevant. Rake and Rimbu were both second sons, while Mapi was a first son whose only inheritance was the power of dreaming, which he got from Rimbu's father! Mapi described this as a sort of succession: 'Wapa was the dreamer in our group before, and when he died this ability passed on to me.' The ability passed on, but by no means on genealogical lines. None of the three men's fathers had been particularly noted, though Wapa had been a *mudu*, a war leader. (Wapa and Gapea, Mapi's father, had achieved some note by living to be so old.) Rake seemed to people to be in a position of high authority, but did not have their trust; his authority was somehow beyond their ken and control, but they were in awe of him. Mapi on the other hand had people's trust and he really did seem to spring from them, although he was also vested with another authority. Rimbu was the most home-grown and therefore the most vulnerable of leaders. He was the most closely bound by the requirement to show that his interests merged with the small community's. And yet, in a sense, being the most intimately linked to his small base he was also the most indispensable. If Rimbu went, the Yakopaita community would be no more; but if Mapi went the Aka community would continue, and certainly Sumbura carried on after Rake's death.

The second question, that of the social significance of the big man, has already been hinted at. A big man holds the group together, in fact guarantees the autonomous status of a group (see also A. Strathern 1971). A big man motivates, co-ordinates and carries through major events. A big man lends credibility to events and takes responsibility for them in situations where no other person would be prepared to take responsibility. Aspiration to bigmanship means that there is always strife and competition within the group, and the 'egalitarian ethic' ensures that a system of checks and balances is worked out in practice and remains in force. There are shades of Hobbes' *Leviathan* (although the level of tolerance of despotism is much lower, and not so formally expressed): it is as if villagers had made a covenant with one man to allow him to have a great part in directing their lives for as long as he was successful and avoided too much strife; as soon as he went too far, or was unsuccessful on too many occasions, they withdrew their support and merely by so doing brought him low. For there is no permanent and secure way for anyone to hold power; when support is lost power is lost, and there is no coercive way to hold on to it. This does not mean, however, that *while in power* a big man does not indulge in coercive or exploitative practices. The difference is between being tolerated and supported and losing support. Support is enjoyed by a man for as long as he seems to the people to be the best bargain they have – the best man for the job.

This discussion may suggest, misleadingly, that the community quite deliberately and consciously chooses a man as its leader, and that this decision is unanimous. This is not so, because the community is not a homogeneous group, always united and ranged opposite the leader who is morally outside or above it. On the contrary, within this community itself there are power blocks and interest groups, especially at the higher levels of power politics which encompass larger groups. Thus in many cases the big man may lose the support of some of his clanspeople, or a sizeable portion of his constituency (in the case of a Member of Parliament), but remain the 'number one man'. It is not always easy, then, to get rid of a man once he has become entrenched in a position of power, especially where his support is large and diverse. But this is more likely to apply to provincial and national politicians than to old-style village big men, who are more vulnerable to local opinion. Yet this is an important point to make here lest it be assumed that because in some reductionist sense 'all power rests with the people' this means that in practice 'the people' will always have the solidarity and organizational ability to topple a leader who becomes too powerful (see Thoden Van Velsen 1973), or even that they will always want to remove him.

The discussion in this chapter has focused on the notions of equality and power as ideology and practice. While an 'egalitarian ethic' was found at the base of Kewa group organization, the extent to which rights could be claimed in practice, or opportunities availed of by all in equal measure, was a function of political influence, which was unevenly distributed. Women and men were not measured with an equal yardstick, as their relationship to group organization was different. The 'egalitarian ethic', modified by the exclusion of women and reinterpreted to refer to 'potential equality', thus achieved a mere Kantian generality in everyday situations where only power can actualize potential.

The question of power, then, is crucial in discussions of social practice. This was wielded inequitably by different people, being most conspicuously concentrated in the hands of the category 'big men'. However, it was the community as a whole which legitimized the position of the big man, and this support was forthcoming only for as long as he seemed to fulfil certain functions. The main function was that of managing disputes and keeping the community running smoothly. Big men were successful to the extent that they could enforce viable solutions to the problems of social organization, requiring in many respects the merging of their interests with group ones in the community's eyes. Thus they personified the group, so that its credit and liabilities became their personal assets and responsibilities. In Chapters 7 and 8 I shall show how the big man organizes the distribution of these liabilities, while as far as possible credit remains concentrated in his hands.

A distinction was made, in passing, between big men with large bases and those with small bases. While big men in general must be careful not to provoke or alienate their supporters, those who have the power to bring them low by withdrawing their support, big men with a large base can afford to be more forceful and are more difficult to dislodge. This is a problem which develops as support groups become less homogeneous and localized, mainly following the dispersal of the group or the concentration of big men away from their home base. While this is most commonly felt in the case of MPs as a result of the parliamentary system, it is a growing problem which must be attended to.

Notes

1 Interestingly, Hagen men think that all mothers die with a grievance, and therefore that their ghosts are always trying to wreak vengeance on the living (A. Strathern 1972: 27).

2 Although the pidgin word *baim*, to buy, is used on these occasions.

3   This compound word is also used to mean 'relatives'.
4   A useful background for this is the collection of essays in Epstein
     1974. However, since these were written before Independence in
     1975, their descriptions of local Village Courts diverge from the one
     given here. For the language of dispute, see Goldman 1984.
5   For a historical account of how this evolved see Gordon 1983.
6   During the divorce proceedings with Lapame, Waliya always
     stressed that he put up with what he termed her 'strange ways' (for
     instance, her habit of keeping her money from coffee pickings in her
     brother's house instead of the marital home) because she was a good
     worker. He never referred to the fact that they had no children, and
     when I once asked him how he felt about this he said it did not
     matter, as long as the woman was a good worker. This reinforces
     the point made in Chapter 5: Kewa men seem in their statements to
     be more concerned with women's value as producers than as
     reproducers.
7   But it must be borne in mind that a man behaving in the same way
     would not find himself in the same predicament. Men often leave
     their wives and children for long periods, especially to go off to
     plantations. This does not by itself give women a case for divorce.
     Certainly men who left their land and gardens for long periods
     would not thereby forfeit their rights to them. Perhaps this will
     happen in the future, when absences become more prolonged and
     land scarce; but it will be a different matter then, and will still not be
     comparable to the position of women which can be stated baldly as
     follows: women do not accrue rights to their husband's land, where
     they remain always permissive residents.
8   In a review of Melpa material, Feil (1982b) traces the origins of
     inequality to this monopolization of pearlshells. Discussing the
     conditions for the development of stratification, Feil argues that big
     men had the edge over others because they controlled shells, which
     only they could produce locally through the manipulation of ex-
     change ties. In other words, 'What is produced . . . are the exchange
     links . . . that facilitate the entry of pearlshells into the Melpa region'
     (p. 294). Thus Feil appears to give credence to the claims of big men
     that their exchanges 'produce' wealth. But this analysis overlooks a
     crucial point: that when the shells entered the landlocked areas they
     were exchanged for something, and that something must have been
     produced locally. Therefore, big men could only 'produce' shells if
     they already controlled the labour that produced the items for which
     the shells were exchanged.
9   His hands were deformed.
10   To marry, *lamula*, refers to all the transactions which are part of the
     marriage settlement. Here the old man meant that his brother did
     not pay bridewealth for him.
11   From younger men, who were just old enough to remember
     pre-contact days, I had a different story: 'In the old days we had to

work very hard and for long years in the gardens of big men before we were given our first breeding sow.' The discrepancy may simply be a different focus; the younger men were referring to an earlier period in men's lives, and were, according to the older men, exaggerating a little.

12 The position with many young men now away on plantations is more ambiguous and unresolved; at present most are unmarried, while some have contracted unstable marriages.

13 For a number of ethnographic discussions on oratory and its relation to political influence, see Bloch 1975.

14 In pidgin, *tumbuna pasin* and *lo bilong gavmen*. It is highly debatable that Mapi was conversant with the latter.

15 So called because they were held from 6 p.m.–6 a.m. String band music was played on these occasions and beer was sometimes drunk illegally. For this reason they were banned by the local Council, which was another reason why the Councillor should not have been patronizing them.

16 The cause of death appeared to be dysentery. His four year old son, however, died in dramatic circumstances the same evening and the two were buried together. A few days later one of his wives also died, so almost the whole family was wiped out in a short time.

Two divination methods were suggested. The first, which was carried out, was the spear method. Rake's body was trussed up on a tree trunk, each end of which rested on a forked piece of wood planted in the ground. A man from his mother's line (*agira*) stood at Rake's head and rested the blunt edge of a spear on his chest, while he whispered the names of various clans. If blood appeared the person responsible for the death would be found in the clan whose name was being whispered at the time. No speck of blood appeared on this occasion. The bamboo divination method was planned for later in the evening. This involves tying a piece of bamboo to the body, and as the bamboo 'pulled', the men carrying the body would follow. The bamboo would disintegrate in front of the house of the murderer. However since on the night of Rake's wake there was a full moon, this parade was not thought proper (as the body would be seen by everyone).

17 Tiarepa tribe, not to be confused with Tiarepa clan of Yala tribe.

18 Rimbu was aware, then, that he was not merely 'maximizing net outgoings' (see Chapter 8).

7
Exchange and the pig kill

Kewa exchanges may be described as a system of total prestations in that they may involve economic, religious, ritual, aesthetic and kinship aspects (A. Strathern 1971: 214). The Kewa *yawe*, however, is different from the Hagen *moka* and the Enga *tee* in that all exchanges are not necessarily fed into it. For Hagen and Enga, it has been said that 'the lesser events are geared to, and culminate in, long-term cycles of large-scale transactions' (Meggitt 1974: 165). Among the Kewa, everyday exchanges may have different functions from the periodic group events.

In the Sugu Valley I did not notice the busy daily exchanges noted by Lederman in Upper Mendi, and especially among women. But there is no doubt that when something special or plentiful is in the possession of one group member it will be distributed as far as possible. Recipients are not obliged to return similar items but simply to redistribute when they have something special themselves. It is one of the basic tenets of Kewa social organization that things be shared within the group.

If members of the same group fall out they must make up by compensating one another, or exchanging some item. This happens most often with clan brothers. When petty disagreements have raged for some time a pair or more of brothers may decide to put an end to the bad feeling (*kone kolea*) by exchanging something. Often this is when some other, larger event has shaken them, as for instance when an older generation agnate falls sick or dies. The idea is that you show your goodwill by giving something of yourself, and your opponent does likewise. If the exchange is disproportionate, a debt is created. If events have progressed so far that one disputant falls ill, this gesture of goodwill will no longer be adequate. The sick person must now be given a pig, or have a pig killed in his name. This is more likely to happen in disputes between different generation agnates, when the older man falls sick. Instances of women being propitiated in this way were noted only between married couples, and then rarely. Women appear less prone to this sort of sickness, and are less likely to receive pigs except for really serious injuries. When they do feel wronged or neglected a more common strategy for them is to leave, or threaten to leave, their husband's settlement.

One incident narrated below, while illustrating how exchanges and gifts ease bad feelings, also shows that duty is owed to elders and that Village Courts support this principle.

'Wapa, the Umba lineage elder, made a habit of quarrelling with his sons' wives. One of these sons, Nasupeli, eventually lost his temper over his father's continual bickering and ill-temper and told him that this settlement (Yakopaita) was not his home, and if he did not like the way they did things he could return to his own house on the ridge. In a huff, Wapa withdrew to Popa. Part of his peevishness stemmed from his sons' tardiness in building him a new house in Yakopaita; his old one was falling apart. For a time he threatened to take his sons to court over the issue, and had many informal hearings in the village with the Magistrate. Finally, he did go to court, and the court ruled that his sons should build him a house. The sons knew this in advance; Rimbu, the second son, told me that if their father went to court they would be able to provide no defence whatsoever: *"Mipela nogat toktok"* (We have no case), he said in pidgin. What their father asks they must do, and although often they did not, that was only an indication of their disobedience; they could never justify it or offer an argument for it.

Some work started on the house, but before it had progressed very far Wapa fell ill. The sons became very worried; they felt that it was their neglect and lack of respect that had filled Wapa with the *kone kolea* that had brought on the sickness. Immediately he was brought down from Popa and deposited into the *tapada* in Puliminia, close to Yakopaita. A pig was killed for him and he was given pearlshells and money. He was too ill to eat any pork and could articulate no response to the gifts. However, the sons assured me that the sight of them made him better. At the same time the sons were settling their own scores among themselves. Two pairs of brothers who had been having disputes for some time exchanged pigs and affirmed their amity. The pigs were a token, representing a part of themselves, I was told. The general climate of goodwill was thought to be beneficial to the health of the patient, who soon recovered.

A few months later, however, Wapa fell ill again, and this time he died. But there had been no bad feeling this time, so the sons, though very aggrieved, were not burdened with the responsibility for the death. They did not have to fear the dead man's *remo*. A group with which Wapa had lived in his youth did in fact try to extort some compensation for his death from his agnates, but his sons ridiculed the suggestion: "It's not as if he died because we neglected him." [This case was discussed fully in Chapter 6.] It was indeed lucky that he did not die the first time.'

People also exchange things to satisfy some present need. A man needing a large pig to give away to his newly married daughter or sister may obtain it by giving two smaller pigs to another man who wants to breed them for a pig kill the following year. Borrowing and lending are also quite common. Money may be borrowed for the immediate purchase of food or cigarettes. Local tradestores operate largely on credit, in spite of the inscription on the door of each store, in both Kewa and pidgin, that no credit can be given. People also borrow in order to gamble at cards; these loans should be returned as soon as possible. Then there is long-term borrowing, which is really part of the political manoeuvring towards the *yawe*. This usually takes place between unrelated men. Perhaps 'borrowing' is an improper term for what happens on those occasions, which people describe as 'helping' a friend because they feel 'sorry' for him or her (*raba* and *yala*). One anecdote, of how Rimbu struck up a friendship with two brothers, will illustrate this sort of relationship.

Koai and Kaporopali were two brothers of Ala tribe living in Roga on land belonging to the Koiari and Kamarepa tribes. Many of their clan had settled in Roga before pacification, when they were chased out of their own land in Katiloma. Most of them returned home after pacification, but Koai and Kaporopali had linked themselves through marriage to both of their host groups and chose to stay. One day, in 1976 or 1977, Koai approached Rimbu in the market and told him he had been given a cow.

Would he come to Katiloma with him the following day and kill it? (it was known that Rimbu owned a shotgun.) Rimbu agreed, and with his younger brother Komalo accompanied Koai and his brother Kaporopali, together with their wives and children, to Katiloma. Koai and Kaporopali had helped two brothers, Roga and Sen, to build a *neada* in Katiloma, and the cow was in payment for this. When the party arrived they found that Sen, the owner of the cow, was away, so they had to spend the night there, waiting for him. Rimbu gave K6 to Komalo to buy food, most of which was offered to the large families of the two Ala brothers, who were suitably appreciative.

The following day they heard that the cow owner was in Kagua getting drunk, and sent the following message: 'I am not looking after anyone's pig or cow. Whoever says so has no shame.' Rimbu very tactfully asked the Ala brothers if they had really been given a cow. They assured him that they had. Rimbu suggested that in any case they should return home, as there seemed to be no point in spending a second night in Katiloma.

Seeing the party leave, Roga, Sen's brother, felt shame, so called them back and offered them a sow of his. With the sow on a rope the brothers again started on their way home, inviting Rimbu and Komalo to eat with them when the sow was killed. They had not gone very far when Roga started shouting after them: 'Where are you going with my sow? Put her down!' In utter disbelief Rimbu turned and asked the man if he was joking. 'No', he said, 'bring my pig back!' Koai's blood was up. 'You two brothers are made,' he said, attacking Roga and knocking him to the ground before Rimbu could restrain him. Then Koai told Roga to take his 'rubbishy pig' and go, and the party returned home.

This incident brought a lot of shame on the Ala brothers, and on Rimbu by extension, because he was their guest. Rimbu felt so painfully sorry for them that when they reached the Wilimi stream near Aka and saw his cow grazing, he said to them, 'Come, we will kill this cow and eat it.' The brothers protested. 'No, brother, you are another man's son and we have already put you through too much.' It had been raining heavily all the while, so Rimbu invited them into his house. Koai and family were billeted with Nasupeli, and Kaporopali with Rimbu. They cooked bananas for them, and Rimbu noticed that they looked at his pigs with interest. So after they had eaten he 'talked sorry' to them, recounting their misfortunes with the cow and the sow, and finishing off with the following: 'I have offered you a cow. But is it pigs you want?' Yes, it was. Rimbu said nothing, directly, of his intention to build a *neada* and kill pigs himself, but spoke thus, in *siapi* (metaphoric speech):

> 'I am giving you two pigs. I don't know if I shall have children in the future; but if I do, you can bring some soap and towels to my house to help wash them.'

Here the *yawe* is spoken of in the idiom of childbirth, where a woman assists in the birth by washing the newborn baby. The message, clearly, was that Rimbu expected the brothers to help when he held his pig kill. Then Rimbu gave Kaporopali one pig, K50 worth of pearlshells, and an *adasekere* ('big shell'). To Koai he gave a pig and K80 in cash. When the two brothers returned home with the pigs other neighbours of theirs expressed an interest in them, and Rimbu ended up giving more away and forging new partnerships. He expected to have his pigs back and additional ones in return when the time came. In the event, these partners had their pig kill just prior to Rimbu's so they could not give pigs. But they returned money instead. On an earlier occasion, Koai had also given Rimbu a pig which his daughter had received in bridewealth. This was now part of an active exchange relationship in which the exact status and value of each gift could not be calculated in isolation and outside the relationship.

The complex of delayed gift exchange described above is exactly the area which offers the possibility for some individuals to appropriate and redistribute products of other people's labour. This is because what is given is not formally 'sold' for an immediate return, and what comes back does not bear the formal character of a payment. It cannot, then, be claimed by the producer of the original gift, whose product was seized by a more powerful person and put into an exchange cycle which blurred the continuity between labour and its product. In this case Rimbu gave away pigs and cash to men that he felt 'sorry' for. Whether Lari, his wife and co-producer, also felt sorry for them does not enter into the discussion (when I asked Lari she said she felt sorry for Rimbu!). Lari could have kicked up a fuss if she disapproved of the gift, and could have created an embarrassing situation for Rimbu. But he would have got his way in the end.[1] In any case, Lari liked having her workload tightened by a few pigs. The real point is that she could not have struck up a similar friendship and given away pigs in her own name. (I shall come back to this below.) By giving the pigs away, Rimbu had created credits in his name alone. As we shall see, when the pigs came back to him, the role of labour in their acquisition was 'forgotten'. Rimbu did not cheat his partners in unequal exchange; he did not receive back more than he gave without the creation of debt; however, in the act of giving he appropriated the product of Lari's labour. I will return to this sort of alienation in the following chapter. Here I want to concentrate specifically on the pig kill, its socio-cultural aspects and political implications.

Kewa killed pigs for a variety of reasons. At the most pragmatic level, sick animals were killed so that the meat would not spoil. (According to a number of informants, this was sometimes used as an excuse to satisfy a desire for pork.) Pigs were also killed as a treat for a special guest, or to placate a relative who had fallen ill as a result of 'bad feelings' or 'bad talk'. At marriage exchanges many live pigs changed hands, but some were also killed by the groom's family to feast the bride's family. Neighbouring tribes' pigs were at times killed as an act of hostility, either seized when found wandering in the bush or after a successful attack on an enemy village. Most importantly, pigs were killed in the name of cult deities and 'for the longhouse'. This is the type of pig killing I shall be concerned with here.[2]

Yawe

The 'longhouse pig kill', *neada yawe*, was the only really central feast in the Kewa social reproductive cycle. It was the long-term goal of all clans, and plans for it started with the inception of any new settlement. The dispersed settlement pattern described in Chapter 2 provides the background to the description of those social endeavours. The founder of a settlement would first build a *tapada* and try to attract people there. It was not taken for granted that others would follow him; he had to woo even members of his own clan and patrilineage. When members of outlying hamlets did join his own it was only for the duration of the pig kill; after the festivities participants dispersed again to their own settlements. The building of the *neada* and the culmination in a *yawe* thus did not follow automatically on the construction of a *tapada*, but success depended entirely on the founder's ability to attract others to him. He proceeded by organizing various small feasts to which he invited everyone who he hoped would later help him in the *yawe*. This was kept up over several years. Small pigs and large pigs were slaughtered, and meetings were held. If helpers in the meantime suffered a death, the aspiring pig killer had to make prestations to the relatives if he wanted to retain their support. The more supporters he gathered around him, the more prestige attached to his name. His closest supporter became known as the 'mother' (*agi*) of the *neada*, while he himself was called the *neada*'s 'father' (*ara*). The 'mother' would try constantly to bring the *yawe* forward (in order to discharge his duties and start planning his own *yawe*), while the 'father' would want to put it off until the line of the pig stakes was long. Apart from spending wealth to propitiate supporters, the 'father' would be incurring debts throughout this period by mortgaging pigs that he might not yet have, in order to buy the pigs or to have solicitory feasts. The creditors in this case would also be pushing for the *yawe* to be held.

The most committed supporters came to work on the building of the *neada*, each constructing his own 'room'. Men did most of this work, although women helped with roofing and gathering *kunai* grass in small bundles. The *neada* 'father' fed the workers at this time. Sometimes men were hired to do this work, for which they were paid with a feast of pigs. These men were called *kaberekeali* and described as 'bought men'. Each door (*poragapea*) of a *neada* represented two major pig killers, while the rounded corners (*neada wako*) belonged to the 'father' and 'mother' (*aragi*). These were expected to kill at least five pigs each and to exhibit many more.

Often other men joined the father of the original *neada* and built *neada* themselves. Sometimes in the past there were as many as eight *neada* in just one or two settlements. However, the original 'father' on whose land the feast was held was considered to be the real 'owner' of the *yawe*. It was his name which was uplifted, although the pig kill was a joint affair.

In the old days *neada* pig kills were accompanied by exhibitions of *rungi*. These were long poles kept in a special spirit house and decorated with the bones of pigs killed over the years. At the *yawe* they were taken out of the house and planted in front of the *neada*, and pigs were killed beside them. The poles were also decorated with pearlshells and other valuables. Pig killers would taunt their enemies with the *rungi*, sometimes parading it within sight of enemy territory and daring them to take the wealth exhibited there. The *rungi* enhanced the reputation of the pig killing clan by showing the number of pigs its members had already killed and the valuables they possessed. Eventually the wealth was distributed by the owners in accordance with exchange arrangements, and the *rungi* was buried.

The *wali karia* ceremony is still held today. Literally *wali karia* means 'breaking of the sugar cane' and takes place a few days before pigs are killed. It consists of prestations of various lengths of sugar cane as well as a showing of pearlshells. The pig killers collect many sticks of sugar cane and distribute different lengths to different people, as a token of the size of pork they will receive when pigs are killed. The pork thus bespoken may be paid for, or it may be a gift. At the same time pig killers display their pearlshells and publicly announce to whom they shall be giving them. At this stage it is still hoped to attract more pig killers. At a recent pig kill one man described to me how on seeing his display of shells people 'greased' him with promises of pigs and money in order to obtain some of his shells. Many shells circulate among pig killers, as well as between them and outsiders. This is a sort of dress rehearsal for the *yawe*. At the end of the day most people should know what to expect, and there should be no surprises. Agreements about sales of sides of pork may also take place at this time (although these may take place at any time). In an article on the Kewa pig kill, LeRoy (1979b) describes how shells are exchanged against sides of pork, two shells being equivalent to one side. He also mentions that such transactions may be made only once in respect of a single pair of shells or side of pork. This prohibition on multiple exchanges was not palpably adhered to in any of the pig kills I witnessed. With the debasement of pearlshells a whole side can no longer be obtained for a pair; K50 or K60 will be paid for such a quantity of pork. Only small cuts can be returned for shells.

On the occasion of the *wali karia*, *kepa* is also given to the hosts by visiting pig killers. *Kepa* are long bamboos on which slits are made where valuables are secured. In the old days these valuables were mainly shells, but now they have been overtaken by paper money. Small pigs, ducks and other animals may also be given. These are to settle small 'food' debts incurred over the *yawe* preparation period.

One day before the pig kill all participants line up their pigs and tether them to the stakes. They decorate, and display, their shells. Full decorations are no longer worn by many men, as most missions disapprove of them. The characteristic hat (*wambe*, or *raguna*) which distinguished those who could afford to give pork to their mother's lineage as well as their wife's and father's, are no longer seen. The shell distribution is a lively and confusing affair, very difficult to follow as so much happens at the same time. Many men stand up simultaneously, hold up a shell and call out the name of the recipient. The recipient collects the shell, in most cases merely to redistribute it again. Thus although one man may start with only thirty shells he is likely to end up distributing double that quantity. Women also receive and give out shells, but with little display. They certainly do not hold their own 'showing' of shells. Each shell transaction may have a different meaning; one may be an affinal payment, another a gift to a member of one's own lineage, a third a return payment to a partner or a payment for pork to be given. Thus many obligations are discharged in just one day. At the end of the day there is a small feast, and at dawn the following day the slaughter begins. Not all the pigs lined up and tethered will be killed, however; some will be given to partners and affines, to discharge debts and obligations.

To show off their wealth and largess, pig killers tried to invite dancers from the south (*kewa*) or the north (*madi*)[3] to the festivities. These dancers received several pigs for their services. However, the practice is now discouraged by the missions as being too provocative, in at least two ways: excessive self-exaltation is the sin of hubris, and may provoke others to violence or competitive destruction (*rawa*);[4] and decoration and beautification of the body may lead to sexual excitement and delict. As one big man, a keen church supporter, told me, 'If I put on full decorations I'll turn women's heads, and encourage them to sin.'

With the exception of the first pig killed, the slaughter on the occasions I attended was unceremonious. There is little variation in the pattern of events. Early in the morning the clan leader makes a speech and clubs the first pig to death with a stick known as the *mena roto*. The rest of the pigs are killed noisily and in an unorganized manner, not always very efficiently. Some young men simply go around clubbing anybody's pigs, and usually have a hard time killing them. Pigs already sold and for which money has been received are touched with a *mena roto* and the buyer's name is called out before they are killed. Before long the noise of squealing pigs is quietened, and the air is heavy with smoke and the smell of blood. While some people singe the pigs on open fires, others dig the pits in which they will be cooked. These are long, narrow trenches about 40 cm deep and 90 cm wide. The pigs are then carved. The head is cut off and the inner organs are removed and given to the women, who make parcels to cook later in the pits, or stuff them in bamboos and cook them on open fires. Blood is collected in bamboo tubes with leaves, and cooked on wood fires. This is eaten by the pig killers and their families while waiting for the main pits to be opened. The carcass is usually broken open, the legs cut off, and the rib cage separated. Stones are heated in the pits, and the meat, together with some vegetables, is put in. The pits are sealed with banana leaves and the food is left to cook for one or two hours. The meat is not normally done by this time, but it is expected that after distribution recipients will take it home and recook it.

Pork distribution is like shell distribution inasmuch as each man distributes many more pieces than he had to start with. Large pieces are given first, with the pig killer holding aloft the pork and calling out the village and name of the recipient. In addition to individual prestations, bowls filled with pork and vegetables are given by name to the villages attending the pig kill. This is considered common courtesy, even if these villages were not officially invited. Women make their own smaller redistributions, quietly and with little fuss.

Since most exchanges are prearranged, many disagreements arise when a recipient considers the pork received not to be equal to the money given for it in advance, or to be an inadequate return for some past debt. Sometimes fights ensue, with disputants playing tug-of-war with pieces of pork. Domestic fights also take place when women are not satisfied with what has been given to them for their own patrilineage. In such cases husbands invariably impose their own decisions, although they may then have to run off to avoid their wives' blows.

Historical function of pig kills

In his first monograph on the Melpa speakers of Mt Hagen, Andrew Strathern defines ceremonial exchange systems as

'crucial institutions by means of which relations of equality or
inequality are established between groups and individuals' (1971:
214). While this 'ranking of clans and men' is an important
function of the Kewa pig kill, in the old days when warfare was
endemic, the building of *neada* and the joint slaughtering of pigs
had a wider significance within the social structure. It facilitated
the amalgamation of individuals into groups, or groups into other
groups, following devastation and dispersal in war. Thus it had a
part to play in group formation. Victors celebrated their victories
by holding pig kills with their allies, whom they compensated for
their help and their casualties. Routed groups, moving from
clanland to clanland, had to be easily absorbable into other groups
if they were to survive. Yet at the same time the exigencies of war
required of the group a solidarity based on some notion of
exclusiveness. A strong ideology of moral duty towards kin,
reinforced by fear of supernatural sanctions, served this function.
But since in the interests of self-survival this 'kin group' had to
keep an 'open door' policy, the acceptance of new groups or
individuals had to be smoothed over and covered up. Thus
groups thrown together following some social upheaval proceeded immediately peace was achieved to build *neada* and kill
pigs jointly. A common story of origin then sometimes began to
circulate, and the groups might even adopt an overarching name.
Their own names they would retain for internal use only, except if
they broke up again very soon. In such a case they would take up
their old names again, and perhaps use the overarching ones on
occasions, for diplomatic reasons. When two friendly, neighbouring tribes acted jointly over a number of years they became
'paired' in the minds of outsiders and were referred to together.
This 'pairing' might then be celebrated by the two groups in a
joint pig kill.

Many examples can be cited to illustrate the points made above.
When the Agema Yala were chased out of their land during the
mena yada ('war over a pig'; see Chapter 1), some dispersed in
various directions, but the bulk went to Wapia in the east. Other
groups calling themselves 'Yala' dwelt there; it was not clear at
which stage they began to call themselves that. Hosts and refugees
built a *neada* together and killed pigs before the next war broke
out. The Yala then acquired a common story of origin, although a
number of inconsistencies befuddle the various versions. After
many wars and wanderings the Agema Yala refugees were invited

back to their own land by a friendly group which had vanquished their enemies. As soon as they were settled a pig kill was held by the following tribes: the Kamarepa, the friendly tribe; the Yala; the Eno and Urupa, neighbouring groups; and some Kambia, Tangerepa and Tepenarirepa, at the time also fugitives from their own land. In an earlier pig kill in the settlements of Mapiame and Agema, many tribes came together, driven by war: the Ala and the Yamu, refugees living with the Koiari; and the Kambia and Tepenarirepa, living with the Yala for the same reason. There was a tendency, then as now, for several pig kills to be held simultaneously in many settlements. On these occasions a man killing pigs at his own settlement would send members of his family to attend neighbouring festivities, so that there were representatives from all clans in all pig killing settlements and no-one felt slighted.

Data from several pig kills, from about 1930 to 1981, show that in pre-contact days there was involvement by a larger number of tribes in a single pig kill than is the case now. With the cessation of warfare, the pig kill has lost its particular function of blending various clans and tribes together, but it remains ideologically important as a group event and a measure of the prowess of individuals and the group. However, *individual* pig kills in Kagua are not as important for the *ruru* as *moka* appears to be for the independent status of a Melpa *rapa*. Although in general and in the abstract pig kills are important, particular ones will not make or break the group. A discussion of contemporary pig kills will highlight these issues and illustrate the kinds of power struggles attending these occasions. An analysis of the exchanges taking place will stress further the complexity of the events; but we shall have to go behind the exchanges, to a discussion of the history of the items transacted, to understand how the relationship between those items and the labour which produced them is denied.

Contemporary pig kills: Yakopaita 1981

Pig kills are held for a variety of reasons nowadays: to inaugurate new churches, to celebrate mass baptisms, or to make war reparations for now very old wars. The last are *mena kiri* ('pig-burnt') prestations, so called because the pigs to be given are first killed and their bristles singed. Pigs are also killed at the death of an important man (*komada*), or to commemorate such a death; to clinch the relationship between two partners; to mark a new settlement; to honour a name; or to ease some man's burden.

All these reasons (and more) may be present simultaneously in any single pig kill, although men and women respectively reduce the major cause to a single one: 'We are following our father's footsteps', and 'It is men's way to do this, and we help them.' Furthermore, each pig kill is a chain in the cycle of pig kills, giving the impetus and the credit for others to follow. A large pig feast invariably creates an artificial settlement in which various groups and individuals come together to build long *neada*, only to abandon them again when the celebrations are over. Although the celebrations were joint, and each *neada* bore the names of the men who built it, used it, and slaughtered pigs outside it, they were at the same time seen primarily as the affair of the group on whose land they took place. Other participants were mere helpers, who would return to their own settlements or perhaps build new ones. Since a new settlement has to be, as it were, consecrated by a pig kill, the hosts in the previous pig kill will be invited to repay their debts, or create new ones.

Although known to the outside community as tribal events, pig kills are in fact initiated and sustained by a small core group of 'strong' men who have a variety of reasons for deciding to hold them. But these men expect to recruit most support from their agnates and kinsmen in other clans within the tribe. However, they will also seek support from unrelated men from other tribes with whom they have struck up a friendship. The main pig killers, most of whom are usually agnates, will form an 'action set' for the organization of the pig kill, but this will not necessarily mean that they will co-operate on other issues or that their alliance will outlive the occasion for which it was created. Yet although a cavalier individualism pervades men's statements concerning their obligation to follow the lead of others, there undoubtedly is a strong pull to participate in group affairs. This is especially the case with close agnates, who may suffer personal loss of name if they do not support events organized in the group name. They will most certainly be derided by outsiders as well as scorned by their own kinspeople. Some of the events leading to the 1981 pig kill in Yakopaita will illustrate this.

Yakopaita was first settled in 1968 by one brother. More brothers followed at regular intervals in the next seven years.

They were living higher up on the ridges before this, and started on the descent only when Patrol Officers had them come down in order to build rest houses and an airstrip in Kagua. They found it too difficult to make this journey every day, so eventually settled in the valley. At first they built only shelters and started making gardens; then they discussed the construction of a *tapada*. Rimbu, the second brother, wanted to build a *tapada* while the others preferred to start with a *neada*. The eldest brother, Nasupeli, recruited the help of other agnates and built a *neada* while Rimbu was working on plantations on the coast. In 1979, however, the *neada* bore Rimbu's name, because (as another agnate put it) 'Nasupeli has no talk.' The significance of having the *tapada* built first (as Rimbu desired) was that it implied that a pig kill would follow shortly. A temporary lean-to longhouse (*pokala*) could fulfil the function of the more elaborate *neada* on these occasions. In spite of this initial setback, Rimbu continued pushing for an early pig kill. He was in a hurry to make his name, especially as he had fallen out with his father's older brother's son, who had joined Mapi, the big man of Yala Tiarepa clan, and had killed pigs with him in his new settlement (part of the story told in the previous chapter).

Rimbu's brothers parried, finding excuses for putting off the pig kill. In the meantime Rimbu was engaging in transactions calculated to bring in more pigs for the projected feast. His reasons for wanting the pig kill were numerous. He wanted to advance his name as initiator of a pig kill; to discharge his duties in connection with the new settlement; to discharge various debts in a public way; and to enhance his reputation by sending off the anthropologist in a spectacular way. He picked up other reasons *en route*; most importantly, his father died, so the pig kill was also a commemorative feast. This is a very common *post factum* justification given for a pig kill, since one does not have to look very far back for the death of an elder or an important man.

A little over a year before the pig kill took place, Rimbu proposed again that a *tapada* be built for the occasion. An older agnate, Rama of Paripa clan, proposed also that Kewa dancers be invited and that the organizers themselves (including the anthropologists) decorate in the traditional way. Rama could suggest this because he was a Catholic, and the Catholic mission had by that time become liberal *vis-à-vis* traditional customs. The members of the Evangelical Church of Papua (ECP), however, could not decorate, nor could they kill their pigs at a feast where Kewa dancers were invited. Heated discussions and factional, almost cabalistic, meetings took place, where the cud was chewed but never swallowed. Each meeting would reverse, ignore, or repeat the decisions of the previous one, just as if they had never been made.

In the midst of this shilly-shallying, Wapa, Rimbu's father, died. This seemed to put a rather different and more determinate face on things. Before dying Wapa had named the most senior Umba clansman, Roga (his older brother's son), to be clan headman. This was the same Roga who had grown away from the rest of the Umba years before following various disagreements and leadership tussles between Umba and Tiarepa. He had thrown in his lot with the Tiarepa, with whom he was now living. He was also a staunch member of the ECP, in fact one of its deacons. Immediately at Wapa's *komada* he stepped in, and standing at the head of the coffin had the following conversation with Rimbu:

> *Roga:* Tell me when you plan to kill pigs. We were enemies before but father [Wapa] brought us together. So now I am asking you to inform me of the date.
>
> *Rimbu:* We planned it for Christmas 1981. We will make a second *neada* and a *tapada* in six months.
>
> *Roga:* But will you keep to the date you fixed while father was still living?
>
> *Rimbu:* The others didn't listen to me while father was alive. I fixed the date in earnestness, and cannot change it now.
>
> *Roga:* That's your problem, but I want to change all this. You've been obstinate and wayward and never saw through your decisions. Now father has died, and I am going to change all your plans again. They are digging father's grave and I am standing at his head. I can't joke, or lie to you. Did you have in mind to invite Kewa dancers?
>
> *Rimbu:* Yes, we agreed to get Kewa dancers.
>
> *Roga:* When father died this died with him. Did you have in mind to build a *tapada*?
>
> *Rimbu:* Yes, we agreed to have a *tapada*.
>
> *Roga:* When father died this died with him. Did you plan to make a second *neada*?
>
> *Rimbu:* Yes, we agreed to make a *neada*.

Roga: When father died this too died with him. These three things I now call off. Instead, you will proceed in the following manner: a *pokala* instead of a *neada* will be built in February next year; in the sixth month you will collect firewood; in the seventh month you will receive your pigs from the Okane [the people from near Ialibu, who owe them pigs]; and in the eighth month we will feast our father. The *yawe* died with father; now we will simply cook food for him. Is there anyone who can oppose ('kill') my talk?

Rimbu: They never listened to me while father was alive, so now I can raise no objections to your proposal.

In the event a small *tapada* was built by Nasupeli, but it was not suitable for dancing. Kiru, another close agnate, dissociated himself from this move. This led to dissension later, when he was asked to 'compensate' Nasupeli for constructing the *tapada*. This 'compensation' was a contribution expected of all agnates, as a sort of indemnification for the labour and expense that Nasupeli had put into what was considered a group event. Kiru's response at the time the building was proposed was that they could not build a *tapada* now that their father was dead and would not sleep in it. 'You build it; I won't sit in it,' he said. Many arguments followed this demand for compensation, and Kiru's final words on the subject were bitter:

'The gulf between us will never close. We will kill pigs now. Outsiders will see us killing pigs together, but inside there will be a rift. When you display shells at the *tapada polo* (porch) I will display mine on my *manadaga* (platform). When you kill pigs at your *tapada* I shall kill mine here at the old *neada*. But when this is over my children and your children will go different ways.'

The ostensible cause of Kiru's coolness, as he stated it to me, involved a valuable shell which had belonged to his father. His father died while Kiru was away, and the shell was given away in Kiru's absence and without consultation with him. Kiru said this was an indication of how little his brothers deferred to him, and his failure to attract the respect he thought due to him was the real cause of his frustration. In fact, Rimbu had recently been taunting him with the suggestion that he would not be able to make a substantial contribution to the wealth showing at the *wali karia* about to take place.

In spite of all his bitterness Kiru had no thoughts of withdrawing support for the pig kill. 'Of course we'll kill pigs,' he said to me. 'There's no reason why we shouldn't kill pigs. But afterwards we'll go our different ways.' Asked where he would go, he replied: 'Oh, I'll stay here. We'll all stay here, just like before. But we'll do things separately.' While competitiveness between agnates is undeniable, Kiru's enraged remarks were unlikely to make any real change to the social arrangements. Their function, rather, was to enforce the 'checks and balances' which maintain the equilibrium in this social system where power is not formally invested in an office held by an individual. Kiru was pleased for the feast to be known far and wide as the Yala *yawe*, and would support it for this reason. He spoke proudly of the long line of stakes – 102 until then, when in many places as few as 25–30 might be killed. But within Yala he liked it to be known that he was 'doing his own thing', and was every bit as good as Rimbu or Nasupeli.

From this and other discussions, three things at least became clear about pig kills in general as well as this one in particular: (a) that there is no doubt that a large pig kill confers prestige on the whole group; (b) that no brother or close agnate would refuse to support the pig kill except in the most dire circumstances; and (c) that Rimbu would not have succeeded in pulling it off without the help of his close agnates.

Point (a) must be qualified a little. Although it is undeniably the case that the whole group shares in the glory of a pig kill held in its name, it may be misleading to describe such an occasion as the triumph of the group over the individual, as Lederman (1982) suggests for the Upper Mendi and LeRoy (1979b) for the South Kewa, both close neighbours of the Kewa discussed here. Personal resentments were seething very close to the surface in the *yawe* just described; the group did not really act as a group (although people sometimes claimed this). Emotionally group solidarity was not achieved for each individual. The reason why Kiru did participate was not so much because he cared for the reputation of the group as that he cared for his own reputation. The two perhaps are not always totally separable; nevertheless they should not be taken to be one and the same. This is again the vexing question of individual interests versus group ones, which was discussed in more detail in the previous chapter. There the suggestion was that a big man succeeded in having his own way only to the extent that he could show that his interests were at the same time those of the group. Kiru clearly could not convince anyone that in his case this was so. And exactly because he was not strong enough to push through his own designs, his reputation would suffer even more if he failed to follow the initiative of others and support the pig kill.

Psychological and cultural imperatives should not be left out of this discussion, although it seems difficult to do much more than mention that they exist, and that people often present them as efficient causes for their actions. A typical remark justifying participation in a pig kill is, simply, that it is 'our fashion', traditional and seemly.

Timing

In spite of Roga's pronouncements concerning final arrangements for the pig kill, events moved somewhat differently. The following September after Wapa died, a number of pigs started coming into the settlement. Some were returns from partners who were having their own pig kills, and this was therefore the time for them to discharge their debts. Others came from men marrying Yala girls; six girls in all married at about this time, and the pigs were part of the bridewealth. The general opinion was now for a speedy pig kill, as delay would be costly in terms of pig fodder, human-power in pig care, and compensation payments for damage caused by an enlarged pig herd for which facilities were lacking. At this stage virtually nothing can put off the event, especially on this particular occasion, when a so-called 'time of hunger'[5] reigned, and bad harvests meant that sweet potatoes for human and pig consumption often had to be bought. The *pokala* was almost completed, as was the small *tapada*, and people were now working on the *manadaga*, the lean-to shelters, so delay could not be brooked.

The tussles now continued in reverse. Rimbu's partners were pressing him to kill pigs in early November while Rimbu tried to put them off to later in the month when Marc Schiltz and I were due to return to the field. Rimbu was not completely successful. His own supporters agreed to wait for our return (we were in any case pig killers ourselves, as well as major exhibits), but the partners who were killing pigs simultaneously at their own settlements and with whom long and numerous meetings had been held for months previously did not wait for Rimbu, but killed their pigs first. It raises the question, then, whether simultaneity was really all that important, especially as nobody seemed particularly dismayed at the new arrangements. Perhaps what was important was not the actual day synchronization but the close social interaction which the various conferences prior to the big event occasioned.

Although 4 December was fixed as the date for the pig kill, it actually took place on 25 November. Because Wapa had died on 24 November the previous year, Rimbu laid great stress on holding the pig kill on a day of the month with the number 4 in it. Yet this was abandoned without a word; so perhaps his real desire was to kill pigs as close to the anniversary as possible. In *The Rope of Moka* (1971), Andrew Strathern describes the importance of the timing of the pig kill, which big men may manipulate to serve their interests. This happens also among the Kewa, well before the event; however, there comes a stage when the occasion has gained its own impetus and can no longer be held off. At the end of November the preparations in Yakopaita had reached that inevitable stage.

Analysis of exchanges

As LeRoy (1979b) mentions in his paper on the south Kewa pig kill, many things can be transacted on this occasion, and the various transactions may have different meanings. Some money and shell distributions are in payment for pork, some are returns for prior debts, some are affinal/child/maternal payments, and some are to contract new debts. In the Yakopaita pig kill all these aspects were present. Sometimes, even when shells or money were received from a person to whom a pig killer gave pork, the pig killer insisted that this money or shell was not payment for the pork; the pork was a free gift, and the money or shell was a free gift on the other side, because the kinsman or woman was 'sorry' for the pig killer. Sometimes exchanges were not thought to cancel out debts, either because a prestation was classified otherwise than intended, or because it was not considered a sufficient return for what was received. A side of pork (*paki*) is priced at between K40 and K60, depending on the size of the pig. When recipients give more or less than this sum they create new debts or remain indebted. It was difficult, in the Yakopaita case, to be sure of the status of each transaction. This was because the pig kill itself may only be one stage in some transactions, so that although I have full records of the exchanges that took place there I sometimes miss out on prior gifts, which were then being returned. In what follows I present tables showing the distribution of pig killers' transactions with various categories of people, and discuss the implications of these.

There were 31 pig killers in Yakopaita; Marc Schiltz and I were one. Our exchanges, being subsumed with Rimbu's, will not be analysed separately. Of the 30 left, 3 were non-Yala: 2 were wives' fathers, one of whom had lived with the Yala for many years, and the other of whom came to stay with his daughter on and off. The third was a partner of Rimbu's (another two partners of his had defaulted, paying him K400 instead of coming to kill pigs). Of the 27 left, 3 were Yala living elsewhere, and therefore not interviewed, and a fourth was a deaf and dumb man whose pork was distributed by his father. So 23 pig killers were interviewed exhaustively about their exchanges. A total of 256 shells, K1,977 and 44½ pigs were given by pig killers while 154 shells, K 2,063 and 22½ pigs were received by them. In the pig transactions I have included live pigs and sides of pork, but not the small pieces which were given away for nothing or for small amounts of money.

Out of 23 pig killers, 22 gave shells to agnates and 21 received shells from them; 16 gave money to agnates, and 13 received money from them; 14 gave pigs to agnates, and 11 received pigs from them. Of the same pig killers, 16 gave shells to maternal kin while 4 received shells from them; 6 gave money to maternal kin, and 3 received money from them; 3 gave pigs to maternal kin, but none received pigs from them. 7 pig killers gave shells to fathers' maternal kin, while 1 received shells; 1 received money from them, while 1 gave pigs to them. 17 gave shells to affines, and 14 received shells from them; 7 gave money to affines, and 5 received money from them; 11 gave pigs, and 6 received pigs.

Before going any further, I must make an important distinction within the category 'affine'. The broad distinction that can usefully be made is between wife givers and wife takers. I call the first category Affines A and the second Affines B. Affines A includes wife's clan; brother's wife's clan; son's wife's father, mother and brother; and father's brother's son's wife's father. Affines B includes father's sister and her husband; father's sister's son and daughter; sister and her husband; sister's son and daughter; married daughter and her husband; daughter's husband's brother; daughter's husband's father and mother.

It is important to make this distinction because a different exchange relationship is involved in each case. When the categories of 'Affine' appearing in *Tables 1–3* are broken down into Affines A and Affines B, we get the picture seen in *Table 4*.

Of the 15 shells received from Affine A by ego, one was from a very distant affine (the daughter, from a previous marriage, of a WFBW), 5 were from wife's sisters to wife, and 7 from the fathers of two women married into the clan. These men had lived at their daughters' husbands' place for some time. One shell came from a SWF. Of the K120 from Affine A, half came from the same wives' fathers mentioned above, and 50 from a FB who had also just became ego's WFB as a result of a marriage. The money was for the purchase of pork, as was another K10 from the same WFBW's

Table 1   *Shell transactions in percentage of total*

Category of other	Ego gave to other	Ego received from other
Agnate	42.2	69.2
Maternal kin	16.8	5.9
F's maternal kin	3.9	.4
Affines	27.3	17.9
other	9.6	6.6
total	99.8	100

Table 2   *Money transactions in percentage of total*

Category of other	Ego gave to other	Ego received from other
Agnate	65.1	69.1
Maternal kin	9.5	5.5
F's maternal kin	0	3.7
Affines	22.8	8
other	2.6	13.7
total	100	100

Table 3   *Pig transactions in percentage of total*

Category of other	Ego gave to other	Ego received from other
Agnate	46.4	61.9
Maternal kin	9.5	0
F's maternal kin	1	0
Affines	33.7	27.4
other	9.4	10.7
total	100	100

Table 4   *Transactions with Affines A and B in percentage of total (whole amounts in brackets underneath percentages)*

Category of other	Ego gave to other			Ego received from other		
	shells	money	pigs	shells	money	pigs
Affine A	25.3	22.1	15.5	6.2	3.8	0
	(70)	(418)	(11)	(15)	(120)	
Affine B	2.0	.7	18.2	11.7	4.2	27.4
	(7)	(20)	(6½)	(18)	(90)	(6)

daughter, who had given a shell.

What this breakdown is meant to show is that in general Affines A received more than they gave, whereas Affines B (usually sisters and their husbands) gave more than they received. The cases where Affines A gave to ego were shown to be special, as when affines lived with ego almost like agnates, or when the relationship was very distant. The following story emerges from this account. When ego is pig killer he makes gifts to his wife givers but receives none in return. With his wife takers he conducts exchanges in which they give him money or shells in return for pork. When ego's wife takers kill pigs he receives pork from them without payment while they conduct exchanges with *their* wife takers. *Figure 8* presents these asymmetrical exchanges. They are symmetrical when the wife giver kills pigs, but asymmetrical when the wife taker kills pigs. What this illustrates is that the wife giver's gift is always reciprocated, while the wife taker always has a debt to pay. This relationship of indebtedness, which may lapse in normal times, is acknowledged at the time of the pig kill, because pig kills make obligations due. At the time of the

Figure 8   *Pig kill exchanges between affines*

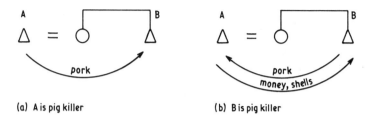

(a) A is pig killer   (b) B is pig killer

Yakopaita pig kill, Rimbu's wife Lari had recently given birth to a
son, her fourth child. Although Rimbu had told me earlier that he
had ceased making child payments after the second child, he had
to make a payment for this one because he was born in the year of
the pig kill. Thus the pig kill is the occasion when the value of
women as wives, their labour power as well as their reproductive
powers, are acknowledged. How much political power accrues to
women in consequence of this recognition will be discussed in the
following section.

The other categories in the exchange tables speak for themselves. Another table which is useful is one denoting the percentage of pig killers who gave at all to the various categories. For the
sake of convenience and space, I shall use Kewa categories: *apara*
for agnate, *agira* for maternal kin, and *ayara* for father's maternal
kin. Finally, we may rank the categories according to the highest number of pig killers transacting with each. 23 pig killers
transacted with *apara*, 17 with Affine A, 16 with *agira*, 13 with
unrelated friends, 10 with Affine B, and 7 with *ayara*. Those
transacting with *ayara* – Rimbu, Nasupeli, Yako, Kiru, Waliya,
Pima and Rero – were of Umba or Paripa clan, and closely

Table 5   *Percentages of pig killers transacting with each category (actual
numbers of pig killers so transacting follows in brackets)*

pig killers giving to		pig killers receiving from	
Apara	100 (23)	Apara	91.3 (21)
Agira	69.6 (16)	Agira	21.7 (5)
Ayara	30.4 (7)	Ayara	8.7 (2)
Affine A	73.9 (17)	Affine A	39.1 (9)
Affine B	39.1 (9)	Affine B	43.5 (10)
other	56.5 (13)	other	47.8 (11)

involved with the pig kill. Rimbu, Nasupeli, Kiru and Waliya were in fact the 'hard core' of brothers involved. Yadi, the 'mother', was the only substantial pig killer who did not give to his *ayara*. Why is this giving to *ayara* important? Because people say that a really big pig killer, a truly important man, will on such occasions give to his *agira* and *ayara* as well as to his *apara* and affines. In fact, only such a man may wear the *wambe* headdress, consisting of two single white feathers from the *tuma naai*, the Papua New Guinea eagle. A man who has once qualified for such a distinction may wear the headdress on all subsequent occasions when he kills pigs, but if anyone sports the feathers without being entitled to them he will be ridiculed. (As a result of mission influence these feathers are no longer worn, although body paint, cassowary feathers, and possum fur are commonly used.)

Although each transaction has a different history, some general comments can be made about the commonest reasons for the transactions with each of the categories discussed. Exchanges with Affine A were almost invariably unreciprocated affinal payments, although sometimes they were returns for pig agistment. Exchanges with *ayara* and *agira* were usually gifts which men made 'for their skin'. With Affine B transactions tended to be purchases, and therefore equalled out more, although slight imbalances were in favour of Affine B. Most of the transactions with 'other' were repayments of loans. Transactions with agnates are worthy of note; these accounted for most wealth and involved all pig killers. Thus my argument in Chapter 1 – that brothers enter into many exchange relations – receives corroborative evidence.

The analysis of these exchanges also provides a link to conclusions drawn in Chapter 3, where I argue that the Kewa have not become capitalists, since locally they operate mainly in a gift economy. Participation in the cash economy has not turned them away from this gift economy; on the contrary, as we see from the tabulations produced, they move most of their cash into these exchanges.

Women's part in transactions

Of all goods given away, 20 per cent were given to the *wenara*, the wife's lineage, and 3.3 per cent of all goods received came from this group. It is as well to be cautious in interpreting these data, however. For many analysts, a common index of a woman's involvement in decision making in such cases is the extent to which her natal group was a receiver of goods, because it is assumed that a wife always wants to give to her own kin. This is of course true to some extent; she does not want her people neglected. On the other hand she may have other, unrelated obligations, or joint obligations with her husband. Earlier I referred to the acknowledgment of the productive and reproductive value of women at the time of the pig kill, when their clan receives wealth and pork. For a fuller understanding of the meaning of these prestations we must be aware exactly how they are conducted in practice. The husband kills the pigs and carves them. He puts aside large pieces of pork and tells his wife to distribute them among her clan. If he is giving live pigs, shells and money as well, he offers these unceremoniously; the shells and money are not displayed on *kepa*.

While she presides over this distribution the wife seems momentarily endowed with the power of the transactor. However, it must be stressed that she is distributing and not transacting. Her power is circumscribed because she cannot use the wealth to transact independently and create debts towards herself, but must give to her clan. The fact that she may want to give to her clan in any case is not the point here; she has no power to do otherwise. Her husband, it is true, has put her at the head of these transactions, but her role is to discharge *his* obligations, to act as his agent. If she attempted to give the wealth elsewhere, both her husband and her agnates would move in to stop her.

Apart from these affinal prestations, how were women involved generally in the pig kill exchanges? The majority of women told me that their husbands decided on the distribution of goods. Only one told me that decisions were always joint ones. But most women did say that their own obligations had to be fulfilled, while many did not disapprove of their husband's choices, although made autonomously. Husbands, with very few exceptions, claimed that only they decided what to do with the pigs. Though men and women in general agreed that men decided how to dispose of the goods, when observed in action or questioned closely this claim was not always easy to uphold. Accurate investigation of this question becomes complicated by the fact that in order properly to understand the exchange transactions at the pig kill one must go back, to exchanges made months or years before the event. I made this thorough investigation in the case of Rimbu's pigs, and obtained the following history. Out of 15 pigs, 6 were from partners in return for 3 pigs which they had received from Rimbu some years earlier. One pig was in payment for a parcel of *aipa* (local salt) belonging to Lari, while another was payment for one year's loan of his shotgun. Three were returns for one pig given three years previously, but also partially a payment for dancing performed at these partners' pig kill. Another three pigs were received in a bridewealth exchange, where Rimbu had traded a large pig. This large pig was received from Rimbu's brother in exchange for another pig, which was given to Rimbu by a partner whose daughter had received it in bridewealth. Both Rimbu and Lari had helped this girl while she was courting, and she asked her father to give them this pig in appreciation of this. The last pig was the anthropologists' contribution.

The unravelling of this ancestry for each pig was a copious business, because men often try to suggest that pigs acquired in this way through a series of exchanges were somehow 'produced' by them and had little to do with their wives' labour. This question will be discussed fully in the following chapter; here I want to pursue Rimbu's reasoning a little further, following his suggestion that his feast pigs came from exchanges. Rimbu reasoned in the following words:

> 'Liame has been looking after this fat pig ever since it was small. Kiru, her husband, is bound to take this into account when the pig is killed and distributed. She must decide what happens to half. However, Lari will have less of a say in how I distribute these pigs of mine. This is because they all come from exchanges; they are *ro mena*, exchange pigs. She has not worked hard looking after them for years, giving them food until they got fat. We remunerate according to work: if I had kept the ten pigs I had in 1978 and Lari had looked after them, then she could talk. But now her clan's share will be small.'

But did this mean in fact that he failed to consult his wife? Not according to my observations. While he was distributing pork Lari was sitting by him, prompting him *sotto voce*, or as he later told me, 'reminding' him to whom they should be giving. Not all husbands behave in this way; during the 1979 pig kill in Aka, Mapi enraged his wife by his neglect of her in his distributions, but the only action she had recourse to was physical assault and frustrated tears, neither of which furthered her cause. Husbands *could* dispense with wifely consultation, even if some do not. A number of men known not to have very good relations with their wives failed to consult them in Yakopaita, to all appearances with impunity.

Yet this is not really the point, and the question of whether men consult with their wives or not has led us momentarily astray. To consult with one's wife about the fate of a pig does not imply a recognition of her role in its acquisition; and the discontinuity between labour and its product is thus not exposed as a strategy. It is exactly for this reason that consultation remains optional.[6]

Pig kill and inequality among men

While the pig kill brought individuals and groups together under a common banner in situations where solidarity and integration were equally necessary for survival, it also ranked clans and men. This function may be more prevalent now, with the cessation of warfare. The *yawe*, then, provides an arena in which power struggles take place and inequalities are created and perpetuated, not only between men and women but also among men. How some men may exploit others is a difficult question to tackle, for while relations between men and women may be openly antagonistic and certainly unequal, inequalities and antagonisms among men are suppressed, and in general ideological terms, unacknowledged. That 'one man is as good as another' is the logic informing payback action, and it would be impossible for a man who flouts this principle to become a leader. In Chapter 6 the question of 'unequal exchange' among men and their unequal access to opportunities (as a function of political influence) was discussed. Chapter 8 will be concerned with bringing out the extractive power behind the political influence, and demonstrate the manner in which some men may exploit others.

Andrew Strathern (1971) describes how Hagen big men can exploit lesser men by conveniently 'forgetting' their contributions in *moka*, and bypassing them when they make their prestations. This may happen sometimes in the Kewa case (see, for instance, the example with Papola in the previous chapter), but it is unlikely that it would work as a regular strategy, especially as social categories here are much more fluid. Unequal distribution of prestige and wealth takes place in more subtle ways here. Influential men may, as in Hagen, push through a pig kill at a time when other men are not ready. But, more importantly, big men are on the whole better able to attract wealth and therefore put up an impressive show, accruing prestige and credit to their names. Because of their standing, acumen and organizational abilities, they are able to enter into many more financial transactions than their less enterprising brothers, and can raise wealth in a number of ways. They will also make arrangements so that labour and expense involved in pig care is shared out to other kin and friends. Years or months before the occasion a big man will 'farm out' pigs and so decongest his own herd. In this way he will pre-empt complaints of overwork from his household, and also lessen the likelihood of his pigs getting out of control and disappearing into the bush, damaging other people's property (which would render him liable to expensive compensation), or generally getting into mischief and injuring themselves. Wives' relations are most commonly used for this sort of agistment, although unrelated friends may also do it. For this service the caretaker is pledged the head of the animal when it is killed.

An important way in which big men raise wealth is by entering into transactions that bring in cash for promised pigs much in advance of the *yawe*. They may, for instance, show a particular pig to a partner and ask for an advance for a portion of it, which they pledge to give to the partner when the pigs are killed. More pigs are then purchased with the money thus received. Earlier I called this 'mortgaging'. Alternatively, and more boldly, they may pledge pigs they do not have, but which they hope to buy with the advance. This can be a precarious undertaking: if it is left too late, live pigs become more expensive (the law of supply and demand seems to operate), and killed pigs may not fetch as much as hoped. This is why it is men of a certain reputation, persuasiveness and pull who are usually successful in these operations.

As a result, these very shrewd transactions that are the trademark of the big man become covered in mystique as magic wealth producers.[7] Yet their crucial function remains unre-marked: that is, they provide a smokescreen behind which the relation between labour and its product is lost, and thus determine how wealth and its acquisition are perceived. These are the main questions to be discussed in the following chapter.

Notes

1 In my discussion of marriage, I described how women could be successful in blocking their husbands' attempts to take more wives by physically pulling away pigs about to be given in bridewealth. They were successful on these occasions not because their husband could not forcibly take the pigs but because would-be affines would not accept them. They took this, quite rightly, as a sign that the proposed marriage would be dogged by contention and dispute and therefore prove unstable. The present case is different: exchange partners are not normally concerned about whether their partners' wives agree with the transactions, although they do not like to be forced to witness domestic scenes in which the extractive aspects become blatant. These aspects, since misrecognized, should remain hidden.

2 Very briefly, however, I should mention the cult house pig killings, which were invariably smaller than the longhouse feasts. These were the concern of men, and women could not participate. The men supposedly killed and ate the pigs by themselves in the cult house area, but many said that they carried some off home, although the women had to remain in ignorance of their actions. Cult house pigs were killed irregularly, whenever it was considered that the sacred stones were dry and in need of pig's grease and blood. This usually coincided with somebody's falling ill or dying. Some cults required the killing of marsupials only, especially if pigs were scarce. This was the case with *kerekaiada*, the only cult I know of in which mothers participated with their sons. No cult house pig killings took place while I was in the field; the missions had long since put an end to them.

3 'Kewa' here simply refers to the distinctive decorations and dancing styles of the people from the south, usually Samberigi. The Madi were the people of the north, from the upper reaches of Kagua to Ialibu. They were famous for a different style of decoration, dancing and drum playing. Pig killers from the Sugu area always aspired to have one or both these groups perform on the big day. At the same time, they themselves, referred to by the people of Ialibu as 'Kewa', were invited by them to dance at *their* feasts.

4 *Rawa*, a sort of potlatch, was the deliberate destruction of property in order to shame a person with whom one was angry. In a small way,

this happens quite frequently. Sometimes shells are broken or tins of fish emptied, out of sheer frustration. During the Yakopaita pig kill (described in this chapter) one man trampled his pigs and smashed two pearlshells. I was told that this was a *rawa* directed at another man who had broken 'mission laws' by making a *mena kiri* (see Glossary) payment. (That *rawa* went against those laws was momentarily forgotten.) A more serious case of *rawa* was recounted to me by Pupula. His daughter Koipame was sitting with a friend, Karupiri, and her sister. The two sisters were having an argument and another girl, Wosu, became angry with them and told them to stop. When they continued, Pou, Wosu's father, killed a pig and invited the two sisters and Koipame to eat the pig's faeces. Agema, Koipame's brother (who was fifteen at the time) became very angry, because his sister had nothing to do with the argument; she was a mere bystander. So he killed a pig and challenged Pou: 'I am paying back your pig's faeces; you come and eat too' (*Nena mena i abulalo, ne page epa mana*). Ragunanu, Koipame's mother, broke up a block of indigenous salt (*aipa*) and threw it at Pou with the words: 'I eat your *rawa*, I am breaking salt and killing pigs' (*Ne rawa nalo aipa lu mena lu pi*). Karupiri's father Ade killed a pig and a dog and invited Pou to eat the faeces of both. This onslaught was too much for Pou who did not have the pigs, dogs or salt to reciprocate, so instead he fetched some dog's teeth to exchange with Ade. This sort of exchange is called *roponale*. The two shook hands and made up.

Clearly all this was not wanton destruction, because the pig meat was eaten. Probably some of the salt was also saved. On the occasions when I witnessed the breaking up of shells these were also eventually retrieved by someone who sewed them back together again. However, what is important is the spirit behind this action, not whether the items sacrificed are totally destroyed. For an extensive treatment of the practice of *rawa* see Leroy 1979a.

5   The pidgin term is *taim hangri*, and the Kewa is *rea pabala*. The usual reason given for this phenomenon by Administration officers is frost, but in my experience the connection was not always easy to make. According to Patrol Reports such periods of food shortage occurred when people for one reason or another neglected their gardens. The Reports claimed that these periods coincided with the pandanus nutting season (January to March), but the local people disagreed. They said, variously, that there was never such a shortage in the past; that when there was, what was meant was that they did not have enough to fulfil their obligations, not that they did not have enough to eat; that bad harvests occurred when the sun dried the ground, or when the worms ate all its good 'grease'. According to many Agricultural Officers, poor harvests were the result of people's failure to fallow.

6   I am grateful to Sacha Josephides for bringing this crucial point to my attention.

7   Modern business may also be seen in this way, which is why many
    enterprises founder. For an extensive analysis of this for the Boroi of
    Madang see S. Josephides 1982.

8
Maximizing control: Alienation and the production of exchange values

In his essay 'Gifts to Men and Gifts to God: Gift Exchange and Capital Accumulation in Contemporary Papua', Gregory (1980) describes a gift exchange system as one in which net outgoings are maximized. This contrasts with a commodity exchange system (such as the capitalist economy), where the aim is to maximize net incomings. According to Gregory, a gift exchange system allows for no accumulation, or the alienation of the product of another person. While Gregory explores the underlying logic of a gift economy, and develops a theoretical framework which is extremely suggestive, enabling him to make a number of exciting observations, he does not provide us with an analytic demonstration of some of his generalizations (see Schwimmer 1984). This in no way attenuates the usefulness of his model, but since it is made up of propositions that are part of the ethnographic data being analysed, its rigorous application to a complete set of data may lead to some self-modification. Here I am particularly concerned with two issues: (1) that a framework for the analysis of gift economy which does not attend to the conditions and circumstances in which gift-items are acquired/created will lead to erroneous conclusions, and (2) that alienation is possible in gift exchange systems.

An entry into this discussion may conveniently be provided by Sahlins' (1974: 83–87) 'domestic mode of production' (DMP), which is characterized by three main elements: 'small labour force differentiated essentially by sex, simple technology, and finite production objectives'. In line with the last characteristic, Sahlins argues that the DMP is geared to producing use values only, 'related always to exchange with an interest in consumption'. It thus 'harbours an antisurplus principle'. Thence 'Chayanov's rule': 'the greater the relative working capacity of the household the less its members work'. However, a reading of Chayanov's work by Donham (1981) does not support Sahlins's interpretation of 'Chayanov's rule'. Donham argues that far from the DMP imposing limitations on production beyond subsistence, peasants do in fact respond to opportunities to produce a surplus. In other words, they produce exchange values. Do Kewa villagers similarly produce exchange values, or are they restricted to use values, as Gregory and Sahlins would have it?

This is a complicated question, for between Kewa production and exchange there lies a contradiction. The logic of the one is not necessarily the logic of the other, and the deepest logic of the system is not reflected in people's perceptions of the conditions in which they produce. While workers in the capitalist economy know that they are producing for exchange, many Kewa producers think that they are working for themselves and their families. However, much domestic production invariably finds its way to exchanges, in such a way that the link between producers and consumers is lost – the broker interposes himself. For the Highlands, it has been demonstrated that there is a correlation between productive intensity and the complexity of exchange systems (see, for instance, Modjeska 1982). More pigs are produced in areas with complex ceremonial exchange systems, and not all of these come back in exchanges to be consumed. Some are exchanged for valuables that are in fact not consumable. So production must, to a certain extent and for some people, be consciously geared to exchange. However, because the *conditions* in which production takes place do not allow for the automatic characterization of products as 'exchange values', their *conversion* is necessary. They must be converted from use values into exchange values. This is a creative enterprise which enables men to construct an exclusive sphere for themselves, a sphere that in fact specializes in this conversion. The question of men's creation of such a sphere is elaborated by Marilyn Strathern in her essay 'Discovering "Social Control"' (n.d.). In the Kewa case this sphere mediates in the conversion of use values into exchange values. The key to this activity is alienation, and I will turn first to the elucidation of this concept.

Alienation

The question of alienation, or alienability, is crucial to the explanation of how inequality is created in the course of wealth exchanges. If alienation is not possible in these gift exchange societies, then we shall have to accept the view that they are egalitarian. If, on the other hand, we can show that alienation does take place, we shall at the same time be able to link this to the creation of inequality.

In Mauss' seminal work, the gift is its own guarantee, which ensures that a return will be received by the donor. Moreover, there is a certain power in things 'which forces them to circulate, to be given away and repaid' (1974: 41). Mauss' explanation of this triple obligation, of the potlatch, and of 'gifts to men and gifts to gods', is undertaken in terms of the perceptions of actors involved in gift exchange systems. It is an 'emic' analysis concerned with transactors' motives and rationalizations, not with the relationship between production and exchange. Because people perceive a mystical link between the gift and the donor, they feel something evil will befall them if they do not reciprocate. A gift, then, is always thought of as being part of the donor (not necessarily the same as the producer, especially where household production is 'generalized'), and although it may – indeed, must – be given away, it must always receive a return. The same thing is not returned, for this would be to give back a person's gift.

In the course of his exposition Mauss coins the phrases 'gifts to men and gifts to gods', but does not differentiate these as two separable spheres of gift exchange. Gregory (1980) takes up this distinction and uses it to construct an analytic framework for the investigation of gift economies, and especially of problems such as alienation and accumulation. His 'gifts to men' and 'gifts to god' systems are ideal types, with the usefulness of such devices. However, they can be seriously misleading when applied to a set of actual ethnographic data, because exchange systems 'on the ground' partake of both aspects. Gregory argues that in 'gifts to men' systems alienation is impossible, not because of the spirit of the gift but because of the social relations that bind people together; so that there can be no accumulation of assets without liabilities (1982a: 345), or the 'appropriation of a worker's surplus without the generation of debt' (1980: 647). Such appropriation and accumulation are possible, however, in a 'gifts to god' system, an extreme form of redistribution in which goods are offered up to the deity in expectation of service in the form of blessings. Following Marilyn Strathern (n.d.), I shall describe relations between transactors within the exchange sphere as 'equalizing relationships'; but following Schiltz (n.d.), I shall argue that 'hierarchical relationships' are always co-present with equalizing ones in exchange systems, whether these systems are typified as 'gifts to men' or 'gifts to god', and that therefore alienation is always possible.

Ethnographic examples cannot provide us with a pure 'gifts to men' type exchange system which has no moral or religious overtones, or hierarchical dimensions. 'Gifts to men' may first have to be alienated from women where domestic production is their source. When the whole household is involved in production it cannot always be demonstrated that transactors are appropriating another worker's surplus; therefore no debt is created when men exchange the products of their wives' labour. The Kewa *yawe* is an example which combines both equalizing and hierarchical dimensions. The occasion itself contains sacrificial aspects, although normally everything is exchanged among people and nothing is destroyed. The exchanges that take place are equalizing in the sense that gifts given are either in repayment of some obligation, or they create one. At the same time, the hierarchical dimension can be seen in the fact that the exchanges are controlled by men, though involving items whose provenance is household production. While there is a reciprocal dependence in production between husband and wife, in these exchanges the conjugal relationship is hierarchical. Men mediate in redistributive or hierarchical relations, and the first step in this is appropriation. When men seize household pigs to kill in the *yawe* or to give away to a man they are 'sorry' for, their success rests on the tacit belief that if things are done well people will prosper. When on the same occasion they chant 'I follow in my father's footsteps', men voice the claim that they are in fact the custodians of the group's prosperity. Women also acknowledge this role of men, both verbally and by allowing them control of their products in this way. This household inequality, with men being in charge of the prosperity and the reputation of the group, has in microcosm most of the elements of chiefly institutions.

If my argument that exchange systems generally contain

both hierarchical and equalizing elements is convincing, then Gregory's distinction between 'gifts to god' and 'gifts to men' systems, the first allowing alienation and the second making it impossible, cannot be sustained. The Kewa *yawe*, where all gifts are given to men and women and nothing is merely destroyed, has ideological connotations involving more than the two exchanging parties, and economic implications in which products are alienated from producers without the creation of debt. But leaving aside religious and moral considerations, I want now to discuss the exchange activities themselves, and elaborate on the way in which alienation takes place in ostensibly 'gifts to men' systems, as Gregory characterizes them.

The *kula*, the *tee* and the *moka* could be cited as 'gifts to men' systems in which gifts are said to be inalienable. According to Gregory's metaphor, 'a gift is like a tennis ball with an elastic band attached to it. The owner of the ball may lose possession of it for a time, but the ball will spring back to its owner if the elastic band is given a jerk' (1980: 640). This would then bring the exchange relationship to an end. While expressing reservations about Gregory's metaphor, Feil (1982a: 341) agrees that items circulating in *tee* roads are inalienable. He cites one example of how, after fourteen steps in one of these roads, a pig was held, killed, and returned through the same fourteen steps to be consumed by its producer and her family. If the suggestion here is that a woman gets back a whole killed pig, this would certainly be different from my experience among the Kewa, where a woman who has looked after a pig will receive a share when it is killed. Although the producer's rights are acknowledged here, this is another way of covering up unequal returns. It is no mere quibble to stress that a part may stand for a whole on these occasions. Marxist theory exactly locates capitalist exploitation in the fact that workers are not paid for part of the commodity they produce. But perhaps a distinction should be made here between 'nurture' and 'production'. Pigs are unlike other items in the Highlands, and their care is classified more as the nurturing of children than the production of objects. What is returned to the women in *tee*, then, could be seen more as appreciation of nurture than acknowledgment of ownership. This is certainly the attitude taken by the Kewa in cases of agistment, where the woman receives the head and entrails of the pig she has looked after.

The term 'producer' is itself not unambiguous. Apart from the fact that within the household there is often joint production involving both husband and wife, pig production is a fragmented process. Ownership, then, defined as based on production, must itself be fragmented. Kewa frequently exchange pigs according to their needs. Very few pigs are brought up in one household, from the day they are born to the day they become big and are killed. They are constantly moving around, being sold or given away, loaned or agisted. Who, then, is the owner of a pig that so many people have fed and cared for while it has been passing from hand to hand? How are all these cares compensated for?

The answer is that they are not, always. This is why I characterize such exchanges as smokescreens, concealing the labour that goes into the care of pigs which are in transit. Feil (1982a: 341) is also concerned about the middle stages of a *tee* chain. After the initial transaction the owner not only loses possession of the pig; he/she does not even know of its whereabouts. Although Feil still claims that the pig will eventually find its way back to its producer, he can see how all along the transaction chain people are using the products of others' labour for their own benefit. In fact, pigs in *tee* chains function 'more like commodities'. The possibilities for exploitation are myriad. In the Kewa case it is men who control exchanges, and the big man is better able than a less prominent one to use for his benefit items circulating in the exchange roads. In an earlier work (Josephides 1982b) I discuss how in the *moka* case a succession of exchanges creates a smokescreen which covers the relationship between the item exchanged and the labour that produced it. This process is certainly at work in Kewa exchanges, where not only can the care of transit pigs be unacknowledged, but so also their link to productive labour can more easily be forgotten. Exchange pigs come in exchanges, this is what is immediately seen.

Though Marx is concerned with the circulation of the products of human labour in capitalist economy, he traces the origin of alienation in barter, and argues that private property in fact depends on this alienation, not the other way round. A 'smokescreen' process similar to the one described above occurs in barter, when the provenance of objects exchanged is lost, so that what was produced as a use value becomes transformed into an exchange value. Unlike Mauss, Marx is not concerned so much with actors' perceptions as with an analysis of the inner logic of the economic system. Nor is he concerned with gift exchange, but with how products (commodities) circulate, in what conditions they are produced, and how they are alienated. In the capitalist economic system that he analyses, separation between capital and labour exists at the outset, for the labour power which produces commodities is itself a commodity which has already been alienated for a wage. But in gift economies where labour power is not sold as a commodity, how does alienation take place?

An implicit assumption must now be explicitly stated: that things can have exchange value *only if* they are alienable. This is why the question of inalienability and use value production are so intricately linked. In some discussions, in fact, demonstration of the one has led to the assumption of the other, so that when a writer has established that a certain society produces use values only, the following assumption is that these values cannot be alienated. In contrast to this, I want to argue that although Kewa production is geared to use values, another activity takes place that converts these into exchange values. Within the capitalist economy, where labour power is itself a commodity, the wage formally buys the workers' claims to the products of their labour. Since (according to Marxist theory) the labour power thus bought produces more exchange values than are necessary for its own reproduction, and since it is on the cost of the latter that the wage is calculated, exploitation takes place when a portion of the commodity produced by the worker is not paid for by the capitalist. This is the basis of the theory of surplus value. But a Kewa woman has not sold her rights in her product, which she can still claim. Her labour power is not a commodity, so alienation of the product is not automatic. Precisely because pigs are not produced as alienable items, their alienation and conversion into exchange values must be carried out in a cloud of mystique. They are not produced for alienation, yet they are alienated. People produce use values, yet exchange values exchange.

This paradoxical situation is probably at the bottom of much of the confusion underlying the debate on alienation. I take my cue here from Marilyn Strathern's (n.d.) characterization of the exchange sphere as one of 'equalization relations' created by men, into which they can 'convert' domestic products, which then circulate as wealth items. Women, being denied ownership of the 'currencies of exchange', wealth and talk, do not participate in these conversions. Further, in their collective representations, men 'eclipse' relations based on production by those based on exchange;[1] thereby (I would surmise) eclipsing the social position of women.

In the Kewa case, women also do not control these conversions. It is at the stage of entering the exchange sphere, not at the point of production, that their products become converted into exchange values and alienated. In this conversion, products gain in value. In Kewa country today, live pigs as exchange items are more expensive to procure than pork for consumption. So while in the domestic domain use values are produced, in the exchange sphere exchange values are produced. Reciprocity between co-operating units – husband and wife, established man and bachelor – does not take place: this belongs to 'equalizing relations' among men. Inequality is right there in the household, because while both husband and wife are engaged in producing use values, only the husband can convert these into exchange values. In addition, the exchange sphere is presented as a quasi- 'gifts to god' system, and exhibits hierarchical dimensions; while they are in charge of the group's 'prosperity', men have much room to manoeuvre in their distributions.

By whatever mechanism alienation is carried out – whether at the point of production or at a later stage when domestic products are converted into exchange values – the underlying activity at work in both gift and capitalist economies is the unequal control of the pool of labour power. When the product of a woman's labour is repeatedly alienated, it is more than an object which is being appropriated: her rights to control her own activities are themselves being denied. This is where the two meanings of the Marxist concept of alienation meet: material alienation of the product of one's labour, and psychological self-alienation of the producer. The important issue is that through the control of things, people and their activities are controlled.

In his discussion of power and reciprocity, Grant McCall (1982) constructs a continuum along which all human societies (or 'associations') can be placed in respect of their control of the pool of labour power. The continuum stretches from the end where control is 'mutual', so that there is perfect equality, to the other where control becomes increasingly unequally distributed, so that it is 'coercive'. Two methods for the control of labour power are elaborated: 'by extracting goods produced by another's labour power', or 'by restricting the distribution of time that another person has for individually productive labour' (p. 312). The first method clearly obtains in the case of Kewa women, as the discussion above has shown. Women cannot convert values from one domain to the other, but at the time of the big slaughter their products are drawn off, and seem to disappear up in a quasi-'gifts to god' system, which in reality is a 'gifts to men' system. Any credit created, material or symbolic, is in the husband's name. The extent to which a wife may share in the returns when she is with her husband, or influence any further decisions regarding the objects returned, depends on her personal relations with him, but ultimately on his discretion. As the owner of the land and the name which his wife uses by virtue of her marriage (itself involving the transaction of wealth), custom supports his supremacy.

The second form of controlling labour ('by restricting the distribution of time that a person has for individually productive labour') does not apply, for in domestic production a wife is not supposed to produce individually for herself alone. Domestic labour can be controlled, however, to the extent that its products are siphoned off from fulfilling the immediate needs of the family, out of the woman's control. Another variant of the first criterion could be 'controlling labour by extracting unequal contributions towards family subsistence'. More products of Kewa women's labour are directly consumed by the family; therefore their contributions towards the physical reproduction of the family are greater than men's.[2] In the old days when men had to fight for the security of the group this inequality in contribution may have been better offset; today there is little doubt that women contribute more.

But how about control of other men's labour power? McCall's second criterion holds only in the case of unmarried men, though in the old days it may have been more widespread. What is more likely to happen nowadays is that a big man, whose display is large because of his wide networks and household production (including his own), gains prestige and attracts wealth at the time of the pig kill. Implicit in this control of wealth is the indirect control of the labour power of many people; however, a big man does not directly control the labour power of any particular man outside his household in the sense that he may force such a man to work for him. He *can* hold working parties (*ki kogono*), and this enables him to boost his production in a way that an ordinary man can not.

The case of boys and young unmarried men merits a separate mention. An illustration from the field will be useful here. Rimbu, the most prominent man in Yakopaita, for a time seemed to control the activities of four such young people, although they did not lodge with him. Two were schoolboys, one had never been to school, and the fourth was a returned migrant. All four were more closely related to other men in the settlement, but Rimbu seemed to enjoy the liberty of sending them off on errands and generally using them for odd jobs. When I arrived on the scene my presence in relation to these young men was, for Rimbu, ambiguous. On the one hand he wanted to offer them to me as persons whose labour he controlled; on the other he was afraid I might become their direct patron and dispense with his mediation. If this happened not only would he become redundant as my patron and labour provider, but would also lose control of the young men, who might become spoiled by my (relatively) generous remuneration. He watched my transactions with them very closely, and he preferred to mediate in them; when he learned that I had given a raise to my young assistant without consulting him, he immediately showed his displeasure. On occasions he asked me not to offer cash for casual services, a request which incensed the young men when they heard of it.

Etali, the young returned migrant who acted as my regular assistant, lodged with Waliya. Waliya was Etali's FBS, and by no means a big man; however, he had a spacious, solid house. For more than a year Etali worked in Waliya's gardens with him and his wives (of whom, by an accident of fortune, he had two) in return for his keep. Eventually he married, and Waliya contributed a pig towards the girl's bridewealth. Although Etali and Waliya lived together and assisted each other, one point about their respective positions must be made clear. While Etali received from Waliya the wherewithal to live, his unlooked-for labour offered to Waliya something extra, which he could use to widen his exchanges. Waliya did not need Etali for his subsistence, whereas Etali needed Waliya (or some other patron) for his. In other words, their exchanges were not of the same kind, and had a different value for each. This difference is, in summary, what characterizes such relationships.

What remains to be pointed out are the similarities between the conditions of young men and women, at least in respect of their labour power. As a result of their economic and social positions both have an 'unlike for unlike' exchange relationship with the householder, but for the young men, this is only a temporary situation. Yet this comparison can perhaps help to bring into sharp relief the sometimes hazy outline of social interactions so that we see that it is in this area of unequal exchange, flowing from a dependent relationship, that control of labour and appropriation of its product can take place. The comparison between young men and women cannot be carried very far, however. For not only is the dependent position of women permanent, it is also more severe. Women are forever sojourners in any group and may never own land, whereas young men, even when unmarried, are the owners of land in their own right.

Another important form of control in the case of men must also be mentioned. A big man must be able to control the *fighting power* of other men, so that he can activate it when he needs to, but keep it in abeyance when he considers it wiser to maintain peace. With pacification also, the ability to control exchanges and decide whether they should be of 'blows' or of 'wealth' (Marilyn Strathern's coinage) is of considerable importance. As has been convincingly argued by Schiltz (n.d.), peace itself is a power relation, forming an integral part of productive relations. A schematic presentation, then, of these 'controllable' powers of women and men could look something like this:

Figure 9   *Controllable powers of women and men*

women	men
labour power (material production)	labour power (material production)
procreative power (of human life)	destructive power (of human life)

By way of conclusion, I want to come back to two points. The first concerns Gregory's (1980: 636) claim that the principle behind gift exchange systems is to 'maximize net outgoings'. He cites the example of the Kwakiutl chief who destroys property without the expectation of a return, and the Trobriand chief who allows yams to rot in his yam house for the glory of his name. Yet the Kwakiutl chief could not produce all the coppers he breaks, nor could the Trobriand chief produce his rotting display. Following my exposition above, I would argue instead that both these chiefs maximize net outgoings of other people's products, and net incomings of gift-credit or prestige to themselves; therefore in the same act they alienate, appropriate and mystify. Because Gregory was interested in the act of exchange rather than in production, he ignores the other process at work at the same time as the competitive destruction or distribution, which in fact maximizes net incomings. This is the power to control the labour of others, openly displayed by the Trobrianders for whom rotting yams, following McCall's (1982: 313) interpretation, 'can show publicly that not only does a man control his own labour power, but demonstrates also that he has abundant resources in the labour power of others'.

The second point is an attempt to tie up some loose ends and at the same time underline the major contribution of this chapter to the argument. Throughout this book sporadic references were made to Mendi and Melpa women, to whom Kewa women were sometimes likened, sometimes contrasted. A final reference here is that, notwithstanding different cultural practices in these three societies, women are in fact subordinated in a similar manner in all three. This follows directly from the analysis of alienation, which demonstrated that in these gift economies men only controlled the convertibility of values from production to exchange. According to Marilyn Strathern's expression, they excluded women from ownership of the 'currencies of exchange'. These may vary from society to society, but what concerns us here is whether women own them. Melpa women do not own 'wealth' and 'talk'. Although Mendi women have their personal exchange networks into which they circulate their own products, they have little public talk or control when it comes to big group exchanges (Lederman 1982), that is, events where the sort of alienation I describe is likely to take place; in their personal exchanges their control over their partners' labour power is mutual. Kewa women have no name, talk, group, or land. As new political and economic forms emerge, these currencies may be changing, or multiplying; my contrast of three Kewa big men in Chapter 6 indicated that each was dealing in a slightly different currency. Nonetheless, all these men had the ability to control the flow of exchanges in their groups in a way no woman could.

Ultimately this book has been concerned with power relations. But while I moved through 'structures' I was particularly concerned with 'practices', so that this itinerary took me from gender and prestige structures to alienation and the control of labour. These are all part of the power relations under investigation; and though I finish with a different set of data and an altered framework from the ones I started with, this is only because I was led there in the course of this investigation into the production of inequality.

Notes

1 This last point was emphasized by Marilyn Strathern in a personal communication.

2 I discuss elsewhere the relative contributions of men and women to subsistence work. While women do most of the day-to-day work in family gardens, their husbands (especially if they are big men) may be working very hard in their large, commercial vegetable gardens, sometimes by holding *ki kogono*. So the suggestion is not necessarily that men are lazy. Men also go hunting for birds or marsupials, sometimes staying away a day or two, but their success and therefore contribution to subsistence in this way is minimal. It is, rather, a sport. The role of men's organizational skills in the reproduction of the group and therefore the family should not of course be denigrated. But it must be seen that it is exactly this role which gives men control over the labour power of women.

9
Conclusion

In this book I have explored relations of inequality in a small-scale society with no hereditary offices and no formal inequalities among men, all of whom possessed their own means of production. Land ownership and the control of one's own labour power were not sufficient to ensure survival and subsistence, however. As well as producers, it was necessary to have warriors, for defensive purposes, and big men who held the group together politically. Warfare and exchange together defined and reproduced the group: alliances and accretions were usually the result of war, but they had to be cemented in pig kills. Men were the warriors, and also the organizers of the pig kills, and all attendant exchanges. The group thus defined was a male conglomerate with an agnatic ideology, and a solidarity which stressed continuity in the male line.

I argued that women did not define the group; attributes conventionally associated with women had no place in male descriptions of their tribe's identity. The tribe was described as strong, fierce, wealthy, land-owning, prestigious, admired and feared – all attributes culturally associated with men. Although women lived at their husband's place on marriage, they were not 'in between', in two senses. First, in their daily existence, politically and personally, women did not have the experience of being torn between two groups, played off by one against the other, or blamed by both for the other's shortcomings. Second, they did not initiate by means of their linkage intricate inter-clan relations. The fact that a man married a woman had no bearing on whether their groups would continue friendly exchanges or go to war. Arguably, if a substantial number of brides were taken from one group this might have affected relations with it but there was no evidence of such a concentration of marriages.

My characterization of women as peripheral to group ideologies and as sojourners in respect of any group should not be taken to mean that their rights of access to land were restricted, or that they passed on no rights to their children. Women always had access to some land, though they could be expropriated from particular land. Their children would never be refused land by their mother's group, and a sister or daughter would give up her gardens only if she was going off in marriage to another group; she would never be forcibly evicted. A wife, on the other hand, might be so evicted, if her husband divorced her. She would also be alienated from livestock and other property from which she had received revenue in acknowledgment for her labour, but could never own. All these things might also be alienated from her by her husband at any time, when he chose to transact them in exchanges. At these times she might receive partial compensation only to 'make her feel good'.

The different relationship that men and women had to groups was matched by the ascription of different potentialities, which in turn defined their social roles and expectations. This appeared culturally as a division of activities and spheres of influence. Women were active in production and in the domestic sphere of social reproduction; men were active in production, and in both the domestic and the public spheres of social reproduction. That is, both men and women had a domestic, private life in which they produced for their family's subsistence, and administered to its needs. Men, in addition, had a political, military, and religious life in which women did not participate, except as reluctant or unconsulted contributors, victims or spectators. Women did not have a corresponding sphere which excluded men. They had their menstrual and birth huts, but no large-scale ceremonies or mystical rites took place there. Menstruation and childbirth were private events, while war, politics and pig kills were public. Such women as gathered together on these occasions shared no binding group ideology, and did not engage in the solidarity activities which were influential for group identity, whereas the men's political and military activities were the base of group identity, and dealt directly with wealth and power.

The gender relations described in this book are part of a gift economy in which exchange is the activity colouring all relationships. Every transaction must be euphemized as a gift, because what is formally stressed is always the relationship between people transacting, rather than the acquisition of goods. This cultural emphasis covers up the unequal exchanges which take place between husband and wife, married man and bachelor, big man and his agnates. Gift exchange persists in the village, in spite of the fact that villagers now produce for a wider cash economy. It is a prestige structure as well as an economic one, in which men must participate if they hope to make a name for themselves. University graduates returning to the village may find their degrees and other social accoutrements handsome embellishments, but although village men may refer to them respectfully as *kadipi* and proudly proclaim their book-learning to outsiders, when they attend public meetings to debate preparations for pig kills they will have no say if they do not have pigs, the currencies of exchange. A home base is really needed for the production of pigs. Mothers may perform this service for their sons, who then convert these pigs into exchange values, for political and matrimonial purposes. Pigs of course may also be bought for cash, but this requires an extremely high outlay.

In the introductory chapter, I suggested, following a review of relevant literature, that though the social expression of power differentials varied from society to society, these were normally to be found in all societies. No society is free of the seeds of inequality. With the collection of people into groups, organizational needs develop, and this makes possible a number of social functions which can bestow rights over the social life of individuals. This is why I defined power as being residual within the group. How far it can be monopolized by individuals, and the extent to which it is coercive, depends on specific cultural variables. In my discussion of the big man complex, I suggested that a power vacuum – that is, the absence of purposeful direction within the group – leads to its disintegration.

The body of the book has been concerned with investigating the specific manner in which power is wielded in the Kewa case, and how resultant inequalities are expressed. Since social groups were male-based, men were the formal forgers of social relations; therefore their power over women was clear and unambiguous. Women depended on them for access to the means of production; fathers and husbands made land available for their daughters and wives, and formally presented them with the digging sticks with

which they were to till it. Male-based groups, the ownership of
the means of production in the male line, patrivirilocality – all
these provided the economic base for the political domination of
women, allowing men to monopolize the convertibility of values
from the domestic into the political sphere. Power differentials
among men, on the other hand, were created as a result of political
advantage. Whereas men's dominance of women was openly
exercised and ideologically validated, relations of inequality
among men presented a disjunction between ideology and social
reality. The agnatic idiom demanded a solidarity based on
equality; but in practice inequalities were engendered. What
mediated this process?

While some bachelors had a dependent relationship with married men which outwardly resembled women's dependent position, this was not the only way in which inequalities among men
were expressed. Peers were productively independent of one
another, yet they were not equally prominent in group affairs. At
the same time, big men were not necessarily wealthier than
politically less consequential ones. This relates to the fact that
powerful men traded in exchange values, not use values; they did
not necessarily produce or consume more than others, but they
controlled more. Inequalities were created among men, then, by
the unequal wielding of social power which resulted from individual men's talents and ambitions; and this differential was
expressed in the direction of group events such as the organization
of large-scale exchanges, and the personal amassing of prestige
following these.

Among peers, there was no direct economic exploitation of
men in the way there was of women. Men could not control other
men's products as they controlled household products. On this
base of female economic exploitation, struggles among men
assumed political expression, and in these some men gained
political advantages which could then be used in a number of
ways. This was mediated by exchange, in which 'unlike for
unlike' was transacted and exchange values were created. Big men
had the power and the means to call up *ki kogono* working parties,
for which they paid with food, a use value, for the creation of
wealth as an exchange value.

The appropriation of the products of women's labour is also
euphemized when these products are circulated within the exchange system. Though husbands have rights in their wives'

products and may seize them forcibly, this euphemization is necessary if exchange is to be presented as the creative producer of wealth. Gift economy, then, disguises unequal exchange and mystifies transactions as free gifts, yet at the same time presents them as wealth creators. Since transacting is the political activity of men *par excellence*, and one which most sharply defines maleness in contrast with femaleness, as well as being the means by which men make their names, the claim that it has a creative function has powerful political implications, both for the status of transactors, and the ease with which they may transact other people's products.

As a conclusion, one may speculate on the long-term implications that a greater participation in the cash economy will have for power distribution in the society. In his discussion of the Baruya of the Eastern Highlands, Godelier (1982b) argues that the traditional practice of marriage by sister exchange obviated the need for wealth accumulation, and therefore the possibility for one man to control the labour power of another, with the result that socially prominent 'great men' could not become extractive. But recent developments in cash cropping and other avenues for individual accumulation of wealth presage for Godelier the emergence of Gorokan-style big men among the Baruya, as bridewealth begins to replace sister exchange. Cash cropping is seen to transform indigenous practices, leading to greater social differentiation. Writing about a society that was already part of the big man complex, Andrew Strathern also saw the development of greater differentiations. Although an earlier individual access to wealth from as yet unmonopolized channels led to a 'democratization' of the system (A. Strathern 1971), a consolidation has now taken place in Hagen, where the biggest men are those who can combine formal offices in development associations with useful government connections (A. Strathern 1982a: 155).

Throughout this book I have given many illustrations of the resilience of the gift economy as the major way in which social relations are reproduced in the village, despite the growing pervasiveness of the cash economy. As a final question then, will increasing participation in a cash economy geared towards development in a capitalistic fashion lead to democratization, or greater power differentials? The inference from the argument underlying the present work is that inequalities will grow, as individual access to wealth and power grows. For inequalities to be entrenched and new status groups to be established, it is not necessary for the local gift economy to be abandoned, for it is not really inimical to alienation, maximization, and the creation of inequality.

Glossary and note on pronunciation

Compared with other Highland languages, Kewa is easy to pronounce for English speakers. *B*, *d* and *g* are always prenasalized, so I never write them as *mb*, *nd* or *ng* (with the exception of the name Rimbu, which I write with *mb*, following local usage. This also distinguishes it from the cult of ribu). *R*, *t*, and to a lesser extent *s*, sometimes slide into one another. The vowels present no problems, apart from *a*, which may be short (as in m*a*n), long (as in f*a*ther), or *u* (as in s*u*n).

ada   house; big; look, see
adali   big man
agi   mother
agira   mother's lineage
ali   man
ali rakia   love potion
ame   brother (male speaking)
amoali   wealthy man, big man
apara   patrilineage
emapu   swidden garden
kadipi   white person; public servant
kalusekere   head pearlshell
kama   open ground, dancing ground
kepa   wealth presented on bamboos
kewa   dancers from the south
ki kogono   'hand work', working party
komada   funerary celebrations
kone   mind, thoughts (cf. Melpa *noman*)
lamua   to marry
lidi   story or myth
mapu   permanent, mounded garden
mena   pig
mena kiri   war reparation payment
muduali   warrior, fight leader

neada   food house, ceremonial feast house
nu   woman's netbag
nuyapara   placenta; a form of magic
oge   small
paki   side of pork
pala   afraid
pokala   lean-to festive structure
polo   porch, especially in men's house
rameada   menstruation hut
re   base, origin
re agele   a true story, a story of origin
repa   clan, lineage
rome   courting song
romo   lethal magic
roponali, roporopo, exchange, swap
ruru   tribe, clan, lineage
siapi   metaphoric speech
tapada   platform house, men's house
tieboali   small man, rubbish man
tupale   metaphoric songs
wena   woman
wenada   women's house
wenali   people, relatives
wena nu laapo   bridewealth
wena ragele   bridewealth
wena yapa   bridewealth
yaari   cassowary (headdress)
yada   war
yada au   war decorations
yada re   cause of war
yada yaari   war reparation payment
yagi   bridal gift, child payment
yaisia   singing; *kununa yaisia* courting songs
yala   ashamed
yamanu   kitchen garden
yapa   possum
yawe   to cook in earth oven; feast in which many pigs are killed and
    cooked this way

Appendix:
Wars involving Yala

Name or description	cause	approximate date
1 Yala expulsion from Aliwi by Perepe	Yala children destroyed Perepe kitchen garden	mythical times
2 Yala driven to Agema	Tiarepa of Yagore waged war on them; not known why	'Yawi's time', c. turn of the century
3 *Mena lo yada*	Killing of Samberigi man by Aburupa	1930s
4 *Mena yada*	Yala men killed pig belonging to the Tiarepa of Yagore; Tiarepa sacked Agema, Yala fled to Wapia	1930s
5 *Wapia rekele pi yada*	In Wapia, Yala was split to help Wabea and Waluaparepa who were fighting each other	1930s
6 *Bala yada*	Yala helped in war between Kamarepa and Waluaparepa on one side, Bala tribes on the other	1930s
7 *Kanada yada*	Perepe, in revenge against earlier killings by Yala, pursued them to Kanada	1930s
8 *Bana yada*	To avenge the killing of Bana	1940s
9 *Kalariki yada*	Following abduction of old woman by Tiarepa man	1940s
10 *Wena kura yada*	Following abduction of young Kamarepa woman by Tiarepa	1940s
11 *Rarupo yada*	Vengeance for Tiarepa killing of Perepe man	1940s

Name or description	cause	approximate date
12 *Moge yada*	To avenge killing of Yala Moge by Waluaparepa	1940s
13 *Peawi yada*	To avenge killing of Paisa by Peawi cult belonging to Eno	1940s
14 *Meleparepa yada*	To avenge killing of Yala Tupa	1940s
15 To assist Meleparepa	To help Meleparepa, attacked by Kamarepa and Waluaparepa	1940s
16 *Kambia yada*	Because Kambia Raisi ridiculed Yala for not demanding compensation for man killed by Meleparepa	1940s
17 To assist Kamarepa	Kamarepa, who had helped Yala return home, was attacked	1950s
18 *Pepeawere yada*	Following disagreement over timing of joint pig kill with Perepe, Yanarepa and Subulu	1950s
19 *Kopayo kaluali*	Following disagreement over payment for spirit cult bought by Yala	1950s
20 *Ragu yada*	Yala assisted Perepe	1950s

References

Allen, M. R. (1967) *Male Cults and Secret Initiation in Melanesia.* Melbourne: Melbourne University Press.

Apea, S. (1975) *Research on Cults in the Ialibu Sub-district SHP.* Lahara Project for the History Department, University of Papua New Guinea.

Barnes, J. A. (1962) African Models in the New Guinea Highlands. *Man* 62: 5–9.

Bloch, M. (ed.) (1975) *Political Language and Oratory in Traditional Society.* London, New York: Academic Press.

Bourdieu, P. (1977) *Outline of a Theory of Practice.* London: Cambridge University Press.

Bus, G. A. M. (1951) The *Te* Festival or Gift Exchange in Enga (Central Highlands of New Guinea). *Anthropos* 46: 813–24.

Collier, J. F. and Rosaldo, M. Z. (1981) Politics and Gender in Simple Societies. In S. B. Ortner and H. Whitehead (eds) *Sexual Meanings.* Cambridge: Cambridge University Press.

Cook, E. A. (1969) Marriage among the Manga. In R. M. Glasse and M. J. Meggitt (eds) *Pigs, Pearlshells and Women.* New Jersey: Prentice Hall.

Donham, D. L. (1981) Beyond the Domestic Mode of Production. *Man* 16, 4: 515–41.

Epstein, A. L. (ed.) (1974) *Contention and Dispute: Aspects of Law and Social Control in Melanesia.* Canberra: Australian National University Press.

Epstein, T. S. (1968) *Capitalism, Primitive and Modern.* Canberra: Australian National University Press.

Faithorn, E. (1976) Women as Persons: Aspects of Female Life and Male-Female Relations among the Kafe. In P. Brown and G. Buchbinder (eds) *Man and Woman in the New Guinea Highlands.* AAA Special Publication 8, Washington DC: American Anthropological Association.

Feil, D. K. (1978) Enga Women in the *Tee* Exchange. *Mankind* 11, 3, Special Issue, J. Specht and J. P. White (eds) *Trade and Exchange in Oceania and Australia.*

References 227

Feil, D. K. (1980) When a Group of Women takes a Wife: Generalized Exchange and Restricted Marriage in the New Guinea Highlands. *Mankind* 12, 4: 286–99.

Feil, D. K. (1982a) Alienating the Inalienable. Correspondence in *Man* 17, 2: 340–42.

Feil, D. K. (1982b) From Pigs to Pearlshells: The Transformation of a New Guinea Highlands Economy. *American Ethnologist* 9, 2: 291–306.

Finney, B. R. (1973) *Big-men and Business*. Honolulu: University Press of Hawaii.

Frankenberg, R. (1967) Economic Anthropology: One Anthropologist's View. In R. Firth (ed.) *Themes of Economic Anthropology*. London: Tavistock ASA Monograph 6.

Franklin, K. J. and Franklin, J. (1978) *A Kewa Dictionary*. Canberra: Australian National University.

Goldman, L. (1984) *Talk Never Dies*. London: Tavistock.

Gillison, G. (1980) Images of Nature in Gimi Thought. In C. MacCormack and M. Strathern (eds) *Nature, Culture and Gender*. Cambridge: Cambridge University Press.

Godelier, M. (1982a) *La Production des Grands Hommes*. Paris: Fayard.

Godelier, M. (1982b) Social Hierarchies among the Baruya of New Guinea. In A. Strathern (ed.) *Inequality in New Guinea Highlands Societies*. Cambridge: Cambridge University Press.

Good, K. (1979) The Formation of the Peasantry. In A. Amarshi, K. Good, and R. Mortimer (eds) *Development and Dependency: The Political Economy of PNG*. Melbourne: Oxford University Press.

Gordon, R. (1983) The Decline of the Kiapdom and the Resurgence of 'Tribal Fighting' in Enga. *Oceania* 53, 3: 205–23.

Gregory, C. A. (1980) Gifts to Men and Gifts to God: Gift Exchange and Capital Accumulation in Contemporary Papua. *Man* 15, 4: 626–52.

Gregory, C. A. (1982a) Alienating the Inalienable. Correspondence in *Man* 17, 2: 343–45.

Gregory, C. A. (1982b) *Gifts and Commodities*. London: Academic Press.

Healey, C. J. (1978) The Adaptive Significance of Systems of Ceremonial Exchange and Trade in the New Guinea Highlands. *Mankind* 11, 3: 198–207.

Herdt, G. H. (ed.) (1982) *Rituals of Manhood*. Berkeley: University of California Press.

Herdt, G. H. and Poole, F. J. P. (1982) 'Sexual Antagonism': The Intellectual History of a Concept in New Guinea Anthropology. In F. J. P. Poole and G. H. Herdt (eds) *Sexual Antagonism, Gender and Social Change in Papua New Guinea*. Special Issue Series Social Analysis 12: 3–28.

Hides, J. (1973) *Papuan Wonderland*. Sydney: Angus and Robertson. First published 1936.

Hobbes, T. (1965) *Leviathan*. London: Dent.

Josephides, L. (1982a) Kewa Stories and Songs. *Oral History* 10, 2.

Josephides, L. (1982b) *Suppressed and Overt Antagonism: A Study in Aspects of Power and Reciprocity among the Northern Melpa.* University of Papua New Guinea.

Josephides, L. (1983) Equal but Different? The Ontology of Gender among Kewa. *Oceania* 53, 3: 291–307.

Josephides, L. and Schiltz M. (1980) Socio-economic Change and Labour Migration among the Southern Kewa, SHP. *History of Agriculture* Paper 43, University of Papua New Guinea and Department of Primary Industry.

Josephides, L. and Schiltz, M. (1981) Current Problems and Prospects: View from the Sugu Valley, SHP. In *What do we do about Plantations?* Monograph 15, IASER, PNG.

Josephides, L. and Schiltz, M. (1982) Beer and Other Luxuries: Abstinence in Village and Plantation by Sugu Kewas, Southern Highlands. In *Through a Glass Darkly: Beer and Modernisation in PNG.* Monograph 18, IASER, PNG.

Josephides, S. (1982) *The Perception of the Past and the Notion of 'Business' in a Seventh Day Adventist Village in Madang, New Guinea.* Unpublished PhD Thesis, London School of Economics.

Kagua and Erave Patrol Reports (1956–80) Mendi and Kagua, Southern Highlands Province, PNG.

Kagua Patrol Reports (KPR): 1, 1958; 1, 1962; 3, 1966; 3, 1968; 1, 1969; 7, 1970; 12, 1970; 14, 1971; 8, 1973; 25, 1973; 17, 1975; 18, 1975.

Kahn, J. S. (1978) Marxist Anthropology and Peasant Economics: A Study of the Social Structure of Underdevelopment. In J. Clammer (ed.) *The New Economic Anthropology.* London: Macmillan.

KEOP (Kagua and Erave Official Papers) (1966, 1970) Mendi and Kagua, Southern Highlands Province, PNG.

Langness, L. L. (1967) Sexual Antagonism in the New Guinea Highlands: A Bena Bena Example. *Oceania* 37: 161–77.

Lederman, R. (1982) *Mendi Twem and Sem: A Study of the Social Relations of Production and Exchange in a Highland New Guinea Society.* Unpublished PhD Thesis, Columbia University.

LeRoy, J. D. (1975) *Kewa Reciprocity: Co-operation and Exchange in a New Guinea Highland Culture.* Unpublished PhD Thesis, University of British Columbia.

LeRoy, J. D. (1979a) Competitive Exchange in Kewa. *The Journal of the Polynesian Society* 88, 1: 9–35.

LeRoy, J. D. (1979b) The Ceremonial Pig Kill of the South Kewa. *Oceania* 49, 3: 179–209.

LeRoy, J. D. (1981) Siblingship and Descent in Kewa Ancestries. *Mankind* 13, 1: 25–36.

Lévi-Strauss, C. (1969) *The Elementary Structures of Kinship.* London: Eyre and Spottiswoode.

Mauss, M. (1974) *The Gift.* London: Routledge and Kegan Paul. First published 1925.

May, R. J. (1982) Micronationalism in Perspective. In R. J. May (ed.)

Micronationalist Movements in Papua New Guinea, Canberra: Australian National University.

McCall, G. (1982) Association and Power in Reciprocity and Requital: More on Mauss and the Maori. *Oceania* 52, 4: 303–19.

Meggitt, M. J. (1964) Male–Female Relations in the Highlands of Australian New Guinea. In J. B. Watson (ed.) *American Anthropologist*. Special Publication on New Guinea 2, 66: 204–24.

Meggitt, M. J. (1965) *The Lineage System of the Mae-Enga of New Guinea.* Edinburgh: Oliver and Boyd.

Meggitt, M. J. (1974) 'Pigs are our Hearts!' The *Te* Exchange Cycle Among the Mae-Enga of New Guinea. *Oceania* 44, 3: 165–203.

Meggitt, M. J. (1976) A Duplicity of Demons: Sexual and Familial Roles Expressed in Western Enga Stories. In P. Brown and G. Buchbinder (eds) *Man and Woman in the New Guinea Highlands.* AAA Special Publication 8, Washington DC: American Anthropological Association.

Meggitt, M. J. (1977) *Blood is their Argument.* Palo Alto: Mayfield.

Mel, M. (1982) Highlands Liberation Front: An Insider's Statement. In R. J. May (ed.) *Micronationalist Movements in Papua New Guinea.* Canberra: Australian National University.

Modjeska, N. (1982) Production and Inequality: Perspectives from Central New Guinea. In A. Strathern (ed.) *Inequality in New Guinea Highlands Societies.* Cambridge: Cambridge University Press.

Molyneux, M. (1977) Androcentrism in Marxist Anthropology. *Critique of Anthropology* 3, 9–10: 55–81.

National Planning Office (1975) *The Eight Aims.* Waigani, PNG.

Notes and Queries on Anthropology (1960) Sixth Edition, Revised and Rewritten by a Committee of the Royal Anthropological Institute of Great Britain and Ireland. London: Routledge and Kegan Paul.

Ortner, S. B. and Whitehead H. (1981) Preface and Introduction: Accounting for Sexual Meaning. In S. B. Ortner and H. Whitehead (eds) *Sexual Meanings.* Cambridge: Cambridge University Press.

Rappaport, R. A. (1968) *Pigs for the Ancestors.* New Haven: Yale University Press.

Read, K. E. (1951) The Gahuku-Gama of the Central Highlands. *South Pacific* 5: 154–64.

Read, K. E. (1954) Cultures of the Central Highlands, New Guinea. *Southwestern Journal of Anthropology* 10: 1–43.

Read, K. E. (1982) Male–female relations among the Gahuku-Gama: 1950 and 1981. In F. J. P. Poole and G. H. Herdt (eds) *Sexual Antagonism, Gender and Social Change in Papua New Guinea.* Special Issue Series Social Analysis 12: 66–78.

Reay, M. (1959) *The Kuma.* Cambridge: Cambridge University Press.

Reay, M. (1968) Myth and Tradition as Historical Evidence. In *The History of Melanesia*, Second Waigani Seminar 1968, University of Papua New Guinea and the Research School of Pacific Studies, Australian National University, 463–75.

230   The Production of Inequality

Rubin, G. (1975) The Traffic in Women: Notes on the 'Political Economy' of Sex. In R. R. Reiter (ed.) *Toward an Anthropology of Women*. New York: Monthly Review Press.

Ryan, D. J. (1969) Marriage in Mendi. In R. M. Glasse and M. J. Meggitt (eds) *Pigs, Pearlshells, and Women: Marriage in the New Guinea Highlands*. New Jersey: Prentice-Hall.

Sahlins, M. (1974) *Stone Age Economics*. London: Tavistock.

Schiltz, M. (n.d.) War, Peace and the Exercise of Power: Perspectives on Society and the State in the New Guinea Highlands. Forthcoming.

Schwimmer, E. (1983) La guerre aux femmes (Nouvelle Guinée): propos et discussion. *Anthropologie et Sociétés* 7, 1: 187–92.

Schwimmer, E. (1984) Review of C. Gregory's *Gifts and Commodities*. *Man* 19, 2: 339–40.

Shanin, T. (1976) Introduction. In *Peasants and Peasant Societies*. Harmondsworth: Penguin.

Sillitoe, P. (1979) *Give and Take*, Canberra: Australian National University.

Sinclair, J. (1969) *The Outside Man: Jack Hides of Papua*. Melbourne: Lansdowne.

Souter, G. (1963) *New Guinea: The Last Unknown*. Sydney: Angus and Robertson.

Standish, B. (1982) Elite Communalism: The Highlands Liberation Front. In R. J. May (ed.) *Micronationalist Movements in Papua New Guinea*. Canberra: Australian National University.

Strathern, A. J. (1969) Finance and Production: Two Strategies in New Guinea Highland exchange systems. *Oceania* 40, 1: 42–67.

Strathern, A. J. (1971) *The Rope of Moka*. Cambridge: Cambridge University Press.

Strathern, A. J. (1972) *One Father, One Blood*. London: Tavistock.

Strathern, A. J. (1975) Veiled Speech in Mount Hagen. In M. Bloch (ed.) *Political Language and Oratory in Traditional Society*. London, New York: Academic Press.

Strathern, A. J. (1978) 'Finance and Production' Revisited: In Pursuit of a Comparison. *Research in Economic Anthropology* 1: 73–104.

Strathern, A. J. (1979) *Ongka: A Self-account by a New Guinea Big-man*. London: Duckworth.

Strathern, A. J. (1982a) Tribesmen or Peasants? In A. Strathern (ed.) *Inequality in New Guinea Highlands Societies*. Cambridge: Cambridge University Press.

Strathern, A. J. (1982b) Death as Exchange: Two Melanesian Cases. In S. C. Humphries and H. King (eds) *Mortality and Immortality: The Archaeology and Anthropology of Death*. London: Academic Press.

Strathern, A. J. and Strathern M. (1971) *Self-decoration in Mount Hagen*, London: Duckworth.

Strathern, M. (1972) *Women in Between*. London: Seminar Press.

Strathern, M. (1974) Managing Information: The Problems of a Dispute Settler (Mount Hagen). In A. L. Epstein (ed.) *Contention and Dispute:*

Aspects of Law and Social Control in Melanesia. Canberra: Australian National University.

Strathern, M. (1976) An Anthropological Perspective. In B. Lloyd and J. Archer (eds) *Exploring Sex Differences.* London: Academic Press.

Strathern, M. (1978) The Achievement of Sex: Paradoxes in Hagen Gender-Thinking. In E. Schwimmer (ed.) *The Yearbook of Symbolic Anthropology.* London: Charles Hurst.

Strathern, M. (1981a) Culture in a Netbag: The Manufacture of a Sub-discipline in Anthropology. *Man* 16, 4: 665–88.

Strathern, M. (1981b) Self-interest and the Social Good: Some Implications of Hagen Gender Imagery. In S. B. Ortner and H. Whitehead (eds) *Sexual Meanings.* Cambridge: Cambridge University Press.

Strathern, M. (1983) Subject or Object? Women and the Circulation of Valuables in Highlands New Guinea. In R. Hirschon (ed.) *Women and Property, Women as Property.* London: Croom Helm.

Strathern, M. (n.d.) Discovering 'Social Control'. Forthcoming in W. E. Wormsley (ed.) *Conflict and Control in the New Guinea Highlands.*

Thoden Van Velsen, H. U. E. (1973) Robinson Crusoe and Friday: Strength and Weakness of the Big Man Paradigm. *Man* 8, 4: 592–612.

Vicedom, G. F. and Tischner H. (1943–48) *Die Mbowamb.* Three Volumes, Hamburg.

Weiner, A. B. (1976) *Women of Value, Men of Renown: New Perspectives in Trobriand Exchange,* Texas: University of Texas Press.

Weiner, A. B. (1982) Sexuality among the Anthropologists, Reproduction among the Informants. In G. H. Herdt and F. J. P. Poole (eds) *Sexual Antagonism, Gender and Social Change in Papua New Guinea.* Special Issue Series Social Analysis 12.

Name index

Adawi 25
Allen, M. R. 93n
Anona 20–1
Apea, S. 76
Areli 25
Awei 22

Barnes, J. A. 61
Bloch, M. 171n
Bourdieu, P. 166–67
Bus, G. A. M. 107

Champion, 68–9
Collier, J. F. 104, 106, 132
Cook, E. A. 62

Department of Business Development 88
Donham, D. L. 204
Duni 22

Epstein, A. L. 90, 170n
Etali 212

Faithorn, E. 98
Feil, D. K. 61, 62, 107, 108, 170n, 208
Finney, B. R. 90
Flint, Leo 68
Frankenberg, R. 91
Franklin, K. J. 5, 6, 12n

Gapea 22, 31, 35, 167

Genoka Pipi 20, 21, 50
Gillison, G. 98
Godelier, M. 107, 111, 112, 114n, 220
Goldman, L. 170n
Good, K. 90
Gordon, R. 170n
Gregory, C. A. 94, 203, 205, 207, 213–14

Healey, C. J. 27, 28, 107
Herdt, G. H. 93n, 97, 113n
Hides, J. 68–9

Josephides, L. 9, 39n, 44, 88, 122, 137, 167, 208
Josephides, S. 201n, 202n

Kabenu 141
Kahn, J. S. 90, 91
Kamarenu 20, 21
Kaporopali 174–75
Karia 35
Karupiri 150
Kegeai 49, 50
Kiru: and death of child 141–42; location of house 46–7 Figs 6 and 7; and pig kill 187–88, 195
Koai 31, 174–75
Kodo 22
Kogalepa 22
Komalo 175
Koya 22

Langness, L. L. 98
Lapame 150–51, 170n
Lari: appropriation of labour
    176–77; and marriage 156; and
    pig distribution 127, 197–98
Lederman, R. 27, 51, 56, 60, 107,
    108, 109, 172, 188, 214
LeRoy, J. 6, 15–17, 39n, 45, 60,
    107, 179, 188, 190, 201n
Lévi-Strauss, C. 65
Likasi 22
Liwa 22, 23

Maisa 34–5
Malinowski, B. K. 104
Malupa 36
Mapi: as big man 158, 159,
    161–63; and compensation
    payments 51; and dreams 167;
    and land 48; and politics 49; and
    wife 198
Mara 22
Marx, Karl 208
Mauss, M. 107, 205, 208
May, R. J. 9
McCall, G. 210–11, 214
Meggitt, M. J. 28, 32, 36, 40n, 61,
    62, 98, 107, 108, 120, 172
Mel, M. 9
Modjeska, N. 92, 107, 111,
    112–13, 116, 118–19, 204
Molyneux, M. 97

Nasupeli: and death of child
    141–42; location of house 46–7
    Figs 6 and 7; and neada 185; and
    pig kill 195; and tapada 187
National Planning Office 91
Noyopa 25

Ongka 83
Oropo 22
Ortner, S. B. 106, 114n, 115,
    130–32, 139

Papola 46–7 Figs 6 and 7, 151
Peawi 35

Perapu 25
Perea 22
Pipi see Genoka Pipi
Pisa 12n
Poole, F. J. P. 93n, 97, 113n
Popanu 22, 26, 48, 54
Poya 22
Pupula 12n, 31
Pusa 148

Raisi 35
Rake 159–61, 167, 171n
Ralu 36
Rama: lineage 22; and pig kills
    12n, 185; on war 31, 39n
Rambe 31
Rappaport, R. A. 43
Rau of Samberigi 20, 21, 23
Read, K. E. 98–9
Reay, M. 38n, 98
Regepea 35, 39–40n
Ribanu 20, 21, 50
Riesi 22, 23, 26, 48
Rika 151–52
Rimbu: and Ala brothers 175–77;
    as big man 163–66; conciliation
    of mother 127–28; council
    candidate 49–50; and death of
    child 141–42; and death of
    Wapa 148; and establishment of
    settlement 185; and labour
    control 212; and Mapi 161–63;
    and marriage 156; payments for
    birth of child 194; and pig kill
    12n, 185–87, 189–90, 191, 195,
    197; position of in settlement
    46–7 Figs 6 and 7; power base of
    167
Roga: and Ala brothers 175; and
    pig kills 12n, 186–87; political
    loyalties of 49
Rosaldo, M. Z. 104, 106, 132
Rubin, G. 97
Rudu 32, 34
Ryan, D. J. 53, 54

Sahlins, M. 203–04

Sawa 32, 34
Schiltz, M. 9, 12n, 44, 88, 191, 206
Schwimmer, E. 136–37, 203
Sen 175
Sepa 22
Shanin, T. 91
Sillitoe, P. 51, 102, 107, 108
Sinclair J. 69
Souter, G. 68
Standish, B. 9
Strathern, A. J. 18, 51, 55, 83, 85, 93n, 94n, 107, 110, 153, 157, 163, 167, 169n, 172, 181, 190, 198, 220
Strathern, M. 67, 97, 98, 100, 102–03, 108, 144, 145, 146, 204, 206, 209, 213
Sumbura 167

Tischner, H. 110, 153
Tupa 34, 35

Ulu 22, 23

Van Velsen, T. 168

Vicedom, G. F. 110, 153

Waliya: and divorce 150–51, 170n; and labour control 212; location of house 46–7 Figs 6 and 7; and pig kill 195
Wapa: ancestry 22, 23, 25; death of 148, 173–74, 186; and dreams 167; illness of 173–74; location of house 46–7 Figs 6 and 7; on war 31, 36
Weiner, A. B. 99, 100, 104
Wenu 20, 21
Whitehead, H. 106, 114n, 115, 130–32, 139

Yadi 12n, 46–7 Figs 6 and 7 195
Yakema 35, 39n
Yaki 76, 77
Yala of Kuare 20–1, 23
Yalinai 22
Yamanu 22
Yamola 25
Yanyali 32
Yawi 22, 23, 48
Yokoto 22n, 32, 39n

Subject index

accumulation, and gift economy
  205–06
ada (big) 134
Ada tribe 34
ada re ali (base-men of the place)
  45
affines 64, 191–95
Agema clans 24–6
Agema settlements 44
Agema Yala, the 182–83
age structure, as a prestige
  structure 138
agira (maternal kin) 51, 194–95
agistment 207
agnates 39n, 188, 191–95, 218
agnatic descent 10, 26–7
agnatic idiom 219
Aka settlements 44
Ala tribe 32, 34, 174
ali (man) 133, 144
alienation 2, 177, 205–15
ali rakia (aphrodisiac) 121
Amburupa tribe 32, 33, *Map 4*, 34
amo ali (big man) 29, 134, 135
antigamous lineages 53
antigamous rules 53–4
apara (patrilineage) 17, 194–95
'appreciation of value' 144
appropriation 11, 205–6, 219
assymetrical exchanges 193
Ausparepa clan: ancestry 19, 21,
  24 *Fig. 3*, 25, 26; and marriage
54; and residence 45; and war
  32, 35
Australian administration 70–1
ayara (father's maternal kin)
  194–95

bachelors *see* unmarried men
barter 154, 208
Baruya, the: big men 112, 220;
  women 114n, 136–37
base-men of the place 45
bias 98–103
big men: among Baruya 112, 220;
  and heredity 167; among Kewa 8,
  11, 134, 135, 154, 156, 157–69;
  and labour 152, 211; among
  Melpa 94n, 107, 153–4, 157,
  170n; and pig kills 198–200; and
  settlement of disputes 146; and
  state administration 82–3; and
  war 29
birth huts 44, 217
body paint 195
borrowing 174
boss boys 71–2, 73, 83
boys, control of labour of 212
brideservice societies 104–05, 106,
  112
bridewealth: and clan support 89,
  94n; customs of 54–5; and
  divorce 55; exchanges 55–60,
  155–56; by instalment 67n

bridewealth societies 105, 106
brotherhood: ideology of 17;
  idiom of 63

capitalism 89, 90, 209
Capuchin mission 74
cash cropping 220
cash economy, effects of 220–21
Catholic church 52, 185
cattle projects 81, 93–4n
Chayanov's rule 203–04
childbirth: attitudes to 120–21;
  idiom of 176
child payments 194
Christianity 77, 79
churches, and tradition 52, 180,
  185
clan brothers, and exchange 172
clans: Agema 24–6; and daughters
  53; defined 17; and marriage 26,
  54, 62–3, 67n; and residence
  patterns 45; and stories of origin
  19–23
coffee: buying 86; introduction of
  79–82; and land dispute 50;
  picking 87; prices 87; and
  women's labour 116–17
collective responsibility 149
colonization 68–73
commodities 90, 94n
commodity exchange system 203
compensation payments: and
  children 141–43; for goods or
  labour 151; for homicide 50–1,
  67n; and women 149
competitiveness, in exchange
  107–8, 109
controllable powers of women
  and men 213 Fig. 9
control of labour see labour
  control
conversion, of exchange value 209
co-operation: between agnates
  39n, 45; between husbands and
  wives 119–20; in residential
  groups 49–52
cult house pig killings 177, 200n

cults 52, 74–5, 76–7
cultural salience, of gender
  categories 131, 133

dancers, at pig kills 180, 185–86,
  200n
daughters, and clan 53
death 140–41
development projects 79–82
disputes: and big men 146;
  domestic 149–50; over land 50,
  66–7n
divination 79, 171n
division of labour 97–8, 112,
  116–18
divorce: and bridewealth 55; and
  children 170n; and land 63; and
  property 150–51, 217
domains model 122; see also
  gender domains
domestic disputes 149–50
domestic mode of production
  203–04
domination of women see male
  domination of women
domination/subordination idiom,
  and gender 115
Duna, the 111, 119

education 91
egalitarian ethic 140–44, 168–69
elections 49–50, 52, 66n
emapu (garden) 7
Enali tribe 34
Enga, the: exchange system 107,
  108; male/female work pattern
  119; marriage and clan 61, 62;
  wars 28, 36
Eno tribe 33 Map 4, 34, 35, 36,
  183
epea ali (men who have come) 16,
  45
equalizing relationships 206–07,
  209
Erave Patrol Report 38n, 70, 74,
  93n
euphemization 218, 219–20

Evangelical Church of Papua 52, 74, 185
exchange: as alternative to violence 111; assymetrical 193; and bridewealth *see* bridewealth; as economy 107–09; and euphemization 218, 219–20; and gender relations and production 1; and gifts 176, 203, 205, 218; and group definition 216; and pig kills *see* pig kills; and political activity 11; and social inequality 110
exchange systems 107, 204; *see also moka*; sister exchange; *tee*
exchange value, and conversion 209
exogamy 93, 136

'false generic' xi
'food' debts 179
food shortages 189, 201n
funerals 51; *see also* death

Gahuku-Gama, the 98–9
gender: and bias 98–103; and cultural salience 131, 133; definition of term 97–8; as a legitimating mechanism 138; as a prestige structure 106
gender categories 130, 131, 133
gender concepts, revised 101–06
gender constructs 139
gender domains 122–30
gender ideology 106, 130
gender idioms 133
gender models 104–06
gender relations: and exchange and production 1; and gift economy 217–18; and political and economic change 91–3; and power relations 10–11
ghosts 142, 169n
gift economy 90, 91, 109, 195
gift exchange 176, 203, 205, 218
gifts 107

'gifts to gods and gifts to men' 203, 205–07
group composition 17
group continuity 18, 39n
group formation: and co-operation 49–52; and pig kills 182; and settlement patterns 41–9; and state power 84; and warfare 27, 36–7
group ideologies 18, 26–7
group prestige 143

Hagen, the *see* Melpa, the
headdresses, ceremonial 180
Hides and O'Malley patrol 68
hierarchical relationships 206–07
Highlands Liberation Front 9
homicide, compensation for 50–1
horticulture, shift to 111, 116
houses 42–4, 66n, 118
hunter-gatherer societies, and labour control 112
hunting 134

ideology, and inequality 66, 106, 144–53; *see also* brotherhood; gender; kinship
idioms: agnatic 219; of gender 106, 133; of kinship 26
illness 146, 172–74
immigrant status 16, 45
inalienability 209
indebtedness 193–94
Independence 73
inequality: and alienation 205; and ideology 66, 106, 144–53; among men 49, 198–99, 211, 219; and power 109–13; and reciprocity 109; use of term 145
initiation rites 77, 93n, 120

Kabia, the 33 *Map 4*, 35
kadipi (European) 134
Kagua 9, 69–70
Kagua and Erave Official Papers 80, 81
Kagua Local Council 72

Kagua Patrol Reports 12n, 71, 72,
    73, 75, 80, 81, 93n, 94n
kai ('cousin' relationship) 21
Kalopo, the 19
kaluali (cult elder) 134
Kamarepa, the: and land 50;
    location of 33 Map 4; and pig
    kill 36, 183; and Tiarepa clan 23;
    and war 29, 34, 35
Kambia, the 34, 183
Kanarepa, the 33 Map 4, 35
Kapauku, the 119
kepa 179
Kewa, the: big men 8, 11, 154,
    156; division of labour 116;
    exchange 107, 172; genealogies
    19; language 2, 4 Map 2, 6,
    222–23; male-female relations
    99; marriages 62; use of term 2;
    women 100–01; but see
    throughout
Kewa Dictionary, A 6
Kewai clan 19
kiap 93n
kiapo (officer) 134
ki kogono (hand-work) 49, 152
kinship ideology 144
kinship, idiom of 26
kinship terms 135
kogono (work) 135
Koiari tribe 29, 33 Map 4, 34, 35,
    50
Koiari village 45
komada (wake) 51
Komarepa tribe 33 Map 4, 34, 35
kone kolea (bad feeling) 172–73
kopayo cult 35
Kopereyala clan 19
kununa yaisia (courting parties) 54
Kwakiutl chief, the 213

labour control, 2, 11, 49, 210–11,
    212, 214
labour, division of see division of
    labour
labour, and gift exchange 176–77
labour, and unequal exchange 152

lamula (to marry) 65, 170n,
land: changing attitudes to 48;
    disputes 50, 66–7n; ownership
    18; purchase 75; and women
    65–6, 92
lidi (myth) 23
Likasirepa, the 25
local councils 70
Lodorepa clan 19
Lutheran mission 71, 74

Mae Enga, the 27, 28
magic 79, 121
Maita clan 21
male/female relations 8, 99; but see
    gender relations
male domination of women 98,
    112, 115, 218–19
male inequality 49, 198–99, 211,
    219
male prestige 131, 136, 138
Malipu clan 21
manliness 133
Mapopidipia clan: in Aka 45;
    ancestry 19 Fig 1, 25, 26; and
    marriage 54
Maring settlements 43
Maring wars 27–8
market economy, effects of 89–91
marriage: antigamous rules 53–4;
    arrangement of 54–5; and
    bachelors 154, 155; and
    bridewealth see bridewealth;
    concentration of 61; and land
    10, 63; prohibitions 26;
    randomness of 62; transaction,
    transcription of 58–9; and
    warfare 31; women's part in
    60–1; see also divorce
marriage settlement 57
'maximization of outgoings' 203,
    213, 214
Melanesian pidgin, use of 2
Meleparepa, the 33 Map 4, 34, 35,
    39–40n
Melpa, the: big men 94n, 153–54,
    170n, 198–99; boss boys 83–4;

exchange 62 (*see also moka; tee*);
warfare 28; women 67n, 100,
104, 214
mena kiri (war payments) 154,
183
mena lo yada (war over pig's belly)
32
mena yada (war over a pig) 32, 34,
182
Mendi, the: exchange 108;
marriage 53, 56; women 214
menstrual huts 120, 217
migration 81, 88
Mirupa tribe 33 *Map 4*, 34
missions 74–9
modo mapu (garden) 7
moka (Hagen exchange system)
62, 107, 110, 153–54, 157, 173,
208
'mortgaging' 199
mortuary payments 51
mudu (war general) 134, 135
myth, definition of 19, 23, 38n
myths of origin *see* stories of
origin

neada (foodhouses) 41, 66n,
183–87
neada yawe (longhouse pig kill)
177
Notes and Queries 17
Noyoparepa lineage 25
nurture and production 207

oratory 157, 171n
origin, stories of *see* stories of
origin

pacification 70
Paisa tribe 34, 35
Palerepa clan 19, 21
pali (wife's brother) 30
Pamarepa tribe 35, 36
Papua New Guinea 2, 3 *Map 1*
Papuan Wonderland 68
paradigmatic shift 103
Paripa clan: ancestry 19, 20–6; and

land 45, 48; and marriage 54,
67n; and war 32, 35, 36
parliamentary candidates 158–59
patrilineages 17
patrilocality 84–5
patrivirilocality 93, 136
patrols 68–74
payback killings 143
Pax Australiana 36, 37
peace, as a power relation 213
pearlshells 153, 170n, 179, 180
Perepe tribe: ancestry 21; and land
50; and local politics 49; and
war 32, 34, 35, 36
peripheral sojourners, concept of
65–6, 67n, 100
pidgin *see* Melanesian pidgin
pig kills: and agnates 184, 188;
analysis of exchanges in
190–95; and cessation of
warfare 85; and churches 52, 78;
contemporary 183–89; cult
house 177, 200n; dancers at 180,
185–86, 200n; and death 51, 79;
and delayed gift exchange 176;
distribution at 196; 'for the
longhouse' 177–81; and gift
economy 90; and group
interests 188–89; historical
function of 181–83; and illness
173–74; and inequality among
men 198–99; and intra-group
politics 8–9, 11, 12n; and land
43; and prestige 188; and
'pulsating' settlements 37, 43,
45; reasons for 177, 183–84; and
siblingship 26; timing of
189–90; women's role in 100–01
plantations: migration to 88–9;
women on 117
pokala (lean-to) 41
political differentiation 82
political influence 11
political power: definition of
99–100; necessity of 110
politics: local 49–50, 52; national
52, 66n

pollution, fears of 120
polygyny 55, 74, 129, 149–50
population movements 44–7
pork: distribution of at pig kills
    181; and pearlshells 179; price of
    190
power: and big men 163, 169; and
    inequality 109–13, 169; political
    99–100, 110; and reciprocity
    210; use of term 145
power differentials, and sex 113
powers, controllable, of women
    and men 213 Fig. 9
prestations, system of 107, 172
prestige structures 130–39
prestige structures model of
    gender 106, 115
producer, use of term 207–08
production: co-operation in 49;
    and exchange and gender
    relations 1; intensification of
    111, 204; and nurture 207; social
    relations of 91
provincial governments 73
'pulsating' settlements 37, 43, 45

raguna (ceremonial hat) 180
rameada (birth hut) 38, 39n
ranking: and ceremonial exchange
    181–82; and division of labour
    98; formal absence of 140, 144;
    and pig kills 198
rawa (destruction) 180, 200–01n
re agele (story of origin) 23
reciprocity: and inequality 109;
    and power 210
rekele exchanges 57, 60
remo (ghost) 142
repa (social grouping) 15–16
reparation payments 154, 183
Repotorepa lineage 25
Ribu cult 76–7, 78–9
romo (magic) 121
Rope of Moka, The, 85, 190
roponali (exchange) 61
'rubbish man' 154–55
Rugialirepa clan 19

rungi (pig kill poles) 178–79
ruru (social grouping) 15–17

sem (group events) 108
settlements 41, 42 Fig. 5, 46 Fig.
    6, 47 Fig. 7; see also 'pulsating'
    settlements
Seventh Day Adventists 74
sexual antagonism 98, 113–14n
sexual division of labour see
    division of labour
sexual domains 117–19
sexual encounters 122, 127
Sexual Meanings 106, 114n, 130
sexual taboos 120
siapi (metaphoric speech) 60, 176
siblingship, and agnatic descent
    26, 39n
sister exchange 112, 220
sisters 53, 64, 67n, 135, 136
'skin' payments 143
'smokescreen' effect 11, 109, 208
social categories 110, 153–57
sojourners see women as
Southern Highlands Province 5
    Map 3, 9–10
stereotypes 128
stories of origin 20, 21, 137–38,
    182
stretim ol samting (ability to settle
    disputes) 153
subsistence activities, hours spent
    by each sex on 119, 211, 215n
Subularepa tribe 33 Map 4, 35
Subulu tribe 33 Map 4, 34
sugar cane breaking ceremony
    (wali karia) 179–80
Sugu River Valley 6, 69
Sugu ruru, location of 33 Map 4
Sularapola clan 19, 21
Sunale clan 19
surplus value, theory of 209
'symbolic' capital 166–67
symmetrical exchanges 193

'talking out' 146
Tangerepa tribe 183

tapada (men's house) 41, 43, 44–5,
   66n, 183–87
tee (Enga exchange system) 61,
   62, 107, 108, 172, 208
Tepenarirepa tribe 33 *Map 4*, 34,
   35, 183
threshold of rights 145, 149
Tiarepa clan: ancestry 19, 21–3,
   24, 25, 26; and land 45, 48;
   location of 33 *Map 4*; and
   marriage 67n; name of 38n; and
   war 32, 34
Tiarepa tribe of Yagore, the 22–3,
   25, 29, 32, 35, 36, 171n
tieboali (rubbish man) 138–39, and
   n, 155
Tolai, the 90
Tombema Enga 61–2, 108
tradestores 81, 85, 117
transaction: chains 208; at pig kill
   190–98; and wealth 110
tribal land 45
tribal names 38–9n
tribe identity 216
tribes 17–18
Trobriand Man 104
Trobriand chief, the 213–14
twem (personal exchange
   networks) 108

Umba lineages 24 *Fig. 3*, 25 *Fig. 4*
Unevangelized Fields Mission 74
universalizing mode 104
unmarried men, control of labour
   of 49, 211, 212
Urupa tribe 33 *Map 4*, 35, 36, 183
use values 204
use value production 209
uxorilocality 64

value creation 133, 139
value of persons 142, 143
valued activities 133
valued statuses 133
valued terms 133, 139
vegetables 88

village constables 70, 71–2, 73,
   80, 84
village court proceedings 145,
   146–52
village courts 73, 170n
village magistrates 73, 93n,
   146–47, 158, 162
virilocality 7, 8, 10, 64, 92

Wabea tribe 34
wage labour 88–9, 117
wali karia ceremony 179–80
Waluaparepa clan: in Aka 45;
   ancestry 24, 25, 26
Waluaparepa tribe: location of 33
   Map 4; and war 32, 34, 35
wambe (ceremonial headdress)
   180, 195
Waparepa lineage 25
Wapia rekele pi yada (war in which
   Wapia was split) 34
Wapia Yala, the 23, 148
Wapiripa clan 22
warfare: cessation of 82, 84, 183;
   conduct of 27–31; and exchange
   216; and land 37, 38n; language
   of, in marriage transactions 60;
   motives for 36–7
wars, among Yala 31–6, 224–25
wena (woman) 133
wenada (*see* women's houses)
wenali (people) 144
wenara (wife's lineage) 195–96
wena ragele (marriage settlement)
   57
wergild 140, 154
widows 8, 63, 64
wife givers/wife takers 54, 57,
   58–9, 60, 191–93
wives, position of: in marriage
   53–64; in warfare 29–30
wok (negotiation) 135
Wola, the 102, 108
womanliness 133
women: and agnatic descent 27,
   37–8; and alienation 206–07,
   209–11, 212–13;

women – *cont.*
anthropologists 102–03; and
coffee gardens 116–17, 139n;
and compensation payments
173; cross-sexual definition of
132, 139; and cults 77; effects of
Independence on 91–3; and
group identity 217; and
horticulture 111–12; and land
65–6, 217; and local politics
117; and marriage transactions
60–1, 62; men's fears of 136–37;
men talking about 127–28; and
pig kills 194, 195–98; and
plantations 117; powers
ascribed to 121–22; and religion
117; as sojourners 10, 65–6,
67n, 100, 217; talking about
themselves 128–30, 135;
unmarried 49, 53; and violence
55–6; and war 30, 37–8; *see also*
daughters; divorce; marriage;
sisters; widows; wives

women's houses 41, 44
'women in between' 67n, 100, 216

yada au (war decorations) 29
yagi (wedding gift) 57
Yaka tribe 34
Yakopaita pig kill 184–88
Yala tribe: crops 6–7; gardens 7;
population 7–8; settlements 42
Fig. 5, 46 *Fig. 6*, 47 *Fig. 7*;
stories of origin 20–1; tribe and
clans 19
Yalapala, the 19
yamanu (kitchen garden) 7, 41, 43
Yamolarepa lineage 25
yapisi (negotiation) 135–36
Yarepa clan: ancestry 19, 21, 24,
25, 26; settlements 45; and war 32
Yatupa tribe 34
yawe (Kewa pig kill) 78, 172,
177–81, 207
yawe kama (dancing ground) 41
Yokorepa lineage 25